XENOPHON

CLASSICAL LIFE AND LETTERS

General Editor: HUGH LLOYD-JONES

Regius Professor of Greek in the University of Oxford

Cicero   *D. R. Shackleton Bailey*

Homer   *C. M. Bowra*

Neoplatonism   *R. T. Wallis*

The Presocratics   *Edward Hussey*

Plutarch   *D. A. Russell*

Hellenistic Philosophy   *A. A. Long*

Xenophon and Socrates. From the edition of Xenophon's Works *by Edward Wells (Oxford: 1703). By courtesy of Mr Arthur Richter.*

XENOPHON

J. K. Anderson

CHARLES SCRIBNER'S SONS
NEW YORK

To Esperance

Contents

List of Plates

Maps

Acknowledgments

I am grateful to Professor Hugh Lloyd-Jones for suggesting me as author of this book in the Classical Life and Letters series, and to Mrs M. A. Littauer, Dr R. Bronson, Professor Crawford Greenewalt, Professor L. A. Mackay, Mr D. A. Russell and Mr D. P. Van Nouhuys for reading it in typescript and improving it in various ways. To Mr Wendell Robie I am indebted for a valuable discussion of Xenophon's professional conduct, as well as for many penetrating comments upon his horsemanship.

Above all, I owe thanks to my wife Esperance, who discussed each chapter as it was written, and typed and re-typed successive illegible manuscripts with unfailing patience. She has more than earned the dedication that is gratefully offered to her.

J.K.A.

Introduction

'XENOPHON was the only philosopher among them all to have adorned philosophy both in word and deed. On the one hand, he writes of moral virtue in his discourses, and to some extent in his historical writings also. On the other hand, he excelled in deeds, and begat generals by the force of his example. Alexander the Great, at least, would never have become "Great" but for Xenophon.' So Eunapius, writing at the end of pagan antiquity, opens his *Lives of the Philosophers and Sophists*, with a proper tribute from a professor of the humanities to an author who had been 'required reading' for centuries.

The consequences of Xenophon's campaigns are not now rated so highly. Certainly Jason of Pherae, lord of Thessaly, was inspired by Xenophon's successes, and those of his friend Agesilaus, to devise a programme for the conquest first of Greece and then of Persia (*Hellenica* vi. 1.4ff.), foreshadowing the actual achievements of the Macedonians, which neither Jason, Agesilaus, nor Xenophon lived to see. Alexander the Great himself encouraged his men before the battle of Issus by recalling Xenophon's victories (Arrian, *Anabasis of Alexander* ii. 7.8–9). But he would no doubt have conquered Persia even if, two generations before his time, in 401 B.C., a Greek mercenary army had not demonstrated Persian weakness by marching nearly to the gates of Babylon and extricating itself after the death of the rebel prince who had hired it. Xenophon held no command at all until some time after the decisive battle, and only achieved the chief command after the worst of the retreat was over. His own account of the affair, the *Anabasis of Cyrus*, makes this quite clear.

Xenophon's philosophy is a mixture of practical common sense and traditional morality, combined with a piety that is too easily dismissed as foolish superstition, or the vain repetition of rituals. But he gives us a picture of one side of Socrates that is not unconvincing, as far as it goes; and though we no longer look to ancient authors for advice on how to run a gentleman's estate or train a wife in household management, our knowledge of Athenian society is enriched by Xenophon's remarks on these topics in his *Oeconomicus*.

In his historical works Xenophon makes mistakes and omissions, and displays his prejudices, though his partiality for Sparta has been over-censured by his critics. But he is, at his best, an excellent story-teller, and, if he offers no profound general reflections on human behaviour, he gives us some good individual portraits. His histories contain many incidents illustrating his notions of honourable or dishonourable conduct, and the standards by which he judges are by no means despicable.

His *Cyropaedia*, a historical novel upon the life of Cyrus the Great of Persia, was written in his old age. In it he tried to sum up his ideas on the training and conduct of a general and statesman, the fruit of a lifetime's contact with great men and public affairs. Modern readers may find it dull.[1] But one must allow merit to a work that during the last century of the Roman Republic seems to have formed part of the education of every future statesman. Cicero, it is true, regrets that rising politicians are brought up on the *Cyropaedia* instead of the more 'relevant' memoirs of Marcus Scaurus (*Brutus* 112), and that they study the great men of Greek history, including Cyrus and Agesilaus, Xenophon's heroes, instead of famous Romans (*Tusculan Disputations* ii. 116). But he himself quotes, twice, a tag from the *Cyropaedia* (i. 2.8) on the self-restraint of the Persians, who ate their bread with no other relish than cress (*De Finibus* ii. 92; *Tusculan Disputations* v. 99). This scrap of nursery morality,

---

[1] 'The *Cyropaedia* is vague and languid: the Anabasis circumstantial and animated. Such is the eternal difference between fiction and truth.' Edward Gibbon, *The Decline and Fall of the Roman Empire*, Chapter 24, note 115 (119 in Bury's edition). I am indebted to Mr Colin Haycraft for this quotation.

recalling Victorian strictures on 'that dangerous luxury, Jam',[1] does not suggest that Cicero was very strongly influenced by the book's contents. In fact, he probably read Xenophon chiefly for his style, which is generally clear and pleasant, though perhaps he does not really deserve to be called the Attic Muse (Diogenes Laertius ii. 57).

But the *Cyropaedia* contains much else, including remarks on the training of recruits, the organization of armies, and military tactics, that must once have been of real practical value. We need not take Cicero seriously when, as Governor and Commander-in-Chief in Cilicia, he writes, after a minor but successful campaign, that he has been putting the *Cyropaedia* into practice (*Epistulae ad Familiares* ix. 25.2). In fact he relied on his brother, who had served under Caesar, and other experienced legates.[2] But he also says (*Tusculan Disputations* ii. 62) that Scipio Africanus 'always had Xenophon the Socratic in his hands, and particularly used to praise that passage of his which says that the same labours are less hard for the general than for the common soldier, because the very honour of his rank makes the general's labour lighter' (cf. *Cyropaedia* i. 6.25).

The practical lessons of the *Cyropaedia*, as well as the influence of Xenophon's historical works, are also apparent in the writings of Arrian of Nicomedia, the distinguished soldier, administrator, and friend of the emperor Hadrian, who is not only our best surviving source for Alexander the Great's conquest of Persia but an authority on tactics. Xenophon and Arrian also had in common a love of field sports, and Xenophon's short pamphlet on hunting inspired Arrian to write notes of his own, under the name of 'Xenophon the Younger', to draw attention to improvements in the science, and in the breed of hounds, that had taken place in the five hundred years that separated them.

Of Xenophon's other instructive monographs, that on horsemanship is still valuable for its sound grasp of basic principles, and regularly receives to this day tributes from authorities on this art.

The high reputation that Xenophon enjoyed in antiquity was

[1] Gwen Raverat, *Period Piece* (London, 1952) p. 54.
[2] cf. D. R. Shackleton Bailey, *Cicero* (London, 1972) p. 122.

renewed in Western Europe with the revival of Greek learning, in England as elsewhere. The virtues—clarity and simplicity of language, and conventional morality—that had made his writings useful to the Romans as school texts, marked them out for the same preferment in the sixteenth and seventeenth centuries. The first direct translation from the Greek into English to which we can give a definite date is perhaps a rendering of the *Oeconomicus* by Gentian Hervet, a Frenchman in the service of Margaret Countess of Salisbury, which was printed in 1532.[1] This version rather delightfully sets the conversation of Socrates and Ischomachus in 'a porche of a churche' instead of the Stoa of Zeus Eleutherius, and makes them swear 'by the faith I owe to God' instead of 'by Zeus'. It was popular enough to run through six editions: 'It may have ranked as light literature or perhaps as a manual for those about to marry, and been considered as a suitable wedding-present for the Vicar of the parish to give to the Squire's daughter in those days'—but one may feel surprised at the suggestion that it 'might be reprinted today (1933) and read with advantage by one anxious to know how to train up a wife and household'.

Xenophon had more distinguished readers than 'the Squire's daughter'. Roger Ascham, the tutor of Queen Elizabeth I[2] and Lady Jane Grey, writes in his *Scholemaster* (p. 51 of the second edition, London, 1571): 'Yea, I have heard worthye M. Cheke many times say: I would have a good student passe and iorney through all Authors both Greeke and Latin; but he that will dwell in these fewe bookes onelie: first in Gods holie Bible, and then ioyne with it, Tullie in Latin, Plato, Aristotle, Xenophon, Isocrates and Demosthenes in Greeke: must needs prove an excellent man.'

Ascham shows familiarity with Xenophon's other works, but makes most use of the *Cyropaedia*, remarking with approval that

---

[1] E. F. Bosanquet in *Transactions of the Bibliographical Society*, NS xiv, no. 2 (Sept. 1933), pp. 178–92.

[2] But it appears that Queen Elizabeth did not write the manuscript translation of the *Hieron* in Cambridge University Library which is sometimes ascribed to her (L. Bradner, in *Journal of the Warburg and Courtauld Institutes*, 1964, pp. 324–326).

Cyrus awaits the consent of his father and mother before announcing his engagement to a most suitable young lady (*Scholemaster* p. 13; cf. *Cyropaedia* viii. 5.19–20), and (cf. *Cyropaedia* i. 4.4) that 'Xenophon doth preciselie note in Cyrus that his bashfulness in youth was the verie true sign of his vertue and stoutness after'. He regrets (p. 12; cf. *Cyropaedia* i. 2.2ff.) that 'we lacke in England of such good order, as the old noble Persians so commonly used: whose children, to the age of xxi yeare were brought up in learning and exercises of labour, and that in such place where they should neither see that was uncumly, nor heare that was unhonest. Yea, a young ientleman was never free, to go where he would, and do what he like himselfe, but under the keepe, and by the counsel, of some grave governor, until he was either maryed or cald to bear some office in the common wealth.'

Ascham also finds support in the *Cyropaedia*'s description of Persian education for his views on school discipline. 'It is hard with ientlenesse but unpossible with severe crueltie, to call them back to good frame agayne. For, where the one perchance may bend it, the other shall surely break it: and so instead of some hope, leave an assured desperation, and shamelesse contempt of all goodnesse, the furthest point in all mischiefe, as Xenophon do most trewly and most wittely mark.' Perhaps we may also trace Xenophon's influence, when Ascham (p. 10) observes that the 'onely cause that commonly the younge ientlemen of England go so unwillingly to schole and run so fast to the stable' is that their masters 'by feare do beate into them the hatred of learning, and wise riders, by ientle allurements, do breed up in them the love of riding . . . And I do not write this, that in exhorting to the one, I would dissuade young ientlemen from the other. Yea, I am sorry, with all my hart, that they be geven no more to riding, than they be. For of all outward qualities, to ride faire, is most comely for hym self, most necessary for his contry, and the greater he is in blood, the greater is his prayse, the more he doth exceede all other therein. It was one of the three excellent prayers, amongest the noble ientlemen, the old Persians. Always to say troth, to ride faire, and shoote well. And so it was engraven upon Darius tombe, as Strabo beareth witnesse,

Darius the king lieth buried here
Who in riding and shoting had never peare.'

Here, besides Strabo (xv. 3.8), and, by implication, Herodotus
i. 136, Ascham might well have referred to Xenophon's *Cyropaedia* (iv. 3.4ff.) and, besides Darius, to Cyrus (*Anabasis* i. 9.2ff.).

A further tribute to Xenophon is given by David Lloyd, who
in his *State-worthies, or the Statesmen and Favourites of England*
(London, 1776), vol. I, pp. 471–2, includes among the books
read by a gentleman of quality, after Cicero (select orations, and
'Tully's Offices, a book which boys read and men understand'),
Caesar, Livy, Tacitus, Curtius, Sallust, and 'prudent and brave
Xenophon, whose person was Themistocles his companion' (a
curious slip) 'as his book was Scipio Affricanus his pattern in all
his wars'. Xenophon is put first in the list of Greek authors, who
include 'ancient and sweet Herodotus; sententious and observing
Thucydides; various and useful Polybius'—but this primacy no
doubt indicates that the schoolboy read him first, not that he was
valued above them all by men of discernment. It is interesting
that, whereas Ascham's reading list includes philosophers and
orators, but Lloyd's historians, both find room for Xenophon.

In the eighteenth century Xenophon was still admired. 'When
Tully informs us in the second book of his Tusculan Disputations,' says Bolingbroke in his second *Letter on the Study and
Use of History*, 'that the first Scipio Africanus' (was it not rather
the second?) 'had always in his hands the works of Xenophon, he
advances nothing but what is probable and reasonable. To say
nothing of the retreat of the ten thousand, nor of other parts of
Xenophon's writings, the images of virtue, represented in that
admirable picture the Cyropaedia, were proper to entertain a
soul that was fraught with virtue, and Cyrus was worthy to be
imitated by Scipio.' This would be more edifying if it came from
an honester man than Bolingbroke.

By this time Xenophon's writings had of course lost their value
as military handbooks. 'The late duke of Marlborough never read
Xenophon,[1] most certainly, nor the relation perhaps of any

[1] Marlborough showed his lack of a classical education when he was proffered
an edition of Anacreon: 'Dear Harry, here's a man comes to me and talks to me

modern wars, but he served in his youth under monsieur de Turenne.' But Xenophon's merits as a moralist and political philosopher were still appreciated, indeed rated too high. 'Read Thucydides or Xenophon,' continues Bolingbroke in his fifth *Letter*; 'you are taught indeed as well as entertained; and the statesman or the general, the philosopher or the orator, speaks to you in every page. They wrote on subjects on which they were well informed, and they treated them fully; they maintained the dignity of history, and thought it beneath them to vamp up old traditions, like the writers of their age and country, and to be trumpeters of a lying antiquity. The Cyropaedia of Xenophon may be objected perhaps; but if he gave it for a romance, not history, as he might for aught we can tell, it is out of the case: and if he gave it for an history, not a romance, I should prefer his authority to that of Herodotus or any other of his countrymen.'

This exaggerated praise from the philosopher of the Tory party drew on Xenophon, in the next century, the thunder of Macaulay,[1] who allows that he 'is commonly placed, but we think without much reason, in the same rank with Herodotus and Thucydides', but gives his own opinion that 'the expedition of the Ten Thousand, and the History of Grecian Affairs, are certainly pleasant reading; but they indicate no great power of mind. In truth, Xenophon, though his taste was elegant, his disposition amiable, and his intercourse with the world extensive, had, we suspect, rather a weak head.' As for the *Cyropaedia*, 'the Life of Cyrus, whether we look upon it as a history or as a romance, seems to us a very wretched performance'. It is pleasant to find an older and more mellow Macaulay noting in his diary for 9 October 1837, after three re-readings of the *Anabasis*: 'One of the very first works that antiquity has left us. Perfect in its kind.'[2]

---

about one Anna Creon, and I know nothing of Creon but Creon in the play of Oedipus, prithee do you speak to the man.' (G. M. Trevelyan, *England under Queen Anne*, vol. II (*Ramillies*), p. 8.)

[1] 'History', *Edinburgh Review*, May 1828, reprinted in *Miscellaneous Writings* (London, 1860), vol. I, p. 247.

[2] George Otto Trevelyan, *The Life and Letters of Lord Macaulay* (London, 1890), ch. 8. I owe the reference to Prof. Gilbert Bagnani, *Phoenix* xv (1961) pp. 230–3.

But Macaulay's earlier harsh judgment has been generally repeated in the present century by scholars, not all of whom, perhaps, have the right to pronounce with Macaulay's authority on their fellow-historians and some of whom even deny those merits that Macaulay allows. In fact, as the Classics have come to be neglected by general readers, and have become the preserve of scholars, Xenophon's faults have become more apparent and his virtues have been less appreciated. We are sometimes tempted to regret the 'accident' of preservation that has given us his writings entire, and left us other fourth-century historians only in quotation or inaccurate summary. But, in fact, no 'accident', like that which preserved the poems of Catullus in a single manuscript, brought about Xenophon's survival. Many scribes, and their employers, in many generations, thought his books worth copying out. They did not pay the same compliment to Ephorus, Theopompus, or, for that matter, Scaurus.

And, since 'his pen copied his narrative from his sword',[1] and any estimate of his worth as a moralist or his truth as a historian must depend on how we judge his own character, this book will chiefly be concerned with his own life, as far as it can be reconstructed from the brief accounts of later writers, and from his own writings, not only the partly autobiographical *Anabasis*, but those passages in his other works where a hint of his own conduct, beliefs or education can be found.[2]

[1] Lloyd, op. cit., p. 552.

[2] It would be ingratitude, if no worse, not to acknowledge at this point my debt to Prof. E. Delebecque's *Essai sur la vie de Xénophon*, for the insight that he has given into this matter. I have not, however, fully accepted his conclusions.

CHAPTER ONE

Childhood and Youth

'XENOPHON was the son of Gryllus, an Athenian, of the parish of Erchia. He was modest and most superlatively handsome. They say that Socrates encountered him in an alleyway and blocked his passage by laying his staff across it, while he asked him where one might buy various products. When Xenophon answered, he again questioned him, and asked him where men might become honourable and virtuous. Xenophon confessed his ignorance, and Socrates replied, "Then follow me, and learn". And from that time on Xenophon was Socrates's disciple.'[1] With this story his ancient biographer (Diogenes Laertius ii. 48) introduces Xenophon as a young man of promise, his education still incomplete, but his age and means apparently both sufficient to allow him to follow his own inclination in completing it.

We are not told the year of his birth. Diogenes (ii. 55) says that he 'flourished in the fourth year of the ninety-fourth Olympiad' (401 B.C.)—not, as such references sometimes imply, his fortieth year, but that of his most famous exploit, which follows directly in the same sentence—'and he marched with Cyrus'. Xenophon seems to have been rather younger than his friend Proxenus, who induced him to accompany the army of the rebel Persian prince, and Proxenus was 'about thirty' (*Anabasis* ii.

---

[1] This is perhaps based on a story that Xenophon himself tells (*Memorabilia* iv. 4.5) of how Hippias of Elis came to Athens and found Socrates telling some of his friends that it was remarkable that if one wanted a man taught to be a shoemaker, a carpenter, a coppersmith or a horseman, there was no lack of teachers to whom to send him. But if one wanted a son or a servant taught justice, one did not know where he could go for the purpose.

6.20; cf. iii. 1.14 for Xenophon's comparative youth). We may place Xenophon's birth, then, a little after 430 B.C.

Erchia, the *deme*, or parish, where Xenophon's family was officially registered, lay to the south of Mount Pentelicus and east of Hymettus, probably near the modern country town of Spata, rather over ten miles from Athens. South of Spata extends the Mesogeia, a level plain surrounded by hills, famous nowadays for its vineyards, but in antiquity perhaps for its grain harvests, since a story was told that Erchieus, the legendary hero for whom Erchia was named, entertained the goddess Demeter on her wanderings.[1] There is no direct evidence that Xenophon's family still owned lands or a house in the parish where it had been settled at the end of the sixth century, when the Athenians were registered by *demes* under the new democratic constitution, but it was certainly rich and well connected, and its position was probably founded on a country estate. Xenophon also shows an interest in the silver mines at Laurium, which are the chief subject of the pamphlet, written near the end of his life (*c.* 355 B.C.?), in which he advises the Athenians how to manage their revenues (*De Vectigalibus*; cf. also *Memorabilia* iii. 6.12). It may be that Gryllus speculated in the mines or contracted to supply them with slave labour.

But, whether his family home was still in Erchia or not, Xenophon was very probably born in the city of Athens. The Peloponnesian War, between Athens and Sparta, broke out in 431 B.C., and the Athenian country-people, who until that time had followed an old-fashioned village way of life (Thucydides ii. 16.1) abandoned their homes and retired within the fortifications. Erchia did not suffer much in the early years of the war, but Gryllus no doubt placed his family in safety, though we must not of course imagine that he was one of the miserable refugees whose hovels crowded the space between the Long Walls con-

---

[1] Stephanus of Byzantium (*c.* A.D. 500) actually refers to the better-known Erechtheus, and a *deme* Erechthia. But Erechthia is not otherwise known, and the emendation Erchia (proposed by Colonel W. M. Leake, *Topography of Athens*, vol. II, *The Demi of Attica* (2nd ed. 1841) p. 199) is confirmed by the fact that Stephanus says that the orator Isocrates, known from other sources to have been from Erchia, came from this *deme*.

necting Athens with its seaport, the Piraeus, and filled all the available open space, even the sacred Pelargikon, within the city. He certainly survived the disastrous plague of 429–428 B.C.

Even before the outbreak of war, Gryllus must often have been called to town by political or business interests, and perhaps he already owned a town house, like Ischomachus, the 'perfect Athenian gentleman' of Xenophon's *Oeconomicus*.[1]

Whether it stood in town or in the country, Xenophon's home must have been built of sun-dried mud brick, on a stone foundation, with a roof of baked tile over wooden rafters (cf. *Memorabilia* iii. 1.7) (Plate 1). These were the usual materials for domestic architecture. Xenophon notes among the natural assets of Attica its fine marble, but this was used for 'most beautiful temples, most beautiful altars, and most magnificent statues to the gods' (*De Vectigalibus* 1.4; he might have added public buildings, like the colonnades, public offices and fountain-houses that already adorned the north, west and south sides of the Athenian market place).[2]

'Beautiful houses are also practical', Xenophon makes Socrates say. So the house should be designed to be warm in winter and cool in summer, and the main range of buildings therefore faced south, and was raised high to serve as a sun-trap. A verandah (*pastas*) was carefully designed to admit the rays of the low winter sun, but to provide shade in summer. Those parts of the building that faced north were built lower, to escape the winter wind. 'In

---

[1] This book was probably written when Xenophon was between fifty and sixty, but must have been based in large part upon memories of his youth, rather than upon the society of contemporary Athens, from which he had been many years exiled. Ischomachus's life is described through a report, put into the mouth of Socrates, of a conversation between them, but there is no reason to suppose that the conversation ever took place.

[2] The Stoa of Attalus, which now, handsomely reconstructed, dominates the site of the ancient market-place, was built some two centuries after Xenophon's death. The Temple of Hephaestus (so-called Theseum), on the Colonus Agoraeus or 'Market Hill' to the west, dates probably from the midde of the fifth century. On the Acropolis, the Parthenon and Propylaea represent successive stages of the Periclean building programme, begun in 447 B.C. and interrupted by the war and the plague in 428, at about the time of Xenophon's birth. The little temple of Athena Nike dates from his childhood; work on the Erechtheum continued throughout his adolescence.

a word, that which provides the master of the house with the
most pleasant shelter in all seasons, and his possessions with the
safest protection, would of course be the most pleasant and most
beautiful form of architecture. But paintings and ornaments take
away more pleasure than they give.' Such adornments (at least
according to the judgment that Xenophon puts into the mouth
of Socrates) were proper for altars and temples, where those
who saw them could make their devotions with pleasure, and
approach them in a reverent frame of mind (*Memorabilia* iii.
8.8–10).

This suggestion that mythological works of art had no place
in the home, because they might not be regarded with sufficient
reverence, is unexpected. Xenophon obviously would not have
approved of a dining-room floor decorated with the Triumph of
Dionysus in pebble-mosaic, like that of the 'Villa of Good
Fortune' in contemporary Olynthus. One wonders whether his
disapproval extended to wine-cups and mixing-bowls decorated
with pictures of the gods, and how far it was shared by other
conservatively brought-up Athenians. It is perhaps significant
that most of the plates, cups and other table wares recovered
from a well in the ruins of the Tholos at Athens, where the
Council entertained distinguished guests, were decorated only
with a handsome, but plain, black glaze. These pieces may represent part of an official dinner service of *c.* 480 B.C.[1]

Ischomachus too says that his house, 'has no fanciful ornaments, but the buildings have been constructed for the express
purpose of holding as conveniently as possible their intended
contents. So these dictated the appropriate form of each part'
(*Oeconomicus* 9.1ff.). He describes how he showed the different
rooms to his newly-wed bride—the strong-room for valuables,
including the best bedding and furniture, the dry store-rooms for
grain, the cool wine-cellar, and the well-lit chambers where the
work of the household was carried on. This work would include

---

[1] For the houses of Olynthus see David M. Robinson and J. Walter Graham,
Excavations at Olynthus, part VIII, (Baltimore, 1938). The mosaics of the 'Villa
of Good Fortune' were first published by D. M. Robinson in *AJA* 38 (1934)
pp. 506–8. For the pottery from the Tholos, see T. Leslie Shear, *Hesperia* 8
(1939) pp. 229–31.

the spinning and weaving of wool, under the mistress's eye (Plate 12), and the daily grinding of grain upon hand-querns. A first-class establishment like Ischomachus's (Xenophon's own home was probably not as grand) would have maintained a number of domestic slaves, of both sexes, superintended by an experienced housekeeper. The men's quarters were separated from the women's by a locked door, 'so that nothing may be carried out that should not be, and so that the servants may not have children without our consent. For if good ones have children they are generally better-disposed thereafter, but bad ones, if they couple, become more inclined to mischief.'

The main feature of the house would be a large dining-room (*andron*: cf. *Symposium* 1.13) where the master would entertain other men. The store-rooms and other subordinate buildings, including, in the house of Ischomachus, and no doubt that of Gryllus, a stable for the master's horse, would probably be grouped round a small square courtyard, so that the house looked inwards, an arrangement which in the country increased security, and in town helped to shut out the noises and smells of the un-drained, unpaved alleyways.[1] Ischomachus's description of the furnishings of the house, which he and his wife next inspected, began (*Oeconomicus* 9.6ff.) with 'those things that we use for sacrifice' (not simply a religious ceremony, but a hospitable occasion, where friends would come in to dine off the victim [cf. St Paul, I Corinthians x. 27.8] or portions of meat would be sent out to them (Plate 2). A cock for the poor; an ox for the rich, says the proverb; but pork was probably the most usual meat.) Then followed 'the mistress's adornments' (jewelry and dresses?) 'for festivals: the master's dress for festivals and for war; bedding in the maidservants' quarters; bedding in the men's quarters; women's shoes; men's shoes'. Armour, instruments for wool-working, for breadmaking, for cooking, each had its own place. So did bathroom necessities (many houses at Olynthus had

---

[1] For general similarities in the plans of a country house of *c.* 420 B.C., a few miles from Athens, and middle-class town houses in Olynthus (destroyed in 348 B.C.) cf. J. E. Jones, L. E. Sackett and A. J. Graham, 'The Dema House in Attica', *BSA* 57 (1962) pp. 75–114, especially p. 105, where Xenophon's evidence is cited.

bathrooms, with small sitz-baths, floors of waterproof cement, and
a drain in one corner emptying directly into the street). A place
for everything and everything in its place, 'shipshape and Sidon-
fashion', like the great Phoenician freighter that had called at
the Piraeus, was Ischomachus's rule—but perhaps here we see
reflected not Xenophon's childhood home but the establishment
of the retired regular soldier who wrote the *Oeconomicus*.

Xenophon's mother Diodora leaves little trace in his writings,
though we may get a glimpse of her in Mandane, the mother of
Cyrus (*Cyropaedia* i. 3–4), who shows a proper concern for her
son's behaviour and upbringing when she takes him to visit his
grandfather. Xenophon's infancy, when he was presumably under
his mother's direct care, must have ended about the time of the
Peace of Nicias (421 B.C.), which closed the first phase of the
war to the advantage of Athens. His memories of these years
must have been very slight, and there can of course be no truth in
the romantic story that Socrates saved his life when he was
unhorsed at the Battle of Delium (424 B.C.: Diogenes Laertius
ii. 22; Socrates's gallant retreat after the rout of the Athenians is
attested by Plato, *Symposium* 221 A, B).

It may be that Xenophon's family, like other Athenians,[1]
moved back into the country in the uneasy interval that followed
the Peace of Nicias, or perhaps Gryllus preferred to keep his
family in Athens and go out regularly to supervise the work of
the farm, like Ischomachus (*Oeconomicus* 11.15ff.). The formal
education of his only son (there is no indication that Xenophon
had any brothers or sisters) might have given him reason to
remain in town. We can imagine Xenophon in early adolescence
being carefully escorted by his pedagogue, a trusted slave whose
job was to prevent the handsome boy from being picked up by
undesirable acquaintances, to a school where, in company with
a small group of boys of his own social class, he would study
Homer, and other improving poets, like Theognis, and learn
suitable sentiments, for instance that

[1] As is illustrated by the 'Dema House' (Plate 1) (Jones, Sackett and Graham,
op. cit.), built at this time and abandoned a few years later when war broke out
again.

'From noble men we learn nobility.
Base friends destroy our natural quality.'
(cf. *Memorabilia* i. 2.20)

He may also have acquired the useful social grace of accompanying himself on the lyre while singing old-fashioned moral or
patriotic songs. But 'music', this side of his education, probably
meant less to him than 'gymnastic'. The Lyceum and the Aca-
demy, lying just outside the city walls, were not yet schools of
philosophy, but exercise-grounds where the well-bred young
Athenian developed his body in healthy competition. Individual
sports—running, wrestling, boxing, jumping and the like—were
favoured; team games did not much interest the Greeks, though
a principal object of this side of education was to produce soldiers
who would drill and fight as a united body.

Xenophon, for his part, could look forward when he grew up
to service in the cavalry—a wealthy and aristocratic body, since
they provided their own horses, though with the help of a state
subsidy. He perhaps received his first lessons in horsemanship
while accompanying his father on visits to the country. Erchia
was rather too far from Athens for them to have followed
Ischomachus's routine (*Oeconomicus* 11.14ff.). 'If I have no
pressing business in the city, my groom leads my horse on to the
farm, and I make the road to the farm my walk, perhaps more
pleasantly, Socrates, than if I were to walk in the exercise-
ground. But when I come to the farm, whether my men are
planting or haymaking or sowing or bringing in the harvest, I
inspect what is going on and make adjustments, if I see room for
improvement. After this I generally mount my horse and school
him in exercises which resemble, as closely as I can make them,
those that are necessary in war. I do not avoid riding across slopes,
or down slopes, or over ditches and enclosures, though I am as
careful as possible not to lame my horse in doing these things.
After this, the groom gives the horse a roll and leads him home,
bringing with him from the farm whatever we need in town.'
(The farm would supply the household with basic foodstuffs, and
the wool whose spinning and weaving occupied much of the

mistress's time, but of course we are not to imagine all this being packed in every day on the master's cavalry charger). 'But I make my way home, alternately walking and running,' continues Ischomachus, 'and then anoint and scrape myself' (the ancient equivalent to a shower) 'and have lunch, just so much as to pass the day neither empty nor too full.'

Ischomachus's farm seems to have been in the suburbs. On the longer journey to and from Erchia, Gryllus and Xenophon probably rode, no doubt practising their horsemanship on the way, like the 'late-learner' in Theophrastus (*Characters* 27), who borrows a horse to ride to his farm. (However, he falls off and breaks his head—a warning to 'be your age'.)

In the early part of the *Oeconomicus* (ch. v), Xenophon makes Socrates praise the farmer's (or rather farm-owner's) life, which brings pleasure, increases a man's property, and trains his body for the activities that befit a free man. The earth bears the necessities of life, and the luxuries too, besides the flowers, sweet-scented and beautiful, with which men adorn the altars of the gods and their own persons. Delicacies and meats in abundance grow from the earth, and are nourished by it. The herdsman's art is conjoined to the farmer's, so that men may please the gods by sacrifice, and have meat for their own use. But these abundant benefits are not to be gained by softness; farming accustoms men to endure the cold of winter and the heat of summer; it strengthens by exercise those who work with their own hands, and makes men of those who employ others by compelling them to rise early and travel hard, for both in country and in town their business is most pressing in its season. Then if a man wishes to defend his city on horseback, farming is most adequate to support a horse; if on foot, it strengthens the body. The earth also encourages a man, through hunting, to enjoy rough living, for it provides the means of keeping hounds, as well as breeding beasts of chase. And so horses and hounds, which are supported by farming, benefit the farm in return, the horse by carrying the master early in the morning to oversee the work and by making it possible for him to leave late, and the hounds by preventing wild beasts from harming the crops and herds, and also by giving security in lonely districts. (It is notable that Xenophon seems to exclude hunting on horseback. The level ground of Attica may have been too closely cultivated for this sport to be practicable.)

Ungrudging hospitality, blazing fires and hot baths in winter, cool water, shade and breezes in summer, are among the delights of country life. Then there are first-fruits and harvest festivals—what life could be more attractive for a man's family, more pleasant for his wife, more desirable for his children, more charming for his friends? Indeed, the earth, who is a goddess, even teaches justice to those who can learn, repaying with most benefits those who care for her best.

But Socrates continues by saying that, if men who are practised in agriculture and brought up in manly vigour are ever driven from their fields by armies which outnumber them, they will be well prepared in soul and body, if God permit, to go to their enemies' lands and provide for themselves. In wartime it is indeed often safer to gather one's food with one's weapons than with agricultural implements. These words are a reminder that in 413 B.C., about the time that Xenophon was developing from childhood to adolescence, the Spartans, taking advantage of the disastrous Athenian involvement in Sicily, and advised by the exiled Alcibiades, renewed the war, and seized Decelea in northern Attica, as a base from which to ravage the countryside far more intensively than they had done before. So Xenophon's pleasant initiation into the duties and pleasures of a country gentleman was cut short—about the time, perhaps, when Gryllus was first allowing him to accompany the grown men after boar, instead of merely hunting hares with nets and greyhounds. Perhaps he had also begun to introduce his son to Athenian society, accepting, on his behalf, invitations to select dinner-parties, where the 'modest and most superlatively handsome' young athlete would be seated next his father, drawing all eyes to him, like a gleam of moonlight in the dark, while the remainder of the guests reclined on couches, according to custom (*Symposium* 1.8; the guest of honour in this imagined banquet is not of course Xenophon himself).

But now this pleasant life was ended. In his old age (*De Vecti-*

galibus 4.25) Xenophon remembered the Spartan occupation of Decelea as a turning-point in Athenian history, perhaps because it had been one in his own life. His family certainly was not ruined by the war (even after the final defeat he was able to accompany Cyrus in some style, with his own horses: *Anabasis* iii. 3.19),[1] but there can have been no more peaceful visits to Erchia. Since we do not know his exact age, we do not know when he first saw military service, but until he took his place in the cavalry most of his life must have been spent within the city walls (Plate 13).

He may possibly have served as a cavalryman in the main theatre of war in Asia Minor, under Alcibiades (restored for a time to popular favour) or Thrasyllus (cf. *Hellenica* i. 2–3, recounting episodes of the campaign of 408 B.C.). It is more probable that he sailed in 406 B.C. with the fleet that was desperately scraped together to rescue the Athenian force blockaded in Mitylene. In this emergency, he tells us (*Hellenica* i. 6.24), many of the cavalrymen embarked on the ships (probably as marines, not as rowers). Philostratus (*Vitae Sophistarum* 1.12), writing in the third century after Christ, upon what evidence we do not know, says that Xenophon was for a time a prisoner in Boeotia, but obtained his release on bail. He was thus enabled to attend the lectures of Prodicus of Ceos, a rhetorician to whom he owed the fable of the 'Choice of Hercules' (*Memorabilia* ii. 1.21). (Xenophon himself acknowledges that Prodicus was the source but quotes it as coming from his writings, and puts it into the mouth of Socrates.)

If Xenophon was indeed for a time a prisoner of war and released on parole, he may have owed this favour to his friendship with Proxenus, the young Boeotian aristocrat who later invited him to join Cyrus. This friendship was very possibly the result of family connections, a further indication that Xenophon, though not a member of one of the greatest Athenian houses, was well-born.

It seems certain in any case that Xenophon was back in Athens

---

[1] The horse that he sold at the end of the expedition (*Anabasis* vii. 8.2–6) must have been acquired in Thrace, since he crossed to Thrace with no more than a single slave-boy (*Anabasis* vii. 3.20).

by the summer of 405 B.C., when the last Athenian fleet was surprised and destroyed at Aegospotami on the Hellespont by the
Spartan Lysander. Xenophon reports (*Hellenica* ii. 2.3–4) the
arrival of the news, brought by one of the state galleys, which
had escaped: 'In Athens the *Paralus* arrived by night and reported
the disaster. And a sound of lamentation went up from the Piraeus
along the Long Walls to the city, as each man passed the news to
the next. So that night nobody slept, because they were mourn-
ing, not only for the men who had been lost, but far more for
themselves, thinking that they would suffer the same fate that
they had inflicted on the Melians (who were colonists of the
Lacedaemonians), whom they had conquered by siege, and on the
men of Histiaea, of Scione, of Torone and of Aegina, and many
others of the Greeks. On the next day they held an assembly, in
which they resolved to block off the harbours, except for one,
and look to the walls, and post guards, and in all other respects to
prepare the city for siege.'

In the many months of hopeless resistance that followed
Xenophon doubtless bore his part, and by the time that the
Athenians were allowed to surrender on terms that stripped them
of their defences, but stopped short of the massacre and enslave-
ment that they had feared, he must have been a seasoned soldier.
But he was not to serve his own city again.

CHAPTER TWO

Further Education

WHATEVER Xenophon's military experiences may have been during the last part of the war, he clearly had plenty of leisure, before the time of the siege, to pursue his education at Athens, and it is in this period that we should place his meeting with Socrates. At least, by introducing into his Socratic dialogues characters who are known to have perished during the war, or under the tyranny of the Thirty, which followed, Xenophon implicitly claims to have known Socrates at this time.

Whether he did in fact associate with Socrates sufficiently, or understood enough of his master's teachings, to deserve to be called a disciple, has been questioned. He probably began to write his *Memorabilia*, or 'Recollections of Socrates', about a quarter of a century after Socrates was put to death, in 399 B.C., and continued working on them over a period of several years, and they no doubt embody ideas that he did not owe directly to his master. But in the indignant defence of Socrates against posthumous attacks with which they open we may see true traditions and the genuine memories of a former disciple, determined to show the world that 'Socrates was not at all like *that*, but like *this*'. As the *Memorabilia* developed (and also in his *Oeconomicus* and *Symposium*) Xenophon seems to have found in the 'Socratic dialogue' a convenient medium for expressing his own opinions, but we may suppose that, if he is not always remembering what Socrates actually said on a particular topic, he is still asking himself 'What would Socrates have said?'

Socrates's methods, as described by Xenophon, do bear at least a superficial resemblance to those shown in Plato's dialogues.

There are the same casual groups, usually including younger men, the same use of question and answer to draw out from the pupil what, afterwards, he seems really to have known already, and the same use of analogies drawn from everyday life and common crafts. But Xenophon does not show Plato's artistic skill in drawing the whole company into the conversation, and developing each man's individual character. Xenophon's dialogues in the *Memorabilia* are for the most part short discussions between Socrates and one other person, aimed at establishing a single point. Moreover Xenophon's Socrates is full of good plain commonsense advice on practical matters—household management, friendship, finance, leadership in war—and does not look deeply into the true nature of 'justice' or 'truth' in the abstract, though (*Memorabilia* iv. 6) he insists on the importance of accurate verbal definitions. In this Xenophon may be influenced by the teaching of Prodicus, whom Plato's Socrates teases more than once for his insistence on distinguishing precisely between words of similar meaning (*Menon* 75E; *Laches* 197B; *Euthydemus* 227E; *Protagoras* 337A–C and 340 A–B).

But though Xenophon may make a show of defining 'economy' (*Oeconomicus* I), it is merely a matter of determining the proper scope of this craft—for that it is a craft, like medicine or carpentry, is speedily agreed—and no metaphysical enquiry follows. It might appear that Xenophon had sometimes amused himself by hanging round the outskirts of a discussion, picking up something of the manner but not the matter. Plato's *Laches* begins with a discussion of the practical value, in actual warfare on the battlefield, of the newfangled art of fencing with shield and spear, and then develops into an examination of the nature of courage. At this point one might unkindly imagine Xenophon (had he been present) becoming bored and wandering off, having got what he came for—the opinion of two leading generals and Socrates, the famous veteran, on a practical military matter.

This is unfair to Xenophon, and perhaps misjudges the scope of Socrates's views on education. We can believe that he did seek out young men who showed signs of leadership and try to direct their studies for the future good of their country, even if they were clearly not interested in philosophy. His efforts were not always appreciated. Meletus, the youngest of Socrates's prosecutors, according to Xenophon, accused Socrates of making young men obey himself rather than their own fathers (Xenophon, *Apology* 20). The son of the senior prosecutor, Anytus, again according to Xenophon (ibid. 29–31), was one whom Socrates tried to improve against his father's wishes. 'After his condemnation, when Socrates was talking with his friends, the story is told that he saw Anytus passing, and said "This man is puffed up, as though he had achieved something great and honourable by my death. It is because I saw that his son was capable of the highest public employments and said that he should not bring him up as a tanner. He is a wicked man, and seems not to recognize that the one of us whose accomplishments prove more enduringly beneficial and honourable is the true victor. But Homer, among other authorities, establishes that some men at the point of death foresee the future, and I myself wish to make a prophecy. For I once associated briefly with the son of Anytus, and he seemed to me to be not without strength of soul. And so I say that he will not continue in the slavish profession that his father has arranged for him. But because he has no good instructor he will fall into some shameful desire and sink to the depths of wickedness." In this he was not mistaken, but the boy formed a taste for wine, drank night and day, and finally became worthless to his country, his friends and himself. And Anytus, through his son's bad upbringing and his own folly, is despised even now that he is dead.'

Whether this story really tells us anything about Socrates or not, it illustrates some of Xenophon's views on education, and the prejudice, which he shared with other Greeks who did not have to make their own livings, against servile trades. It does not seem to have occurred to him that an honest tanner may be more use to 'his country, his friends, and himself' than a discontented unemployed intellectual. Poor Anytus may, for his part, have believed that his son took to drink because his mind had been unsettled by the meddler who gave him ideas above his station.

For boys who did not have to be brought up to a trade, the

traditional education was now beginning to seem inadequate. 'Music', including the study of Homer and other approved poets, to develop the mind and morals, and 'gymnastic' for the body; the example and precepts of one's elders and betters—all these were no doubt very necessary for the future statesman and general. But they were not enough. Niceratus, son of the conservative Nicias, had, by his father's desire, learned the whole of the *Iliad* and *Odyssey* by heart, and claimed in consequence to be able to advise on all practical matters, from cooking to chariotry, by quoting appropriate tags of poetry. It was at once pointed out to him that to recommend onions as a relish with wine, though authorized by Homer, was not seasonable after-dinner advice, especially for a man who was going home to kiss his wife (*Symposium* 4.7ff.).[1]

Since technical knowledge was necessary to the future leader, he could evidently benefit from formal instruction in mathematics, tactics—the art of marshalling men in order of battle—and (even more important) rhetoric, the art of arranging words and arguments to persuade assemblies or juries, even if the speaker had a weak case and knew it. But the teaching of these skills was not yet regulated by formal academies, or by the state. The gymnasium had not yet become (as it became throughout the Greek world in the Hellenistic age) a state-regulated boys' high school, and higher education in the new arts, and in the philosophical speculation that went with them, was not entrusted to regular professors, but left to travelling experts, many of them evidently men of great ability in their fields, who charged high fees to private pupils whom they attracted, and undertook to furnish them with particular useful skills rather than to make them better men.

The moral emptiness of these teachers, and especially of their rhetoric, is strongly criticized by Plato. Xenophon characteristically finds fault with the failure of would-be orators (and by

[1] For Anytus's views on education, compare also Plato, *Menon* 89E–95A. The dramatic date of this dialogue must be well before Menon's joining Cyrus early in 401 B.C., and so more than the two years before the trial of Socrates. But we may suppose that Socrates's observation (90 B) that Anytus has succeeded in his own son's education is intended to be ironical.

implication, their teachers) to master practical matters. He tells a somewhat malicious story (*Memorabilia* iii. 6) about Plato's brother Glaucon, who wanted to be a political leader before he had reached his twentieth birthday. None of his friends could stop him from making himself ridiculous, except Socrates, who began with ironical congratulations upon the nobility of his aims. 'Of all human achievements this is the most honourable. Certainly, if you attain it, you will be able to realize your own ambitions, to assist your friends, to augment your father's house, and to enlarge your country. You will gain a reputation, first at Athens, then throughout Greece, and perhaps, like Themistocles, even among the barbarians. Wherever you may be, you will be admired by all eyes.' But Glaucon's complacency was soon dashed when Socrates continued by asking him to disclose the particular field in which he would benefit the state. Would it be in finance? Glaucon had no idea of the city's revenues, or of its expenditure. 'But, Socrates, one can enrich the state at its enemies' expense.' Here Socrates pointed out the necessity of understanding the state's own military resources, and those of possible enemies. 'Good heavens!' said Glaucon, 'I haven't got the information at the tip of my tongue.' 'Well, if you've got it written down,' said Socrates, 'bring it along. I would very much like to hear it.' 'But as a matter of fact,' said Glaucon, 'I haven't got it written down yet either.' Socrates allowed that a statesman at the outset of his career might not yet have mastered the whole field of major strategy. But how about such details as the siting and strength of the frontier posts? Had Glaucon ever inspected them himself, or how did he know that they were badly garrisoned? 'I conjecture that they are.' 'Well, on this point too we will give our advice when we stop conjecturing and know the facts.' 'Perhaps,' said Glaucon, 'that would be better.' So on other topics also. Glaucon had not visited the silver mines to see why their revenue had decreased. He had not calculated the quantity of home-grown grain and the necessary imports. Yet the knowledge of income and expenditure was the first essential in managing a single household. If the task of managing the city, which consisted of more than ten thousand households,[1] was too hard, could he not begin with a single household, namely his uncle's, and work up to more, if he proved capable? Glaucon said that he would help his uncle, if only he would be persuaded by him— drawing the reply that, if he could not persuade his uncle alone, how could he hope to persuade the entire body of the Athenians? And so Socrates closed the discussion by emphasizing the importance of knowledge as the foundation of a reputation in any field, including politics.[2]

But Socrates certainly did not intend his associates to withdraw from public affairs, if they were qualified to take part in them, as a conversation with Glaucon's cousin Charmides shows (*Memorabilia* iii. 7). An athlete who could have gained glory for his country but was unwilling to compete in the Olympic games was soft and cowardly; so also the man who was unwilling to use his qualifications as a statesman.

Nor was rhetoric, for all its insufficiency, to be neglected. Xenophon repeats (*Memorabilia* iii. 3) a conversation between Socrates and a newly-elected cavalry captain, which began with a discussion of practical matters, such as the elimination of unfit horses and the training of the men. The commander, to win the obedience of his men, was to inspire confidence in his leadership by showing himself superior in all aspects of horsemanship. But this in itself was not enough; he must also practise the arts of speech, unless he thought that he was to command his troop in silence. The lessons of the law, and all other honourable precepts, were verbal; the best teachers spoke best; and those who best understood important issues were most able to discuss them.

Nor (according to Xenophon) did Socrates try to keep his friends from the professionals. 'What was fitting for a gentleman to know, to the extent of his own knowledge, he used to teach with the greatest readiness. But for subjects with which he himself was comparatively ill acquainted, he sent his friends to the experts. And he used to teach them the extent to which a properly

---

[1] We have no accurate information on the actual population of Athens.

[2] cf. Plato, *Protagoras* 319B–323A. The people demand expert knowledge of their leaders and have no patience with those who waste their time with empty words.

educated man should be familiar with each subject'—geometry as far as was necessary to enable a man to measure land, for purchase or sale, distribution, or the allotment of work; astronomy, as far as was necessary for navigation, or the calculation of the night watches and of the seasons. With the more abstruse branches of both sciences he was himself familiar; but what was the use of them? A man might spend his life in them and be kept from much useful knowledge (*Memorabilia* iv. 7.1–5).[1] But the professionals did not escape his criticism. When Dionysodorus came to Athens, professing to teach the art of war (*Memorabilia* iii. 1), Socrates 'said to one of his associates, whom he perceived to be desirous of gaining this distinction in the city, "It would be a shame, my boy, for a man who wants to be a general to miss the opportunity of learning his business. Justice would require his punishment by the state, even more than that of a man who contracts to make statues without having learned the art of sculpture. For in the perils of war the whole city is entrusted to the general, and great consequences for good or evil follow upon his success or failure. So it is only just to punish a man who neglects to learn the art but puts himself forward for the office." ' Socrates's advice seems to be sincere enough, though somewhat ironically expressed and followed by some gentle teasing of the young man when he returned from his course in generalship. He returned with a more lordly bearing, like Homer's Agamemnon, and, just as a musician who did not play was still a musician, and a doctor who did not practise was still a doctor, so he was from henceforward to be considered a general whether he ever actually held the office or not. But Socrates also directed more serious criticism against the insufficiency of the course itself, which consisted only of 'tactics' (i.e. formation drill). The 'general' should be taught to recognize the best soldiers, who, like the tile roof and stone foundation of a mud-brick house, were to form the front and rear ranks, with the mediocre mass in between. He should learn not

---

[1] Is this Socrates in old age, disillusioned with the scientific studies of the 'Thinking Shop' that Aristophanes had ridiculed in the *Clouds* twenty years earlier, or Socrates regulating the studies of a pupil whose abilities he recognized to be practical, rather than theoretical?

merely formations, but how and where each was to be used. If Dionysodorus gave no instructions on these points he had not earned his fee properly.[1] (Socrates himself never took fees, and elsewhere (*Memorabilia* i. 6.5) Xenophon represents him as saying that 'those who take money must perform the task for which they are paid. But I am unpaid and so under no compulsion to converse with anyone unless I want to.')

From the evidence of the *Memorabilia*, we may suppose, then, that Xenophon in his twenties was at least on speaking terms with many of the political and military leaders of Athens, and that, in the intervals of active military duty, he was preparing himself to take his place among them, by paying for technical instruction in the necessary skills. At the same time, he was profiting by the criticism of Socrates, or at least by listening to the criticism that Socrates directed against others. (He only introduces himself by name once into these 'Recollections'—*Memorabilia* i. 3.8–15; a warning against beauty's kisses, which is repeated in *Symposium* 4.10ff.).

But is this evidence reliable? It may be that Xenophon's 'Socrates' has little to do with the real philosopher, and that the so-called 'Recollections' are not really recollections at all, but a device for making Xenophon's own views, based on his experiences as a soldier of fortune, a landowner in Southern Greece, and a confidant of Spartan kings, palatable to an Athenian public. One of the conversations reported (*Memorabilia* iii. 5), between Socrates and the younger Pericles (son of the great statesman: put to death in 406 B.C.), must have been composed with reference to the military situation following the Theban victory at Leuctra in 371 B.C., and, even if none of the other 'Recollections' contain such obvious anachronisms, we must allow that they were composed late in Xenophon's life, perhaps at different periods. Nor is it likely that they were based on written notes made in his youth. Even if he had taken any (and there is no evidence that he had

---

[1] Dionysodorus is also known to us through Plato's *Euthydemus*, in which it appears that Dionysodorus and Euthydemus (they were brothers) taught 'rhetoric' as well as 'tactics'. Euthydemus 'the Fair', of *Memorabilia* i. 2.29, iv. 2.1ff. and elsewhere, is a different person—a fashionable young Athenian. Xenophon repeats the points made here in *Cyropaedia* i. 6.12–15.

any thought of a literary career at this time), written notes would probably not have survived his later wanderings and adventures. The advice to the would-be general and newly-elected cavalry commander would come well from a distinguished retired soldier, and some of the points made about the training of cavalry are repeated in the *Hipparchicus*, a monograph on the duties of Athenian captains of horse composed in Xenophon's old age. What, we may ask, did the real Socrates know about training cavalry? But the points made in the *Memorabilia*—as that the horses should be adequately schooled and fed, and that the men should be taken out of the riding-school and made to exercise across country—are good common sense, that might have come from any old soldier. Moreover it seems that Xenophon did in fact draw in the *Hipparchicus* upon memories of his youth at Athens as well as upon his experiences in foreign service, because he gives advice on the conduct of the review and gallop-past at the Panathenaic procession, in which he had certainly not taken part since he was a young man. There may well be genuine memories of his youth in the *Memorabilia* too. It is, I think, no injury to the memory of Socrates to suppose that he may have benefited, and permanently impressed, many young men who were incapable of understanding metaphysics. A teacher at a great modern school will not hope to turn all his pupils into scholars, and may well be proud of those who distinguish themselves in other forms of service. These pupils' memories of their teacher will be incomplete, in that they fail to convey his quality as a scholar or original thinker, but they will give one side of his character which a description that concentrates on his scholarship may miss. I believe, then, that Xenophon was a pupil of Socrates, and was deeply moved throughout his life by his teacher's advice and example.

With Plato and his friends Xenophon evidently had very little to do. It has often been observed, by ancient as well as modern writers, that Plato and Xenophon have nothing to say about each other, and scholars of the Roman Imperial period deduced from this a hostile rivalry. But it is absurd to talk, as Aulus Gellius does (*Noctes Atticae* xiv. 3) of 'equality of like virtues' and 'the twin stars of Socratic charm'. Xenophon himself probably knew that he was not in the same class as Plato; at least, the one time that he does name him, he seems to acknowledge that Plato had a special place in Socrates's regard. In the account, already mentioned, of how Socrates dealt with Glaucon's political ambitions, Xenophon says (*Memorabilia* iii. 6.1) that Socrates bore kindly feelings toward Glaucon, 'for the sake of Charmides and Plato'. Of course, the story can be taken less generously, as an attempt to hit at Plato through his brother.

Of Xenophon's hatred and contempt for Menon of Pharsalus, after whom Plato named his dialogue *Menon*, we are left in no doubt. But Xenophon writes about the man when he was commanding a brigade of mercenaries under Cyrus, not when he was Plato's friend and Socrates's pupil. We may leave it open to doubt whether Xenophon (cf. especially *Anabasis* ii. 6.21ff.) was moved by spite against one who had been admitted to the inner Socratic circle from which he himself was excluded, or whether, more probably, Menon displayed on active service faults that he had kept hidden in Athenian intellectual society.

Plato himself never mentions Xenophon, though at the end of his life he allowed himself (*Laws* 694C; cf. Diogenes Laertius 3.34) a sidelong hit at Xenophon's *Cyropaedia*.

Antisthenes (cf. *Memorabilia* ii. 5.1; iii. 11.7; *Symposium* 3.7; 4.34ff.) was another associate of Socrates who certainly influenced Xenophon, though, as his writings have not survived, we cannot determine the extent of Xenophon's debt to them in his own Socratic books. Antisthenes was midway in age between Socrates and Xenophon, being born in about 455 B.C., and was later regarded as the first of the Cynics, though the sect was actually named after his pupil Diogenes.[1] His doctrine of self-sufficiency, that riches and poverty are found not in men's possessions but in their souls (cf. *Symposium* 4.34), is shared by Xenophon's Socrates, but this does not prove that the portrait is in fact drawn from Antisthenes. Temperance and fortitude we may suppose to have been a major part of Socrates's moral

---

[1] Not, of course, to be confused with Diogenes Laertius, the biographer, who lived five hundred years later.

teaching. It was, at least, a lesson that deeply impressed Xenophon, who emphasizes, in the defence of Socrates's character with which the *Memorabilia* open (i. 2.1–8), that, so far from corrupting young men, 'he was of all men the most continent as regards sexual pleasures and those of eating and drinking. Moreover he was best able to endure cold and heat and all bodily hardship, and so schooled in the moderation of his needs that, though his possessions were extremely small, he very easily had sufficient. How, when his own character was like this, could he have made others impious or law-breakers or luxurious or sexually incontinent or too soft to endure hardship?' We may suppose that Xenophon, like other rich and good-looking young men, sometimes over-indulged himself. His *Symposium*, written, he says, because 'not only the serious activities but the amusements of honourable gentlemen deserve to be recorded', shows that he enjoyed food, drink, and the homosexual love-affairs that were an accepted part of Athenian social life, and, as has already been said, he makes a personal appearance in his own *Memorabilia* only to receive a warning from Socrates in connection with this last subject, though not such a rebuke as is directed against Critias, who is accused of wanting to rub himself against his beloved Euthydemus like a pig scratching itself on a rock (*Memorabilia* i. 2.30). Diogenes Laertius (ii. 48–9) quotes 'Aristippus in the fourth book of his *Luxury of the Ancients*' on Xenophon's passion for Clinias. But the evidence is a quotation from Xenophon's *Symposium* (4.12) where the praise of Clinias is actually put into the mouth of Critobulus.

It seems unnecessary to follow those modern scholars who suppose that Xenophon is simply dressing up a dummy in Cynic rags, since the austerity of Socrates is confirmed by other testimony from his pupils and contemporaries.[1] To a young soldier, the stories of Socrates's endurance in the winter siege of Potidaea a generation earlier must have doubled the force of the philosopher's teaching (cf. Plato, *Symposium* 219B). And his austerity must have been the more impressive, because, unlike that of the

---

[1] Though the evidence of the *Clouds* of Aristophanes, produced while Xenophon was still a child, is perhaps not admissable in this case.

Cynics, it stopped short of bad manners. Though normally threadbare and barefooted, he could appear in a new cloak and sandals at a friend's dinner party (Plato, *Symposium* 174A). Xenophon's Socrates, too, could relax at a party, and confess to drinking his host's Thasian wine for enjoyment, not because he was thirsty (*Symposium* 4.41). Usually he ate no more than he could eat with appetite, and trained himself to regard hunger as the best sauce. All drink was pleasant to him, because he only drank when he was thirsty. 'Most people,' says Xenophon revealingly, 'when they are asked to dinner have their work cut out to guard against over-eating, but Socrates found it easy. He advised those who were unable to do this to be on their guard against dainties which enticed them to eat when they were not hungry and drink when they were not thirsty. He called these things the ruin of digestions, heads and souls'—and drew a useful moral from Circe's swine[1] (*Memorabilia* i. 3.5–8).

What were these delicacies against whose temptations Socrates warned his friends? Simple fare, by Roman standards, or even by our own. Dinner, for Xenophon, was divided into two parts, bread (coarse-ground wholemeal) and 'cooked food' (*opson*). Xenophon still uses the word *opson* at times (*Cyropaedia* ii. 2.1–5) in the old Homeric sense of roast meat. But the 'cooked food' was not, as it might have been to us, the principal part of the meal—in fact Xenophon records (*Memorabilia* iii. 14.2ff.) the rebuke delivered by Socrates to an acquaintance who neglected his bread and ate the *opson* only—sure proof that he was eating for the pleasure of eating, not to satisfy his hunger. *Opson* in fact included many 'relishes', which were intended to make the bread palatable. The bread was not simply their accompaniment; hence to try several relishes on a single piece of bread was a piece of greedy bad manners, besides being a denial of the art of the master-cooks, who knew which flavours should be combined and which kept separate.

---

[1]   'Who knows not Circe,
The daughter of the Sun, whose charmèd cup
Whoever tasted lost his upright shape,
And downward fell into a grovelling swine?'

But *opson* included, besides cooked meat and elaborate confections, the cress of the ideal Persian children in the *Cyropaedia* (i. 2.8)—a great restraint on greed, says Xenophon, is that they dine with the schoolmaster, and not with their mothers. Cheese and onions were proverbially the 'relish' of the soldier on active service (Plutarch, *Moralia* 349A; Aristophanes, *Peace* 1129). In Plato's *Republic* (372C), Socrates and Glaucon allow plain and wholesome relishes to the men of the primitive model city that they construct—salt, olives, cheese, onions and green vegetables, boiled together after the fashion of rustic cookery. This might be followed by a simple dessert—peas, beans, figs, myrtle-berries, and roasted acorns. Fish, Plutarch says in his *Convivial Questions* (*Moralia* 667F), eventually became the *opson par excellence*; but Xenophon does not expressly mention it, or the delightful meals by the sea shore which were one of the features of life in Greece in Roman times, as they are today.

We must not of course suppose that Socrates used to rebuke his fellow-guests across their host's dining-table. The setting of his lectures on manners seems to have been a sort of Socratic Club, meeting perhaps in a public eating-house, at which the diners were supplied with bread, and some frugal communal relish, but each also brought with him a further *opson*. Xenophon describes how Socrates checked greed and extravagance (*Memorabilia* iii. 14.1). 'Whenever some of those who met for dinner brought a small relish, and others a large one, Socrates used to tell the waiter either to add his small portion to the common stock or to share it among the diners. So those who had brought large portions were ashamed not to take a share of what was placed in the common stock, and not to add their own portion to it in return. So they added their own portions also to the common stock, and when they got no more than those who brought small contributions, they stopped spending large sums on delicacies.'

But of course virtue is not just a matter of good table manners, temperance and continence. We have already seen that Socrates condemned the athlete, or statesman, who did not put his good qualities to use. Effort was needed as well as abstinence. 'The labour we delight in physics pain', and Xenophon again makes

Socrates hold up as an example of voluntary endurance hunters, who bear hardships with pleasure in the hope of taking their quarry (*Memorabilia* ii. 1.18). He quotes Hesiod on the smooth and short way that leads to vice, and the steep ascent to virtue, and (*Memorabilia* ii. 1.21ff.) expands this in the fable, borrowed from Prodicus, of the Choice of Hercules. 'Of those things that are truly good and honourable, the gods have given none to mankind without toil and care.'

CHAPTER THREE

Religion and Politics

I. RELIGION

XENOPHON'S education in religion and politics, whatever it
may have owed to Socrates, was, like his moral instruction, not
complicated by abstract speculations. Throughout his life,
Xenophon remained the sort of conservative whose acceptance of
the doctrines and principles that he has inherited seems either
unintelligent, or dishonest, or both, to those who do not share
them. Xenophon repeatedly represents himself as sacrificing
before military operations, in order to determine, from the entrails of the victims, whether a projected operation would succeed
or fail. At least once (*Anabasis* vi. 4.12ff.) he repeatedly delayed
what seems to have been an absolutely necessary movement
because the sacrifices had not turned out well, and noted that
those who acted without waiting for the proper omens encountered misfortune, while after a favourable sacrifice was at length
vouchsafed everything went splendidly. The episode bears some
resemblance to one which he recounts of the campaign of 397 B.C.
in Asia Minor (*Hellenica* iii. 1.17) when the Spartan Dercylidas
lay inactive for four days outside the town of Cebron, 'much
against his will', for want of favourable omens. The Persian
satrap Pharnabazus was expected to appear at the head of a
relieving force, and the delay seemed inexcusable to the professional officers in Dercylidas's army, one of whom attempted
to act on his own initiative and was duly repulsed with loss. But,
sure enough, the omens changed in time, and, just as the be-
siegers were being led to the assault, the gates were flung open
and the governor surrendered, his hand forced by a mutiny of his
Greek mercenaries. One cannot help suspecting that Dercylidas

(nicknamed Sisyphus for his cunning) had been arranging the mutiny during the four days' delay, and used the 'omens' as an excuse to keep the soldiers quiet. But if so, did he really hoodwink Xenophon?

It is perhaps too easy to suppose that nobody can be sincere in professing belief in things which we do not believe ourselves, and the present tendency, even among writers not wholly unsympathetic to Xenophon, is to regard his religion as the vain repetition of empty formalities, at the best. At the worst, he is charged with dishonesty, not merely towards the gods but to his comrades in arms. It is more charitable to suppose that Xenophon's acceptance of the gods and religious practices of his ancestors was sincere, and at least one of his stories suggests a genuine, if uncritical, belief in the power of sacrifice. After the remnant of Cyrus's army had been transferred to the Spartan service, Xenophon was forced to sell his favourite horse to pay for his passage home. At this point he encountered a seer, Euclides of Phlius, who, after inspecting the entrails of a sacrifice that Xenophon had just made to Apollo, told him that to change his luck he must sacrifice, after the manner of his ancestors, to Zeus Meilichios,[1] whom he had neglected since leaving home. On the next day Xenophon followed this advice, and obtained good omens, which were immediately followed by the arrival of agents, who not only retained him in the Spartan service, but gave him back his horse and refused to take any of the fifty gold pieces that he had received for it (*Anabasis* vii. 8.1–6). Here, if anyone was being fooled, it was Xenophon himself, and the seer's motive, if he was deceiving, is not obvious. Xenophon can only have thought the story worth telling as an instance of the power of sacrifice, both to make the gods' will known and to turn aside their displeasure. It would seem that he really did believe in Zeus

---

[1] Zeus Meilichios ('Gracious Zeus') was worshipped with 'country offerings' outside the city by the whole people of Athens, at the Diasia, the greatest Athenian festival of Zeus (Thucydides i. 126). One of his altars still existed in the second century after Christ 'after the crossing of the Cephisus' (i.e. about 1½ miles from the Dipylon Gate) on the way to Eleusis (Pausanias i. 37.4, with Sir James Frazer's note). Besides being a protector of those who propitiated him with offerings, he was purifier in cases of guilt (cf. Pausanias, ii. 20.1).

Meilichios, and in Apollo, and in the other gods whom the city held lawful, but that his belief did not prompt him to speculate about their nature.

That the earth and its fulness, sun, moon and stars, day and night, and the changing seasons, had all been created by the gods for the express benefit of mankind, Xenophon makes Socrates affirm to the young scholar Euthydemus. The objection that not only man but the brute creation profited from these blessings was met by the assertion that the animals also were created for man's sake (*Memorabilia* iv. 3.2ff.). To prove the existence of the gods, Xenophon's Socrates relied upon the argument from design (*Memorabilia* i. 4.2ff.). Xenophon reports a dialogue that he heard on religious matters between him and Aristodemus, called 'the Little', who, as Socrates had learned, 'neither sacrificed to the gods nor used divination, but ridiculed those who did these things'. Socrates first asked whether Aristodemus admired any men for their wisdom, and received in reply the names of Homer, Melanippides the dithyrambic poet, Sophocles, Polyclitus the sculptor and Zeuxis the painter. He then asked whether those who made lifeless idols were more to be admired than the makers of intelligent and active living creatures. Aristodemus allowed the superiority of the latter, 'if, of course, they do not come about by mere chance but by design', and Socrates now drew from him the admission that things that plainly served some purpose were the work of design, and argued that eyes, ears, and the other parts of the body, each so evidently fitted to its purpose, 'were like the contrivances of some craftsman, wise and a lover of living creatures'. What of the natural instincts for child-rearing and self-preservation? These also looked like the contrivances of One who had purposed that living things should exist. But Aristodemus said that he could not see the heavenly powers, as he could see the craftsmen who created works of art. But, said Socrates, could he see his own soul, which controlled his body? By his argument, all his own actions were by chance, not by design. Socrates then dealt with other objections, as that the gods had no need of human worship, or that they took no thought for mankind. Aristodemus would believe that they cared for him when they sent him counsellors to advise him in his conduct, as Socrates said they did. But, replied Socrates, they made their will known by divination and portents to the Athenians, to all Greece, to all mankind. Why did Aristodemus regard himself as the sole exception? Did he not know that the oldest and wisest human institutions were also the most pious? Let him reflect that his own eyes could see for a great distance, and his own mind consider simultaneously the affairs of Sicily and Egypt. Why should not God's eye see, and his mind consider, everything? Let him make trial of the gods by worshipping them, and see if they did not repay him by advising him about the unseen.

'And to me,' concludes Xenophon, 'he seemed by saying this to make his associates refrain from impious, unjust and shameful conduct not only when they were seen by men, but when they were in solitude, since they thought that not one of their actions would ever be unseen by the gods.'

Though Xenophon believed that the gods watched over, rewarded and punished the actions of men in this life, he shows (unlike Plato) little concern for the possibility of life after death. Xenophon's Socrates (it must be remembered that Xenophon was not present at the trial, as Plato was) faces death after his condemnation with courage and cheerfulness, but looks forward to surviving through the permanence of his beneficial and honourable actions (*Apology* 29) rather than through his own continued existence. Men still sang the praises of Palamedes, the Greek hero who, like Socrates, had been unjustly condemned to death, with more honour than those of his judicial murderer, Ulysses. He would testify to Socrates's innocence—but before what ghostly judges Xenophon does not make clear. Xenophon considered that the fate of Socrates was a blessing from the gods, not because he was translated to paradise, but because he escaped the hardest part of life, did not outlive his own mental and physical powers, and enjoyed the easiest of deaths (*Apology* 26, 32; cf. *Memorabilia* iv. 8, where Xenophon gives as his source for Socrates's last days a certain Hermogenes, son of Hipponicus).

This need not mean that Xenophon rejected the conventional belief—supported by Homer, though even the Homeric tradition was inconsistent—in the immortality of the soul. But he seems to have given the matter little thought, until his own old age turned him to consider his latter end. In the *Cyropaedia* (viii. 7), Cyrus's peaceful death at a ripe old age[1] is carefully described. A super-human being appeared to him in a dream as he lay sleeping in his palace, and warned him to prepare to depart to the gods. On awakening, he realized that the end of his life was approaching, and sacrificed 'to Ancestral Zeus and the Sun and the other gods', for the accomplishment of many noble actions, and in thanks for their divine guidance. On his return home, he took to his bed, and after three days, during which he refused food, he sum-moned his sons and his friends to his bedside. In his dying speech he spoke of his own uninterrupted prosperity, which he had never dared to count complete until now, for fear it should be cut short (compare Solon's speech to Croesus: Herodotus i. 32); bequeathed his empire to his elder son Cambyses, and to the younger the rule of great provinces: advised them on their con-duct, and begged them to honour each other, if they had any thought of still pleasing him (*Cyropaedia* viii. 7.17ff.). 'For you do not, of course, suppose that you know clearly that I shall no longer exist, when I finish my human life. For you do not now see my soul, but from its achievements you infer its existence' (the same argument that Socrates had used to Aristodemus). 'Have you never perceived what terrors the souls of those who suffer unjustly inflict upon their murderers, or with what remorse they visit the ungodly? Do you think that the honours paid to the departed would persist, if their souls had no power over any of them? My sons, I have never yet been persuaded that the soul, as long as it is in the mortal body, lives, but when it departs from the body, it is dead. For I see that even mortal bodies, for as long as the soul is in them, are rendered alive by it.' (This seems to be a faint echo of the argument worked out in detail by Plato in the *Phaedo* (100Bff.) that the soul, being the vital principle, cannot admit death.) 'Nor' (continues Cyrus) 'have I been persuaded that

---

[1] Quite unhistorical: the real Cyrus fell fighting the nomads in Central Asia, though the picturesque details supplied by Herodotus (i. 205ff.) are no doubt embroideries.

the soul will become senseless, when it is separated from the senseless body, but that when the mind is set apart, unmixed and pure, then it will naturally be most rational. At a man's dissolution, each part of him can be seen to return to its like, except the soul. For it alone is seen neither when it is present not when it departs. And consider, that of all mortal activities none is closer to death than sleep. But the soul of man is then indeed revealed at its most divine, and then foresees something of the future. For then, it seems, it is most free. If, then, these matters are as I think, and the soul departs from the body, bear reverence to my soul also and do as I request.'

Xenophon does not make clear—no doubt he was not clear himself—where he supposed the soul would go. Cyrus was to prepare to depart to the gods, but no doubt he was a hero, a special case for whom no ordinary fate was reserved. What did Xenophon hope for himself? He mentions the Eleusinian Mysteries more than once in his history—the bold stroke by which Alcibiades led out the whole Athenian army in 407 B.C. and conducted the procession to Eleusis by land for the first time since the Spartan occupation of Decelea; the beautiful voice in which Cleocritus, the herald of the mysteries, called upon the Athenians to end their civil war; the speech in which Callias the torchbearer rebuked the Spartans for ravaging the land 'where Triptolemus our ancestor is said to have revealed to Hercules your leader, and the Dioscuri, your fellow-citizens, before all other strangers, the secret rites of Demeter and the Maiden, and to have given the seed of Demeter's harvest to the Peloponnese before all lands' (*Hellenica* i. 4.20; ii. 4.20–2; vi. 3.2–6). None of this proves, or even suggests, that he was himself an initiate, though we may be sure that he would have been careful, if he was one, to say nothing that might be construed as revealing the sacred mysteries.

Perhaps Xenophon's real hopes of immortality were those which Virtue holds out to Hercules as the reward of her followers (*Memorabilia* ii. 1.33). 'When their appointed end has come, they do not lie dishonoured in oblivion, but flourish in remembrance, and their praises are told for ever.'

'Only the actions of the just
Smell sweet, and blossom in the dust.'

II. POLITICS

Xenophon's political views were also based on 'sound' inherited
conservatism. There is a hint of up-to-date political theorizing in
Xenophon's characterization of Critias, 'in the oligarchy the most
ambitious and violent of all', and Alcibiades, 'in the democracy
the most incontinent and insolent of all' (*Memorabilia* i. 2.12).
But Xenophon, though he discusses the actual conduct of these
two men at some length, in order to clear Socrates from blame
for the misdeeds committed by his supposed former pupils, does
not develop the view that every different constitutional form
produces its own typical man, or attempt to characterize fully the
abstractions 'oligarchic' man and 'democratic man', as Plato does
in the *Republic*.

His political ideas reflect the inherited traditions and prejudices
of his class, rather than advanced critical theory. A century earlier,
the tyrants had been driven out of Athens and a new republican
constitution drawn up by Cleisthenes. Under this the landowning
class, consisting mostly of small farmers who worked their own
land and were able to equip themselves for service in the ranks of
the infantry, were politically and perhaps also numerically the
most important part of the citizens. Special privileges, including
the right to hold certain important offices and to serve in the
cavalry upon their own horses, were reserved to the proprietors
of larger estates,[1] among whom we may suppose Xenophon's
ancestors to have been included. It was a fundamental principle,

---

[1] The fourfold division of the citizens into 'property classes' is ascribed by
Aristotle (*Ath. Pol.* 7) to Solon, earlier in the sixth century B.C. It was retained by
Cleisthenes, but it is supposed by most modern scholars that it had been altered,
so that an income, or capital sum, expressed in money had been substituted for the
original qualification of land producing five hundred, three hundred or two hundred measures, 'wet' (oil or wine) or 'dry' (grain). It seems to me more probable
that the qualification was never altered, but that when a respectable burgess swore
that he belonged to the zeugite class nobody objected that his money came from
trade and not from land.

and one that Xenophon seems to have accepted without question, that political rights went hand in hand with obligation to serve the state in person and with one's property.

By the second half of the fifth century B.C., though the basic 'Constitution of Cleisthenes' had only been modified in details, affecting chiefly the powers and manner of election of the magistrates, the balance of political power had shifted from the countryside to the city, and in favour of the landless poor. This was, in large part, the result of the Persian Wars and the development of Athenian seapower. The poor man, who could not pay for his own shield and spear, was at least able to pull an oar in the wargalleys, and so had a vital part to play in the armed services. At the same time, by driving the Persians from the islands and the rich Greek cities on the coast of Asia Minor, the Athenians had built up an empire of dependent allies and acquired large revenues which could be devoted not only to the upkeep of the fleet, but to public works like the buildings on the Acropolis. This of course created employment for the craftsmen of the city—'smiths and carpenters, moulders, founders and braziers, stone-cutters, dyers, goldsmiths, ivory-workers, painters, embroiderers, turners'— together with the men who transported their goods—'merchants and mariners and ship-masters by sea, and by land, cartwrights, cattle-breeders, waggoners, rope-makers, flax-workers, shoe-makers and leather-dressers, road-makers, miners' (Plutarch, *Pericles* 12.6–7, in 'Dryden's' translation). This public works programme was continued, by the building of the Erechtheum, even in the later years of the war.

Pay for attendance at the assembly and for jury-service helped to support the poor, especially the elderly, who were not kept away from the courts by other employment. The dependent allied cities were even bound by treaty each to supply an ox for sacrifice at the Great Panathenaic festival, so that whoever wanted to might carry away the meat. In this way the Athenian poor were provided at the allies' expense with a meat meal, a luxury that most of them probably had few other opportunities to enjoy.

Among Xenophon's writings is preserved a so-called *Constitution of the Athenians*, a clever, bitter political pamphlet upon the dealings between the Athenian democracy and its allies. Xenophon was certainly not the author, if for no other reason, because this work must have been composed in his childhood, before the Athenian power was ruined by the disasters in Sicily, the Spartans established a fixed base in Attica, and the Athenian confederation began to break up, when the revolts of the allies could no longer be contained. But Xenophon, like, it would seem, most of the young men of his age and social background, was brought up in the doctrines which the unknown writer expresses. Democracy had gone too far; the respectable classes, who served the state in person and with their purses, must be restored to their rightful position. The grievances of the allies must be redressed (that is, their revenues must no longer be used to subsidize an Athenian welfare state).

The war with Sparta and the expansionist maritime and commercial policy that had precipitated it, by bringing Athens into conflict with Sparta's allies Corinth and Megara, were to be deplored for many reasons. The war ruined the farmers, whose olive trees were cut down and barley fields flattened by invading armies, and drove the population of the countryside into the town. Defeat cost the Athenians their overseas possessions. Xenophon must often have met impoverished gentlemen, like Eutherus (*Memorabilia* ii. 8.1ff.). He had lost his property abroad (many Athenians in the days of the city's greatness had been settled on the lands of allies who had been reduced to subjection after trying to secede from the Athenian confederacy). His father had left him nothing in Athens. He must now work as a labourer while his strength lasted, and look forward to a poverty-stricken old age. Critobulus, in the *Oeconomicus*, was still a rich man, with estates in Attica, but his expenses outran his income, especially as so many relatives—ladies too well brought-up to help support themselves—were left on his hands. Other Athenians put the best face they could on things, like Charmides (*Symposium* 4.29ff.). In the days of his prosperity, what with the fear of burglars and the reality of taxation, he had been no better than a slave. Now he had lost his foreign investments and could no longer cultivate his estates, and the fine furniture had been sold up, and he could sleep secure. Better than that, he no longer had to abase himself before popular leaders; it was his own turn to be feared and courted by the rich, who rose from their seats at his approach and stepped aside for him in the street.

The war—fought by Athens defensively on land, offensively at sea—increased the importance of the rowers on the benches and decreased that of the hoplites, close-ordered spearmen who made up the bulk of the army (though by this time this list of those able to equip themselves, and so liable, for hoplite service included not only yeomen, but craftsmen, like Socrates, a sculptor by trade, and resident aliens). The war destroyed the unity of the Greek world. Sparta and Athens should pull together as 'yoke-fellows', as they had done at the time of the Persian wars. Moreover the Spartan State, at least if one did not examine it too critically, embodied much of the aristocratic ideal. It stood for government by gentlemen, trained from childhood to set service above self-interest, not for mobs misguided by ambitious politicians. Of course, even in the heroic times of the Persian invasions there had been highly-placed Spartans who disgraced their upbringing, like the Regent Pausanias who would have betrayed Greece to gratify his ambition. But the Spartans had themselves punished these regrettable deviates. Again, it was true that, if civilization were to be judged by creative achievement in literature and the arts, Sparta stood very low. But even that could be turned into a virtue by determined admirers. If Sparta had no fine public buildings, at least the Spartans had not bedizened their city like a courtesan at their allies' expense (cf. Plutarch, *Pericles* 12.2 on the Athenian building programme).

When Sparta finally got the upper hand the reality proved to be very different from what her admirers had expected. But perhaps this also was the consequence of the war, and the Spartans of 431 B.C., slow to anger against Athens but bowing to necessity and the will of their allies, would have been shocked to find that the result of a generation's fighting was not a Greece secure under a system of aristocratic alliances but a network of petty tyrannies supported by the bullying strength of the Spartan army.

However illusory the vision of Sparta may have been, it was

shared by many of Xenophon's contemporaries,[1] and of course
any young man who displayed admiration for the Spartan system
was suspected by good democrats. But it was one thing to wear
one's hair long in the Spartan manner, quite another to betray
one's country (cf. Lysias xvi. 18—a speech composed shortly
after 394 B.C. for a young man of the cavalry class).

Unfortunately, while most of the upper classes were no doubt
honest patriots, some of the advocates for peace and constitutional reform were in fact ready to commit treason, as appeared
when an attempt was made in 411 B.C. to bring back the good old
days by 'restoring the laws of Draco and Solon', as the party
propagandists expressed it. The absence of the fleet, based on
Samos because the main theatre of operations was now the
eastern Aegean, allowed the 'reformers' to gain control of Athens
for a time, but they proved incapable of either conducting the war
or concluding a reasonable peace, and some of their leaders would
have betrayed the defences of the Piraeus to Sparta. The fleet
would not recognize the authority either of the Four Hundred who
were supposed to be drawing up the new roll of Five Thousand
fully-enfranchised citizens, or of the Five Thousand, even when
it was allowed by common consent after the collapse of the Four
Hundred that all who were qualified to serve as hoplites also
qualified for the assembly. The sailors, who had not abandoned
the struggle with Sparta to engage in civil war, had every reason
to feel that their own patriotic service was far more deserving.

Xenophon represents Socrates as sharing the view that privi-
lege should be the reward of service, though he is careful to give
the sentiment a democratic twist (*Memorabilia* i. 2.58–9). He says
that 'the accuser'[2] alleged that Socrates frequently quoted Homer's
description (*Iliad* ii. 188ff.), of how Odysseus restored order in
the Achaean assembly by courteously requesting the kings and

---

[1] Compare the half-humorous account of Spartan 'philosophy' in Plato,
Protagoras 343.

[2] 'The accuser' when Xenophon is answering is not so much one of the speakers
at the trial of Socrates as some writer who later attacked his memory, most
probably a certain Polycrates, who is known (Isocrates, *Busiris* 4–5) to have
attacked Socrates for teaching Alcibiades—one of the charges that Xenophon
(*Memorabilia* i. 2.12ff.) sets out to refute.

nobles to resume their seats, but striking the commons with his staff, and telling them to sit quiet and listen to their betters. 'For you are unwarlike and without valour, and count for nothing either in battle or in council.' Xenophon is careful to explain that Socrates was not urging his friends to strike the poor and the common people, for this would have amounted to acknowledging that he himself should be struck. 'But he meant that men who are useless in word and deed, who are incapable of giving assistance in time of need either to an army or to the city, or to the people itself, and especially if they add impudence to uselessness, are to be restrained by all means, even if they happen to be very rich.' Despite this last saving clause, we may suppose that it was usually the poor whom Xenophon and his friends regarded as 'useless', especially in the military sense. In the *Symposium* (2.11ff.) after a dancing-girl has given a display of somersaults into and out of a circle of sword-blades (Plate 3), Socrates calls out that the spectators will not now deny that courage can be taught,[1] since the performer, though a mere woman, has been trained to go so boldly among the sword-blades. This gives occasion for various remarks by the other members of the party, including a sneer by Philippus, a gate-crasher who makes his living by playing the buffoon at rich men's parties: 'I would like to see Pisander the demagogue taught to somersault among the swords, the man who refuses to join the army because he can't bear the sight of spear-points.'

To sum up, one cannot claim for Xenophon any profound moral or political insights. But piety, self-discipline and the ideal of service are not bad guides, and if Xenophon's own best service was not to be to Athens, the cause was not so much want of patriotism on his part as bad judgment and plain bad luck.

In passing, it is interesting that Xenophon and Isocrates ignore each other, though they both belonged to the deme of Erchia and must therefore have met (though Isocrates was about ten years older) at the religious and social meetings of its members, and probably also served in the same cavalry squadron (Pseudo-Plutarch, *Lives of the Ten Orators* 839B). Diogenes Laertius (ii. 55) does, however, say that Isocrates was one of the many who composed encomiums upon Xenophon's son Gryllus, who was killed at the battle of Mantinea in 362 B.C.

[1] On this question cf. *Memorabilia* iii. 9.1–3.

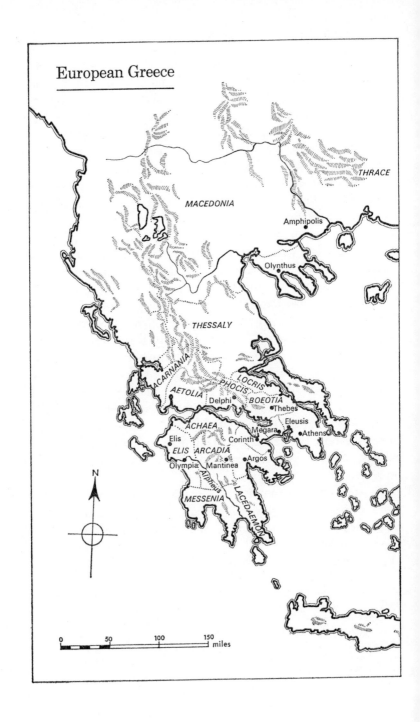

European Greece

THRACE

MACEDONIA

Amphipolis

Olynthus

THESSALY

ACARNANIA
LOCRIS
AETOLIA PHOCIS
Delphi BOEOTIA
Thebes
Eleusis
ACHAEA Megara
Elis Corinth Athens
ELIS ARCADIA
Olympia Mantinea Argos
Alpheus
LACEDAEMON
MESSENIA

N

0   50   100   150
                                miles

CHAPTER FOUR

The Counter-Revolution
at Athens

THE destruction of the Athenian fleet at Aegospotami in 405 B.C., and the surrender of Athens to Lysander next year, led to a second and far more violent attempt to overthrow the democracy. Xenophon gives us in his 'History of Greece' (*Hellenica* ii. 3–4) a detailed narrative of the subsequent events, which tells us indirectly a great deal about his own beliefs and prejudices. It shows how he and others like him were inevitably drawn to take the wrong side, and how they gradually came to recognize that they were in the wrong, without being able to change. He does not mention himself once by name, but no doubt his own personal actions were unimportant. It should be remembered that he was still in his early twenties. He was only one among hundreds who behaved in the same way and obviously history could not record each of them individually. He does not disguise the side from which he is writing, and the assumption that he does not mention himself because he wishes to conceal the part he played is unjust. Nor does he mention Socrates at this point in his history, though he describes his honourable confrontation with the tyrants and refusal to join in shedding innocent blood at some length in the *Memorabilia* (i. 2.29–38; iv. 4.3).[1] This again seems to be because Socrates's behaviour, though most creditable to himself, and therefore to be recorded in a work whose object

---

[1] Socrates had been ordered to arrest Leon of Salamis, one of the men whom the tyrants had marked for death in order to seize their riches, and refused (Diogenes Laertius ii. 24). Socrates did not save Leon; Xenophon (*Hellenica* ii. 3.39) makes Theramenes refer to his death in his defence before the Council—but without mentioning Socrates. The killing was notorious; cf. Andocides, *De Mysteriis* 94.

was, in part, to clear his name, did not influence the main course of events. It is not necessary to suppose that Xenophon did not learn of Socrates's conduct until after the second book of the *Hellenica* had been written and published, and that this proves that he did not really know Socrates at all but picked up scraps of 'Socratic' gossip to help out his own invention.[1] Similarly, Xenophon mentions only briefly in the *Hellenica* (i. 7.15) Socrates's equally honourable conduct as a member of the Council (and therefore a public figure, though his behaviour only affected the course of events slightly) in 406 B.C., but gives extra details in the *Memorabilia* (i. 1.8; iv. 4.2). And in his *Life of Agesilaus* Xenophon gives details which he omits from the *Hellenica*, to illustrate the King's character.

In the *Hellenica*, then, Xenophon describes how Athens was starved into surrender by the Spartan army under King Agis and fleet under Lysander. The fortifications of the Piraeus and the Long Walls that connected it to the city were demolished, and the people elected thirty commissioners 'to compile the laws of their ancestors, under which they would be constitutionally governed'. Agis then withdrew his army, and Lysander sailed to Samos to crush the last resistance against Sparta (*Hellenica* iii. 1.3). Xenophon does not suggest that the Thirty were elected under compulsion, probably because he and his friends in fact voted freely for a measure that they honestly believed would lead to necessary reforms. There must have been at this time a large number ready to believe that democracy had proved a failure, even if we allow that the majority of Athenian citizens did not share this view. Diodorus Siculus gives a different version.[2] He

---

[1] In the same way it is not necessary to suppose (as does Athenaeus, v. 215cff.) that, because Thucydides does not mention Socrates's fortitude at Potidaea, or his courage at Delium, which did not change the issue of the battle, Plato must have made these stories up.

[2] Diodorus, who wrote in the time of Augustus, used, generally in preference to Xenophon, other fourth-century historians now lost. The most important of these was Ephorus of Cyme, whose history covered the period from the Return of the Heraclids, three generations after the Trojan War, to the siege of Perinthus in 341 B.C. Ephorus (born *c.* 405 B.C.) obviously had no first-hand knowledge of the Thirty Tyrants. He may in his turn have used the unknown historian of whom a considerable fragment, now known as the *Hellenica Oxyrhynchia*, was found on a

says (xiv. 3.4–4.1) that the election was forced by Lysander and the Spartan fleet, over the opposition of the moderate politician Theramenes, who claimed that the terms of the peace granted to the Athenians their ancient constitution. Lysander terrified the opposition by replying that the Athenians had already violated the peace by failing to demolish their fortifications before the date stipulated. But this account is distorted, at least as regards the part played by Theramenes himself. After he quarrelled with the other leaders of the Thirty and was put to death by them, he was pictured as a man of the people and a martyr. But in 411 B.C. he had shown himself in favour of limiting the franchise, and his election to the Thirty was probably not merely a device to reassure the people.

The Thirty, once elected, 'kept putting off the compilation and publication' of the constitution, and in the meantime 'arranged the Council and other offices to suit themselves'. Here (*Hellenica* ii. 3.11) Xenophon betrays inexperience of committee work, if he and his friends really expected the whole business to be settled in a few days. Clearly what they were looking for was a republican constitution with the franchise strictly limited to property owners, and in the meantime they did not object when 'first of all those who were commonly known to have made their living by laying false information under the democracy, and who bore hard on the gentry, were arrested and put to death. The Council voted gladly to condemn them, and all those who were conscious that they themselves were not like that were by no means displeased.' This is at least an honest self-revelation. It must be remembered that Xenophon and his contemporaries were a 'post-war genera-tion', hardened to violent death. They had seen, or knew from the first-hand report of their elders, atrocities and judicial murders authorized by popular vote,[1] and no doubt felt that in the present

---

papyrus from Egypt. The surviving fragment deals with the years 396–395 B.C., but the unknown probably, like Xenophon, began his work where Thucydides left off. (A fragment of papyrus in Florence, probably from the same work, describes Lysander's victory at Notium in 406 B.C.) On Theramenes, cf. also Lysias xii. 62–80.

[1] The execution of the six generals after the Battle of Arginusae in 406 B.C. (*Hellenica* i. 7) impressed Xenophon himself deeply. The professional informers

crisis, since the old laws were suspended and the new were still pending, the provisional government was justified in dealing summarily with notorious offenders.

But the Thirty now persuaded Lysander to send a garrison from Sparta—not of course, citizen regiments, but 'Laconians', helots enfranchised and enlisted for military service. Matters began to wear a different face when, with the help of the garrison commander, they began to arrest, 'not as hitherto wicked and worthless men', but probable opponents. This policy led to a split in the leadership of the Thirty themselves, between the extremist adventurer Critias and the moderate, but not wholly trustworthy, Theremenes. Theramenes objected to killing men merely because they were honoured by the people, if they had done no harm to the gentlemen ('the honourable[1] and good', the stock phrase used by the oligarchic party for men of their own political views and social position). He and Critias had both in the past acted and spoken to please the people. But Critias replied that it was inconsistent for men ambitious for power to refrain from putting out of the way their most able opponents. It was foolish to suppose that their government was not to be maintained by tyrannical methods because it was headed by thirty men, not one. The killings continued, and 'when many were being unjustly put to death, many were plainly coming together and wondering what the constitution would be'. Xenophon himself and his friends, who were not, of course, in the inner councils of the Thirty, were evidently beginning to feel doubts. Hitherto, they had genuinely believed it their patriotic duty to support the lawfully elected commission that was going to introduce a fairer system of government.

The publication of a list of three thousand, 'who were

(sycophants) had been troublesome since the beginning of the war (e.g. Aristophanes, *Acharnians* 818ff.), though it seems (*Hellenica* ii. 3.22) that they could often be bought off. Citizens of the allied states were also in danger of the Athenian law (cf. Antiphon, *On the Murder of Herodes*), quite apart from the large-scale massacres at Mitylene and Melos that had been voted by the people.

[1] *Kalos*, the word translated 'honourable' is often used simply of physical beauty. But the notoriously ugly Socrates is included (e.g. *Symposium* 1.1) in the number of *Kaloi Kagathoi*.

supposedly to share in public business', no doubt helped to reassure those who were chosen, though Theramenes, who perhaps
looked for a wider franchise, complained that the number had no
special property to ensure that none but the 'honourable and good'
would be included, and none but the 'base' left out. His further
objection, that they were inconsistently attempting to govern by
force while reducing the strength of the ruling class below that of
the ruled, was met by disarming all the citizens except the Three
Thousand, with the help of the Laconian garrison. But this
garrison had to be paid, and Critias's suggestion that the Thirty
should find the money by each choosing rich resident aliens to
kill[1] led to a final breach with Theramenes, who was now openly
accused by Critias in front of the Council. Here he would have
saved himself by an able defence, but Critias could not afford the
escape of a victim (*Hellenica* ii. 3.50–6). 'At the conclusion of his
speech, the Council was visibly moved in his favour. Critias
realized that if he allowed them to divide on Theramenes's case
he would be acquitted, and considered that this would be fatal to
himself. So he approached the Thirty, and after a few words went
out, and ordered the men with daggers' (young ruffians with concealed weapons whom he had placed in readiness in case the
situation took its present turn) 'to station themselves at the bar
of the House in full sight of the Council. He then re-entered, and
said: "I consider, members of the Council, that it is the work of a
proper political leader, when he sees that his friends are being
deceived, not to permit it. I shall therefore act accordingly. Furthermore, these bystanders say that they will not permit us to
dismiss a man who is evidently injuring the oligarchy. It is laid
down in the new constitution that no member of the Three
Thousand shall be put to death except by your vote, but that
those who are not on the roll may be condemned by the Thirty.
Very well; I hereby strike the name of Theramenes from the roll,
by our unanimous consent, and we condemn him to death." On
hearing this, Theramenes sprang to the sacred hearth with the
words: "I implore you, gentlemen, in the name of all that's

---

[1] Lysias the orator (*Against Eratosthenes* xii), gives a first-hand account of his
own narrow escape and the murder of his brother.

lawful, not to leave it to Critias to strike out my name, or the name of any one of you whom he wishes. They have written the law upon enrolled citizens; by it let you and me alike be judged. Heaven be my witness, that I know that not even this altar will protect me, but I wish to show that they are not only most unjust in their dealings with men but most impious towards the gods. But I am amazed, right honourable gentlemen, that you do not act to save yourselves. You must be well aware your own names can be struck out as easily as mine."

'Thereupon the herald of the Thirty summoned the Eleven' (the officials responsible for executions) 'against Theramenes. When they entered with their agents, led by Satyrus, a man of unmatched boldness and shamelessness, Critias said: "We commit to you this man, Theramenes, condemned according to law. Members of the Eleven, arrest him, lead him to the place appointed, and do your duty." After these words, Satyrus began to drag him from the altar, and the agents assisted him. Theramenes of course called upon gods and men to witness these deeds, but the Council kept still, seeing at the bar men of the same character as Satyrus, and the space in front of the Council Chamber full of mercenaries. And they were well aware that they had their daggers with them. So the Eleven led the man away through the market place, while he proclaimed his wrongs at the top of his voice.[1] The following saying is reported of him. When Satyrus said that he would suffer for it if he did not keep quiet, he asked "And if I do keep quiet, shall I not suffer?" And when he was compelled to die and drank the hemlock, they say that he tossed out the dregs with a toast to "the fair Critias". I am well aware that these sayings are not worth mentioning, but I judge that it was remarkable in the man, when death was upon him, to lose neither his presence of mind nor his wit.'

After this of course there were no more illusions about the nature of the regime. But Xenophon's narrative shows how he

---

[1] Diodorus Siculus (xiv. 5.1) says that Socrates and two friends ran forward to intervene, but Theramenes told them to hold back. This is probably an invention intended to show Socrates as a good Democrat and Theramenes as a good Socratic.

and other decent men were forced to countenance actions which evidently horrified and shamed them. The democratic reaction that Theramenes had expected was hurried on by new confiscations (*Hellenica* ii. 4.1ff.), the victims this time being the smaller landowners. The Thirty first banned from Athens itself all who were not on the roll of the Three Thousand, then drove them from their villages, in order to seize their farms for themselves and their friends. The dispossessed gathered in the Piraeus, and when many of them were again harried away, escaped over the borders to Megara and Thebes.

Thebes was the base from which Thrasybulus, a distinguished soldier and democratic statesman, set out in the winter of 404–3 B.C. with about seventy men to overturn the tyrants.[1] The small fort of Phyle, under Mount Parnes, had evidently been left unguarded, and Thrasybulus seized it, probably intending to use it as a base for guerrilla warfare. The Thirty immediately marched out from the city 'with the Three Thousand and the cavalry' (presumably this means 'the Three Thousand, including the cavalry'; it would appear that the entire body of cavalry, on paper a thousand strong, was enrolled in the Three Thousand, while the rest served as hoplites). Now followed what was later (*Hellenica* ii. 4.14) remembered as a divine judgment. The weather was extremely fine, but when the Thirty and their supporters, whose first rash attacks had been beaten back with loss, encamped for the night, a sudden heavy snowfall came down and continued all next day. The storm drove them back to the city, frustrating their plans of throwing a wall round Phyle and starving the defenders out, and on their retreat Thrasybulus and his men captured many of the baggage animals.

The tyrants now determined to send the greater part of their

---

[1] Diodorus Siculus (xiv. 32–3) misplaces the overthrow of the Thirty, putting it in 401 B.C., after the expedition of the Ten Thousand. His main source (Ephorus?) is at this point inferior to Xenophon, especially in its account of military operations. Lacking Xenophon's eyewitness authority, it gives quite a different version (Diodorus xiv. 33.1) of Thrasybulus's surprise of the tyrants' forces, and it seems to have turned the fight at Munychia into a protracted set-piece. By adding this to Xenophon's account of a single sharp onslaught by the democrats, Diodorus (xiv. 33.3–4) makes two battles out of one.

Laconian garrison, together with two of the ten tribal squadrons
of Athenian cavalry, to encamp about a mile and a half from
Phyle and contain the democrats. They were afraid of raids on the
countryside, and had evidently quite underestimated the speed
with which the exiles would rally. Thrasybulus had already been
joined by some seven hundred men, and resolved upon a surprise
attack, which was favoured by the fact that the enemy were encamped among scrub and woods. Xenophon's account reads like
that of an eyewitness; at least it seems certain that if his own tribe
was not one of the two that took part in the affair he heard first-
hand accounts immediately afterwards.

Thrasybulus and his men came down under cover of night,
grounded arms some five or six hundred yards from the enemy,
and lay quiet. 'As the day was breaking, and the men had separately left their arms for necessary purposes, and the grooms were
making a bustle in currying the horses, Thrasybulus's men
picked up their arms and fell upon the enemy at the double. Some
of them they struck down, and they routed the whole force and
pursued it six or seven stades' (over half a mile). 'They killed more
than a hundred and twenty of the hoplites, and, of the cavalry,
Nicostratus who was nicknamed "the Fair" and two others, surprising them still in their bivouacs. Then they fell back again, and,
after setting up a trophy and collecting the weapons and equipment that they had taken, went back to Phyle. When the cavalry
from the city came to support their friends, they found none of
the enemy still in the field. So they waited until the relatives of
the dead had taken up the corpses, and returned to the city.'

Critias now resolved to secure a fortified refuge conveniently
placed to receive help from Sparta, and at the same time to involve
the members of the cavalry personally in the guilt of the Thirty.
He therefore led them to Eleusis, where he arranged a review of
the inhabitants, on the pretext of seeing what extra garrison the
place required. 'As each man was marked off on the muster roll,
he was ordered to leave through the postern leading to the sea.
But on the beach they had drawn up the cavalry on either side,
and as each man came out the agents bound him. When they had
all been taken, Lysimachus, the commander of the cavalry, was

ordered to commit them to the custody of the Eleven. On the next day the Thirty summoned to the Odeum the hoplites on the roll' (of the Three Thousand) 'and the rest of the cavalry. Critias rose and spoke as follows: "Gentlemen, we are establishing the constitution for you, no less than for ourselves. Accordingly, as you will share in the rewards, you must also share the dangers. A verdict of Guilty is to be brought in against the arrested Eleusinians, so that you may share our own hopes and fears." He then pointed out a place in which they were to give their votes openly. And in the other half of the Odeum were the Laconian garrison, drawn up under arms. These measures also won approval even among the citizens, those of them who were only interested in their own ambitions.'

Xenophon does not expressly draw attention to his change in attitude since the election of the Thirty and the first killings which had been approved not only by the ambitious and greedy but by 'all those who were conscious' of their own moral superiority to the victims. But it would appear that he was among those who now voted under compulsion, and that he was thoroughly ashamed. One would gladly suppose that he found some means of changing sides, as 'about seventy' of the cavalry did shortly afterwards (*Hellenica* ii. 4.25). But his story (*Hellenica* ii. 4.10ff.) still contains details suggesting first-hand observation from the tyrants' side, and it seems likely that he stood by them to the end.

The tyrants' party must by now have been thoroughly demoralized, and Thrasybulus, with forces grown to about a thousand men, was able to gain the Piraeus by a night march. Critias and his friends still had a great advantage in numbers, and even greater in armament, and marched down to the attack. The democrats did not attempt to defend the whole unfortified circuit, but concentrated at Munychia, where they could only be attacked uphill on a narrow front. Those of them who had proper equipment were drawn up in front, ten deep; they were supported by a crowd of missile-throwers, some with improvised shields and light javelins, some only with stones. The tyrants massed their men fifty deep, with their mercenaries on the right, and themselves on the left, 'so as to fill the road that leads to the temple of

Munychian Artemis and the sanctuary of Bendis', but did not lead them up the road to attack the democrats' position.

The two armies paused, facing each other. Thrasybulus ordered his men to lay down their shields, laid down his own, and coming out in front of the ranks, turned towards his own men. Xenophon's account reads as though he was watching, but we must regretfully suppose, from the wrong side. In a short and effective speech (*Hellenica* ii. 4.13–17) Thrasybulus encouraged his men with hopes of success, reminded them that this fight, 'if God will, will restore to us our country, our homes, freedom, honour, and children, to those who are parents, and wives', and added that happy were even those who might fall, for no man, however rich, could buy as fair a monument as theirs. He would himself give the signal for the attack by beginning the paean.

'After this speech he turned about towards the enemy and remained silent. Moreover the prophet told them not to fall on, before one of their own side was either killed or wounded. "But when this happens," he said, "we will lead ourselves, and to you who follow will come victory, but to me myself death, at least as I see it." Nor did he speak falsely, but when they took up their shields, he himself, as though some fate led him on, leaped out of the ranks and charged foremost against the enemy, and was killed, and lies buried at the crossing of the Cephisus. But the others were victorious, and pursued as far as the level ground. In this fight were killed Critias and Hippomachus, of the Thirty, and of the ten governors in the Piraeus, Charmides, son of Glaucon, and of the rest about seventy. The victors took up the weapons of the dead, but did not strip a single citizen of his tunic. Afterwards the bodies were returned under truce, and many men approached each other and conversed. But Cleocritus, the herald of the mysteries, who had a very fine voice, called them to silence, and said: "Fellow-citizens, why do you drive us out? Why do you want to kill us? We have never done you any wrong in the past. We have participated with you in the most sacred rites and sacrifices, and in the fairest festivals. We have joined you in choruses, and been your schoolmates, and your fellow soldiers, and with you we have encountered many dangers by land and by sea for the common safety and freedom of both you and us. By the gods and goddesses of our ancestors, by our kinship and ties of obligation and association, by all that many of us hold in common, in reverence for gods and respect for men, cease from these sins against our country. Do not obey the unholy Thirty, who for their private ends have in eight months killed more of the Athenians, almost, than did all the Peloponnesians in ten years of war. We might have enjoyed our city in peace, but these men are involving us in civil war—a war that is most grievous and unholy and hateful to gods and men. But know well that, of those whom we have now slain, there are some who are greatly lamented, not by you alone, but by ourselves."

'Such were his words. But the surviving magistrates' (members of the Thirty), 'partly because their supporters were paying attention to such speeches, led them off to the city' (*Hellenica* ii. 4.18–22).

Xenophon seems to have gone with them, for his story continues to be written from the side of 'those in the city', not 'those in the Piraeus'. 'On the next day the Thirty, utterly despondent and bereft of hope, held a session in their meeting place. But, wherever the members of the Three Thousand were posted, everywhere they differed among themselves. Those who had committed some exceptional outrage, and were afraid, declared emphatically that they should not submit to the party in the Piraeus. But those who were confident that they had committed no crime themselves reckoned, and told the others, that there was no need for these miseries, and said that they should not obey the Thirty or allow them to ruin the city. Finally, they voted to depose them, and choose other magistrates. And they elected ten, one from each tribe. So the Thirty went off to Eleusis. But the Ten, seeing that the men in the city were in a state of confusion and mutual distrust, consulted with the cavalry commanders. And the cavalry slept out in the Odeum, having their horses and their shields' (for service on foot) 'with them. And in their mistrust they patrolled, after sunset on the walls with their shields, and at dawn with their horses, always fearing that some of the Piraeus party would fall upon them' (*Hellenica* ii. 2.23–8). The Piraeus party meanwhile were improvising shields of wood and wicker-work, whitened to distinguish them from the enemy, and were soon strong enough to make sorties to gather fruit and firewood. From the city only the cavalry dared come out against them, and Lysimachus was responsible for one more outrage when he butchered some farmers, taken on their own land, searching for provisions, 'though they made many entreaties for mercy, and many of the cavalry took it hard'. If Xenophon was one of these, our own age has seen enough men pleading the orders of higher authority as a reason for acting against their moral convictions to understand, if not to excuse, his conduct.

The democrats felt strong enough to kill, in reprisal, a cavalry-man whom they took on his estate, and were even planning to attack the walls. Xenophon notes (with his characteristic eye for practical examples and military stratagems) that the engineer in the city ordered all the draught teams to bring stones large enough to load a waggon (a much smaller waggon than those of modern times) and to throw them down wherever each teamster chose in the road by which the attack was expected. But it was never delivered. The city party turned again to Sparta for help, but, though Lysander showed himself ready to crush the demo-crats by force, the King Pausanias intervened. Pausanias was prepared to use Spartan arms to hold the democrats in check, but he showed himself favourably disposed to them, even after they had killed a number of Spartans, including two senior officers, during a reconnaissance in force, and compelled him to fight and win a regular battle to restore Spartan prestige. Through his mediation, the Athenian parties were reconciled on good terms; every man was to enjoy his own again, except the Thirty and the Eleven and the Ten who had governed the Piraeus. Those of the city party who feared the democrats might withdraw to Eleusis. Then, when the Spartan army had retired, 'the men from the Piraeus went up under arms into the Acropolis and sacrificed to Athena. After they had come down, the generals called an assembly, and Thrasybulus spoke: "Men of the city party, I advise you to know yourselves. And you may know yourselves best, if you reckon upon what grounds you think yourselves superior, so as to attempt to rule over us. Are you just? Though the people are poorer than you, they have never once done you any wrong for the sake of your money. But you, though you are richer than all of us, have committed many atrocities for gain. Since you have no claim to justice, consider whether you are to claim superiority in valour. What fairer proof of this could there be than the issue of the war that we fought against each other? Would you in reason claim to have the advantage, you who had a fortress and weapons and money and Peloponnesian allies, and were overcome by men who had none of these assets? Are you, then, to claim superiority by reason of your Spartan friends? How can this be, when, like men who muzzle biting curs before handing them over, they have handed you over to the people whom you have wronged, and taken themselves off? But I do not expect from you, gentlemen of the democratic party, any breach whatsoever of the oaths that you have sworn. On the contrary, I expect you to display, in addition to your other noble qualities, respect for your oaths and for your religion." After saying this and more in the same strain, he added that there was no occasion for disturbance, but that they should observe the old laws' (that is, of the democratic constitution), 'and so dismissed the assembly. And then they appointed magistrates and were constitutionally governed' (*Hellenica* ii. 4.39–42).

We need not doubt that this represents the substance of what Thrasybulus actually said. His words sank in because they did in fact sum up the moral, economic and military standards by which the oligarchic party would have liked to claim superiority, and the consciousness of its members that they had fallen short in every way. This is not the attempt of a defeated aristocrat to write himself into the favour of the victors by debasing himself in front of them, and at the same time to remind them that they had promised to spare him. For that, at least, there was no need. Xenophon rounds off his account of the Thirty Tyrants as follows (*Hellenica* ii. 4.43):

'At a later period they heard that the men at Eleusis were hiring mercenaries, and marched against them with the whole citizen body. When the generals of their opponents came out to parley, they killed them. But they sent in to the remainder their friends and relatives, and so persuaded them to a reconciliation, and swore solemn oaths that they would not harbour old grudges. And to this very day they share the government of the city, and the people abides by its oaths.'

CHAPTER FIVE

Xenophon's Early Historical Work

'THE people abode by its oaths', but to Xenophon it very probably seemed that all prospect of high elective office was at an end. This was not in fact so. In a speech delivered some time after 394 B.C. (Lysias xvi. 8) the speaker, though he is careful to prove that he himself had not served in the cavalry under the Thirty, is able to show that many who had served had since been chosen for the Council, or had been elected generals and cavalry commanders. But in 403 B.C. Xenophon may have felt that the career for which he had trained himself was over before it had started.

The *Hellenica* break off after the restoration of the democracy, and pick up the thread again four years later with the outbreak of war in Asia between Sparta and Persia after the suppression of Cyrus's revolt. The story of that revolt and its aftermath is related in the *Anabasis*, but Xenophon tells us nothing about what he was doing between 403 B.C. and 401 B.C., when he attached himself to Cyrus. No doubt, during that time he 'enjoyed his own' at Athens in reasonable comfort, and possibly it was now that he began to write history. Diogenes Laertius (ii. 57) says that 'the books of Thucydides were lying unpublished, and he brought them into esteem, when he could have taken the credit for himself'. We have no supporting evidence for this statement, except the bare fact that Thucydides died with his histories unfinished, breaking off in the middle of a paragraph, and that Xenophon (as did other writers) began where he ended. We do not know when Thucydides died, only (on his own evidence—Thucydides v. 26) that he lived to see the end of the Peloponnesian War. We do not know for certain where he died; most

probably Athens; at all events he outlived the sentence of twenty
years' exile that had been imposed upon him for losing Amphipolis in 424 B.C. If he died before 401 B.C., and Xenophon knew
of his unfinished work, the first two books of the *Hellenica* might
have been written at this time, which would explain the imme-
diacy of personal recollection shown in the account of the Thirty.

But Xenophon's account of the last years of the war (*Hellenica*
i–ii. 2) is less detailed, less straightforward, and in places inaccurate. It reads as though the author were drawing upon his
memory, and the memories of others, years later; not as though
he had taken notes while events were still fresh in his mind.
Xenophon himself presumably had no reason for note-taking, and
if, as is sometimes suggested, he was working from Thucydides's
notes, they must have been neither full nor accurate. In fact, there
is no evidence that he inherited anything of the kind, and the
internal evidence certainly suggests that Xenophon did not know
how Thucydides intended to develop his narrative. Thucydides's
History breaks off with an account of how the Persian satrap
Tissaphernes quarrelled with the Spartans, with whom he was
supposed to be co-operating, and, on his way to a conference
with them, came to Ephesus and sacrificed to Artemis. Xenophon
does not continue the story, but begins: 'After this, a few days
later, Thymochares came from Athens with a few ships.' Came
where? Not to Ephesus, where Thucydides leaves the reader, but
to the Hellespont. Tissaphernes makes his appearance at *Hellenica*
i. 1–9—but we hear nothing of the intended conference, only of
his dealings with the Athenian Alcibiades, though some of the
Spartans' grounds of complaint are mentioned at i. 1.31. It would
seem that (unless we accept the desperate suggestion that the real
opening of the *Hellenica* is lost) Xenophon had no notion of what
Thucydides was going to write next, but, having determined to
provide a continuation, simply set down the next incident that
he had been able to discover, with the imprecise 'after this' to
serve as a link.

Moreover, it has been doubted whether all the incidents that
Xenophon introduces in this way did in fact take place 'after this'.
Thucydides (viii. 80) describes how Clearchus, son of Ramphias,

whom he has previously (viii. 8.39) mentioned among the Spartan commanders with the fleet, was sent with forty ships to join the satrap Pharnabazus in the north, where the Byzantines were offering to revolt from Athens. Clearchus himself was driven by storms to Delos and returned eventually to Miletus, but ten of his ships under Helixus of Megara[1] did reach Byzantium and won it over. Byzantium was a strong fortress, whose later siege and recovery by Athens is described at some length by Xenophon (*Hellenica* i. 3.14–22, where Helixus is named as commander of the Megarians in the garrison). But in the meantime (*Hellenica* i. 1.35) he has told us that 'Agis from Decelea saw many corn-ships running into the Piraeus, and said that it was no use that his men had barred the Athenians from their fields for a long time already, if their supply of seaborne grain' (from the Black Sea) 'was not also cut off. So it was best to send Clearchus, son of Ramphias, who was the honorary representative of the Byzantines, to Calchedon and Byzantium. This was approved, and fifteen ships were manned from Megara and the other allies, transports rather than men-of-war, and he sailed. Of his ships three were destroyed in the Hellespont by the nine Athenian ships that were on permanent convoy duty there; but the others escaped to Sestos' (*sic*; but Sestos was in Athenian hands; a slip for Abydos?) 'and thence came safely to Byzantium.' Is Xenophon here writing in ignorance of the account of the revolt of Byzantium that Thucydides has already given? There is no real reason to suppose so: he does not say that Byzantium revolted to Sparta when Clearchus arrived, and his narrative can easily be reconciled with the supposition that Byzantium was in Spartan hands throughout, but that the forces there were too weak to cut off the Athenian cornships (eight ships from the squadron that caused the revolt had later been taken by the Athenians at Cyzicus in the Sea of Marmara; Thucydides viii. 107). Xenophon did not insert a direct reference to Thucydides's story; he took for granted that the reader would have read it and known that Byzantium had revolted from Athens but that Clearchus was not yet there.

Xenophon can perhaps be blamed for not noting that Cyzicus,

---

[1] Byzantium was a Megarian colony.

which Thucydides (viii. 107) left in Athenian hands, apparently passed back into Spartan control before *Hellenica* i. 1.11, when the Peloponnesians under Mindarus, defeated by the Athenians in two major actions in the Hellespont (the battle of Cynossema; Thucydides viii. 101–6, and the action off Abydos; *Hellenica* i. 1.2–7), withdrew there. But Thucydides describes Cyzicus as unfortified, and we may suppose that its people had simply given in to the Spartans upon the arrival of their fleet—as they did a few days later to the Athenians after the Peloponnesian ships had been captured or destroyed and the survivors from the crews had withdrawn with Pharnabazus (*Hellenica* i. 1.19). Xenophon may not have known how Thucydides intended to continue, but we need not suppose that he did not know, or disregarded, what Thucydides had written already.

In this section of the *Hellenica*, but not in the later books, Xenophon does try to keep the Thucydidean annalistic pattern, in which events are recorded year by year, though his chronology is not wholly accurate and was complicated by some later scholar who repeatedly inserted into the text references to the chief magistrates of Athens and Sparta, to the Olympic games, and to the number of years since the beginning of the war, in a misguided attempt to achieve precision.

Xenophon is also criticised for introducing a number of incidents which are apparently described for their own sake, and not for their ultimate bearing upon the main course of events, at least as he sees it. An often quoted example is his account of how Hermocrates, one of the heroes of the defence of Syracuse against the Athenians, who had been sent with a Syracusan squadron to help the Spartans, received the news that he and his fellow-generals had been exiled (*Hellenica* i. 1.27). They displayed their loyalty by calling a meeting, where Hermocrates, though protesting against the injustice of their banishment, told the men to maintain their past good conduct (of which Xenophon (*Hellenica* i. 1.26) records a striking example just before this story) and to choose temporary commanders to serve until the new generals elected by the people arrived from home. At this the men clamoured for their old generals to retain the command, though

Xenophon notes that the captains, marines and helmsmen—that is, the representatives of the upper and middle classes—were most enthusiastic. Though reluctant to cause political trouble, Hermocrates and his colleagues did as they were asked, requesting only that when their supporters came home again they would not forget their former commanders and the successes that they had won, but would do all they could to have the sentence of exile repealed.

The affair in fact marks a significant moment in Syracusan political history, but Xenophon does not develop this important theme. He throws a glance towards Sicily (*Hellenica* i. 1.37; i. 5.21) to note the progress of the Carthaginian offensive against the Greek cities and (ii. 2.24) the establishment of Dionysius's tyranny as the result of the political and military crisis. But he gives no details, and Hermocrates, apart from a brief re-appearance at Sparta (*Hellenica* i. 1.31), is out of Xenophon's story. For his fall, and its significance in Dionysius's career, we must turn to Diodorus (xiii. 75.2–8), who, himself a Sicilian, drew upon Syracusan authors now lost.

Xenophon's story seems, in fact, to be introduced simply to provide an example, not only of how a patriotic gentleman should set his country's interests above his own, but also how a general should earn such love and respect as Hermocrates's officers showed to him. 'Those who spoke privately to Hermocrates' (at his departure from the army) 'particularly regretted the loss of his prudent care, zeal, and familiarity. For of those whom he knew, of the captains, helmsmen and marines, he gathered the best at his own tent morning and evening, and disclosed what he intended to do or say. He also used to instruct them and tell them to speak, sometimes on the spur of the moment, sometimes after deliberation. This conduct gained Hermocrates the highest reputation in the assembly, and he was considered the best speaker and counsellor' (*Hellenica* i. 1.30–1).

Here a new consideration arises, bearing upon the date at which Xenophon wrote these books of the *Hellenica*. Obviously he could not have got this story from an Athenian source—nor, does it seem, from reading a Syracusan history, which would have informed him on the sequel. He seems to be relying on a Spartan informant, who knew and liked Hermocrates when he was with the fleet, knew that he had presented a case against Tissaphernes at Sparta, and did not know about his later career. From 399 B.C. onwards Xenophon, as a mercenary in the Spartan service, was in touch with Spartan generals and statesmen—from 396 B.C. with King Agesilaus himself—and so his use of information from the Spartan side seems to point to a date in the 390s for the composition of these books.

On the other hand, the clear break between *Hellenica* i–ii and the rest of the work, in structure (the annalistic pattern is abandoned in the later books), style and continuity (the events recorded at the beginning of Book iii are several years later than those at the end of Book ii) might indicate that Books i–ii were written separately, and we cannot exclude the possibility that Xenophon met and talked with important Spartans in 403–401 B.C. He is less likely to have associated with the officers of the garrison that the Spartans had earlier sent to support the Thirty Tyrants; Plutarch (*Lysander* 15.5) notes that its commander Callibius quarrelled with Autolycus, the athlete whom Xenophon celebrates in his *Symposium*. Autolycus tripped Callibius from behind,[1] whereupon Callibius would have struck him with his staff, if Lysander had not rebuked him for not knowing how to govern free men. But later the Thirty killed Autolycus to gratify Callibius. We may suppose (quite apart from the general tone of Xenophon's references to the garrison) that Xenophon had few dealings with the men responsible for his friend's death.

Some other important passages, especially those describing the characters of the Spartan admirals Lysander and Callicratidas,

[1] This sounds like a boy's trick, and several indications (including Xenophon's own presence at the dinner) suggest that the 'dramatic date' of the *Symposium* is intended to be shortly before the end of the war. But Athenaeus (v. 216D) says that the *Autolycus* of the comic poet Eupolis, produced in 421 B.C., satirized Autolycus's victory, which would then have taken place in 422 B.C. Since the play has not survived, we cannot be certain that Athenaeus has not been misled by a coincidence of names. If he is right, Xenophon's dialogue is full of anachronisms, and we do not know why he chose to celebrate an athlete whose success was gained in his own childhood, rather than someone younger.

and their dealings with the Persian prince Cyrus, also show influence from Spartan sources. The renewed war between Athens and Sparta gave the Persians the opportunity to break the Athenian hold on the Greek cities of Asia Minor and re-establish their own control, lost two generations earlier. But the great satraps, Tissaphernes and Pharnabazus (Plates 4–5), had not worked well together, and Tissaphernes considered that Persian interests would be better served by drawing out the war and using the Greek powers to weaken each other than by defeating Athens as quickly as possible. The appointment of Cyrus in 407 B.C., with an overriding command over the western provinces, and his wholehearted cooperation with Lysander, were therefore decisive factors in the final Athenian defeat. Xenophon describes (*Hellenica* i. 5.1ff.) how Lysander, after taking over the command and bringing his fleet to Ephesus, went up to Sardis to complain against Tissaphernes and ask for Cyrus's full collaboration. 'Cyrus replied that these were his father's instructions, and that he himself had no other intention, but would do all that Lysander asked. He had brought five hundred talents with him. If this sum was insufficient' (to support the Spartan fleet until the final victory) 'he would use his own revenues, which his father had given him. If these too failed, he would cut up the very throne on which he sat, which was of gold and silver. The Spartans applauded these words and told him to fix the sailor's daily pay at one Attic drachma, demonstrating that, if this rate of pay was established, the Athenian sailors would desert their ships, and his expense would be reduced. Cyrus replied that their advice was good, but that it was impossible for him to act contrary to the King's instructions. The agreement was to pay thirty minae a month[1] for each ship, for as many ships as the Spartans wished to maintain. At the time, Lysander kept silent. But after dinner, when Cyrus drank to him and asked what was the greatest favour he could do him, he replied "If you were to add an obol to each

---

[1] Thirty minae (= 3,000 drachmae or half a talent) a month implies a rate of pay of half a drachma for a ship's complement of 200—an approximate round figure. On the crews of triremes, see Lionel Casson, *Ships and Seamanship in the Ancient World* (Princeton, 1971) pp. 300 ff.

sailor's pay." So from then on the rate of pay was four obols, having been three obols previously. And he paid up the arrears and gave a month's advance pay in addition, to the great encouragement of the fleet.'

This anecdote must come ultimately from a Spartan source. But Xenophon continues (*Hellenica* i. 5.8): 'When the Athenians heard this they were despondent, and sent ambassadors to Cyrus through the agency of Tissaphernes. But Cyrus did not receive them, though Tissaphernes requested him to do so, and recommended the policy that he himself had adopted by the advice of Alcibiades, that he should see to it that none of the Greeks were strong, but all weak, through their internal quarrels.' Here it is evident that the Athenians were in possession of the essential facts almost instantly, since it was in the interest of the Spartans and Cyrus to let the world know that Cyrus was paying high wages to the Spartan fleet. Did they also spread the story of the personal relationship between Cyrus and Lysander, or did Xenophon learn it later from another source? In the *Oeconomicus* (4.20ff.) Xenophon makes Socrates tell a story of Cyrus and Lysander, which (supposedly) Lysander had himself told to a man who had been his host in Megara. 'He said that Cyrus had shown him the paradise[1] at Sardis. And Lysander admired it for the beauty of its trees, the symmetry of its plantations, the straightness of the rows, the exactitude of the angles, and the many sweet scents that accompanied their walk, and in his admiration said, "Certainly, Cyrus, I admire all this for its beauty, but I admire even more the man who measured out and planned all the details for you." When Cyrus heard all this he was delighted, and said, "But all this, Lysander, I measured and planned myself, and some of the trees I even planted." Lysander looked at him and saw the beauty

---

[1] 'The Persian gallants . . . maintained their Botanicall bravery. Unto whom we owe the very name of Paradise: wherewith we meet not in Scripture before the time of *Solomon*, and conceived originally *Persian*. The word for that disputed Garden, expressing in the Hebrew no more than a Field enclosed. . . While many of the Ancients do poorly live in the single names of Vegetables, all stories do look upon *Cyrus*, as the splendid and regular planter. According whereto *Xenophon* describeth his gallant plantation at *Sardis*' (Sir Thomas Browne, *The Garden of Cyrus* (London, 1658) pp. 92, 94).

of his robes, and smelled his perfume and noted the beauty of his torques and bracelets and other adornments, and said, "Cyrus, what do you mean? Did you plant some of this with your own hands?" Cyrus replied, "Are you surprised at this, Lysander? I swear to you, by Mithras, that when I am in health I never dine before I have sweated in the practice of some military or agricultural exercise, or at all events some one honourable pursuit".'[1]

At first sight, it would seem that we need look no further for an explanation of how Xenophon was able to report information from the Spartan side soon after 403 B.C. A prominent Megarian (for instance, Euclides the philosopher, who introduces the *Theaetetus* of Plato; see also Diogenes Laertius ii. 106ff., for his Life) who had perhaps entertained Lysander at the time of the Spartan intervention between the City and Piraeus parties in Athens, was also in touch with the Socratic circle. Here is Xenophon's immediate source for information from the Spartan side. But on closer examination the 'prominent Megarian' seems to vanish. Immediately before telling his story of Cyrus and Lysander, Socrates has praised Cyrus, saying what a fine ruler he would have been, had he only lived, and adding that a proof of his quality was that none of his friends deserted him, though 'many tens of thousands' deserted to him from the King. On the decisive battlefield, all his friends, except Ariaeus, who was wounded, preferred death to surviving their master (*Oeconomicus* 4.18–19). Here Xenophon is putting into Socrates's mouth a paraphrase of his own *Anabasis* (cf. especially 1.9., 29–31). It seems likely that the 'Megarian' is invented, to allow Socrates to tell a story that Xenophon had himself learned from someone else. This does not mean that it is not true. In fact, it is not impossible that Xenophon had it directly from Lysander, whom he could well have met in 396 B.C.

Of course, Xenophon need not have heard both anecdotes at the same time. It is still possible that the story of Cyrus's generosity was deliberately spread at once, and that the more intimate

---

[1] So in *Cyropaedia* viii. 1.38 Xenophon says that his (imaginary) elder Cyrus never dined before he sweated, or gave grain to his horses without exercising them'.

conversation in the garden is not recorded in the *Hellenica* because Xenophon only learned of it through personal contacts years later. But the *Hellenica* contain other stories of Lysander, and of his successor Callicratidas, that are unlikely to have been deliberately put out by the Spartans during the war. Lysander had won a partial success over the Athenian fleet that from its base at Notium had been blockading him in Ephesus.[1] He boasted that at the time of his handing over the command he was master of the sea and victor in a sea-fight. Callicratidas replied that he would believe him if he sailed from Ephesus round Samos (where the Athenian fleet was stationed) to Miletus before handing over. We might imagine this story circulating among the staff of King Agesilaus after Lysander's fall from favour in 396 B.C. The story (*Hellenica* i. 6.6ff.) of how Callicratidas quarrelled with Cyrus, who kept him waiting two days for an audience, might also have been repeated with more approval at this time than when the Spartans needed Persian subsidies. Callicratidas lost his temper and went off, 'saying that the Greeks were most miserable, because they flattered barbarians for money, and that if he got safely home he would do his best to reconcile the Athenians with the Spartans'. Xenophon (whose sympathy with Callicratidas extends up to his defeat and death) represents his position as the reverse of that of Hermocrates; he is shown as a patriotic gentleman, loyally accepting a command for which he has no ambition. Agesilaus too was, in 394 B.C., to set the orders of the Spartan authorities above his own inclinations (*Hellenica* iv. 2.1–3), and to regret the quarrels of the Greeks, who, led by traitors suborned by Persian gold, had in one battle wasted the lives of enough Greek soldiers to have conquered all the barbarians (*Agesilaus*

---

[1] The affair, which is more important because it led to the final disgrace of Alcibiades at Athens than for its direct military consequences, is reported by Xenophon in *Hellenica* i. 5.11ff. (followed by Plutarch, *Lysander* 5.1–2; *Alcibiades* 35.4–6; see also *Alcibiades* 10.1 for the story of how Alcibiades made the acquaintance of Antiochus, the helmsman whom he left in command of the fleet during his absence). Diodorus (xiii. 71; cf. also xiii. 73 for the subsequent affair at Cyme, omitted by Xenophon) gives an independent version, differing in important details. Xenophon was not himself present, and probably did not write down what he heard from other people until years later, when memories were uncertain.

7.5; cf. Plutarch, *Agesilaus* 16.4). It does not follow that Callicratidas did not express similar sentiments in 406 B.C., but Xenophon is likely to have heard them quoted with approval by his Spartan friends twelve years later.

Cyrus's character in the *Hellenica*, it has been suggested, could not have been drawn after Xenophon had served under him in 401 B.C., and idealized him as a model ruler. But, though the Cyrus of the *Hellenica* is consistently the enemy of Athens, he is not on that account represented as a villain. Nor is Pharnabazus, also a friend of Sparta, treated unsympathetically in comparison with the shifty Tissaphernes. Pharnabazus is represented as a gallant soldier, riding into the sea as far as his horse would take him and urging on his men to defend the Spartan ships at Abydos. After the loss of the fleet at Cyzicus, he is again shown to advantage, telling his allies, at a time when the secretary of the dead Spartan admiral was writing despairing dispatches, not to lose heart for the sake of timber, which the King's country could easily replace, so long as they themselves were safe (*Hellenica* i. 1.6; i. 1.24–6).

The characters of Tissaphernes and Pharnabazus in the early books are not inconsistent with what Xenophon says about them in the *Anabasis* and later in the *Hellenica*. It does not follow that Xenophon must have written *Hellenica* i–ii after his service with Cyrus and Agesilaus, but there is nothing in the portrayal of the satraps to prove that these books were written before 401 B.C. Nor is the Cyrus of *Hellenica* i–ii totally different from the Cyrus of the *Anabasis*. His generosity is highly praised in both works. Moreover, Xenophon does not fail to note (*Hellenica* i. 6.18) that when Callicratidas had put to sea and driven the Athenian fleet under Conon into Mitylene 'money came to him from Cyrus'. Of course Xenophon intends the main credit to go to the Spartan admiral, whose victorious actions had gained the subsidy for which he was too proud to beg, but Cyrus, who did not let a personal affront turn him aside from his established policy, also deserves credit for statesmanship.

Xenophon also (*Hellenica* ii. 1.7ff.) mentions Cyrus's part in securing Lysander's return to the fleet, nominally, in order to comply with the law, as the admiral's secretary, in fact as commander. Cyrus, called to the deathbed of his father King Darius, left Lysander in charge of his revenues and so ensured that he had enough money to carry the war through to victory. This is of course an essential part of Xenophon's main narrative, but he also notes that Cyrus killed his father's sister's sons for refusing to pay him royal honours. This incident has no bearing on the war between Athens and Sparta. It is significant in the light of Cyrus's later rebellion, and the fact that Xenophon mentions it suggests strongly that he was writing in full knowledge of Cyrus's later career.

Xenophon does not allude directly to the rebellion, either in writing of Cyrus, or in his references to Clearchus (*Hellenica* i. 1.35; i. 3.15ff.), though Clearchus was to become the greatest of Cyrus's Greek mercenaries. He does not allude, in his mention of Coeratidas the Boeotian, Clearchus's lieutenant at Byzantium, to Coeratidas's abortive attempt to take over Cyrus's mercenaries in 400 B.C. (*Anabasis* vii. 1.33ff.). This might suggest, but certainly does not prove, that these events had not yet taken place when the last two books of the *Hellenica* were written.

On balance, it seems most likely that Xenophon wrote his account of the last years of the Peloponnesian War when, though events were no longer fresh in men's minds, he had access to Spartan information to supplement his own memories of the Athenian side. He must have known of Thucydides's history, and he certainly came from the same social class, and, to some extent, had a similar political outlook, but Diogenes Laertius is not a sufficient witness to establish that Xenophon was Thucydides's literary executor, or that the two men collaborated directly. Whatever the truth of this may be, it is possible that Xenophon in 403–401 B.C. had some thoughts of writing history, and had set down some notes, including much of his account of the Thirty Tyrants. But he was not the sort of man to content himself in his late twenties with a purely literary career, and at this point new prospects opened abroad.

CHAPTER SIX

Xenophon Joins Cyrus

KING DARIUS of Persia had died in 405 B.C., leaving four sons, of whom the first and second disputed the throne. Artaxerxes, the eldest, succeeded, but Cyrus claimed the better right because he had been born while his father was actually reigning. Xenophon came to regard him as courageous, generous, everything that a prince should be. But seen through other eyes, he appears selfishly ambitious, a traitor who continued to plot after a first attempt against his brother had been forgiven. Curious details are given by Plutarch (*Artaxerxes* 2–3), who drew upon the writings of Ctesias, a physician at the Persian court, and a notorious liar, but perhaps a sufficient witness for palace intrigues. Artaxerxes, after the custom of Persian kings, was to enter the temple of 'a warrior-goddess whom one might compare to Athena' at Pasargadae, there to partake of the simple food of his ancestors, to strip off his own robe, and to assume that of Cyrus the Great, the founder of the empire. His brother concealed himself in the temple, planning to strike down Artaxerxes and himself come forth as king. The very priest who had instructed him in the Magian religion denounced him, and he was on the point of execution when his mother saved his life by flinging her arms about him. Of this affair Xenophon (*Anabasis* i. 1.2–3) says only that Cyrus had gone up from his province to attend his father's deathbed, accompanied by the satrap Tissaphernes, officially his subordinate, supposedly his friend. After Darius's death, Tissaphernes falsely accused Cyrus of plotting against his brother. Cyrus would have been put to death but for his mother's entreaties. Xenophon no doubt got his information from one of the three hundred Greek mercenaries who had gone with Cyrus, but these men were certainly not placed, as Ctesias was, to hear the secret history of the Court. Cyrus may very well have put about his version in order to cover his present disgrace and excuse his future rebellion; on the other hand, Ctesias may be inventing an oriental romance for Greek readers.

Not only was Cyrus spared, but he was restored to the government and military command that he had held in Western Asia Minor during his father's lifetime, when, by financing Lysander's naval operations, he had made an essential contribution to Sparta's victory over Athens. He now set about raising an army with which to overthrow his brother. As 'general of all the forces who muster in the plain of Castolus'[1] he commanded a considerable Asiatic army, though he clearly no longer had an over-riding command over the two great satraps, Tissaphernes and Pharnabazus. In any case, Tissaphernes had shown himself the King's man, and Pharnabazus was also to prove loyal. But Cyrus, though he courted the officials whom the King sent to him, can have had little hope of attracting enough Persian support to match his brother's armies. His plan was to collect a large number of Greek mercenaries to add to his own men. His province was favourably situated on the borders of Greece; the victorious Spartans were his friends; and the war had filled Greece with experienced soldiers who were ready to seek their fortunes at the spear-point, now that their cities no longer required their services.

The Greeks, though there had been no major battle between Greeks and Persians since 'Cimon triumphed both on land and wave' half a century earlier, were confident of their own superiority to the 'barbarians' whom their ancestors had routed at Marathon, Salamis and Plataea. Greek mercenaries had served the kings of the East for three centuries, and for at least a generation

---

[1] Xenophon says (*Oeconomicus* 4.5ff.) that each of the tributary nations of the Persian empire was required to furnish its quota of horse and foot, and that these forces (except for the fortress garrisons) were required to muster once a year at appointed places, in order to be inspected. The King in person inspected those near his own residence, and sent trusted officers to examine the rest.

'Pactolus', the famous gold-bearing river of Sardis, has been suggested with some probability for the otherwise unknown 'Castolus'.

(cf. Thucydides iii. 34.2—an incident of 428 B.C.), small contingents of mercenaries, drawn mostly from the uplands of Arcadia, had provided the satraps of Western Asia Minor with better heavy infantry than could be recruited locally (Plate 6). There had even been an earlier attempt (about 420 B.C.) to use Greeks against the central government, by the satrap Pisuthnes of Sardis. He was betrayed by Lycon, an Athenian who commanded the Greeks, and Tissaphernes owed his rise to the part he played in the affair (Ctesias, *Persica* 52).

Cyrus had his Greek bodyguard, but his enemy Tissaphernes also employed a Greek drillmaster, Phalinus, whom he held in honour because 'he professed to understand tactics and hoplite fighting' (*Anabasis* ii. 1.7, 18). The Persians, though now many generations removed from their nomadic ancestors, were still excellent horsemen and archers; their Asiatic subjects provided them with slingers, bowmen and javelinmen, but they had no soldiers who could stand against the Greeks when it came to close combat on foot. The Greek superiority was not, of course, merely a matter of high morale and better equipment. Indeed the Persian noble, clad in scale armour of proof under a long surcoat (cf. Herodotus ix. 22), armed with bow, slashing sword and two javelins, and well mounted on a barded horse, was certainly better equipped for individual combat than the Greek hoplite, the most important part of whose equipment (*hopla*) was his great round shield, which guarded not only himself but the man on his immediate left when hoplites were driven up in close order (Plates 6–7).

Apart from his shield, the hoplite was now more lightly equipped than his ancestors had been a hundred years earlier, as it had been realized that full protection must be sacrificed to mobility, in order to meet the attacks of light infantry on broken ground. Xenophon describes the review order of Cyrus's men as bronze helmets, red tunics, greaves, and shields; in action many of them also wore leather jerkins (*spolades*), but his own horseman's armour, including a plate cuirass, was far heavier (*Anabasis* i. 2.26; iii. 3.20; iii. 4.47–8; iv. 1.18).

The hoplite's offensive weapons remained what they had been

for centuries—a heavy spear, probably usually about eight feet long, furnished with a spike at the butt end as well as a point, and a sword. Both were intended for hand-to-hand fighting, though retreating soldiers sometimes threw their spears at their pursuers (e.g. Xenophon, *Hellenica* iii. 5.20; iv. 6.11; v. 4.52). Men who intended to fight it out would not begin by stripping themselves of their chief weapon. The sword was secondary; the Greek said 'taken by the spear', not 'won by the sword'. Several forms were in use, including a straight, broad-bladed cut-and-thrust and a curved slashing sword which Xenophon (*On Horsemanship* 12.11) recommended especially for cavalry. The Spartan infantry were equipped for the press of close combat with short, straight weapons; jugglers' blades for sword-swallowing, said a mocking Athenian, to which the King replied, 'But long enough to reach our enemies'. Not all Spartans were satisfied; one is said to have complained to his mother, who told him to add one pace forward to its length (Plutarch, *Moralia* 191E, 216C, 241F).

But the strength of a hoplite army did not lie in the superiority of each man's personal equipment or in his individual valour and skill at arms. 'Without good order, the hoplite arm is worthless,' said Aristotle (*Politics* ii. 1297b 17). It was effective because it was not merely an armed mob, 'like a crowd pouring out of a theatre' (Xenophon, *Hipparchicus* 2.7—of untrained cavalry), but a disciplined mass of men, moving, whether on the march or in battle, in regular formation. As the strength of a building depended upon the laying of each individual brick and the observation of the bond between each course, so in an army exactitude in drawing up each man and each company made the whole strong (Polybius x. 22).[1] Numbers and physical strength, thirst for glory, pride of ancestry, courage and patriotism, could not make up for want of discipline, as Xenophon makes Socrates point out (*Memorabilia* iii. 5).

To deploy from a column into a phalanx, a line normally

---

[1] Quoting the late-fourth-century Athenian statesman Demetrius of Phalerum. Xenophon (*Memorabilia* iii. 1; *Cyropaedia* vi. 3.25) employs a similar metaphor, adding that the picked front- and rear-rank men are the tile roof and stone foundations.

between eight and twelve men deep, by bringing up successive files, each close to the left of its predecessor, was the essential manoeuvre; perhaps the only one when battles were settled by the clash of two hoplite armies front to front. But the altered conditions of warfare required not merely more mobility in the individual but more flexible formations. The Spartans, whose citizens, alone among Greeks, were permanently mobilized; the quick-witted Athenians, who at the time of their invasion of Sicily had been regarded by their enemies as the most 'experienced' of the Greeks (Thucydides vi. 72.3); and professional drill-masters and teachers, like Phalinus and Dionysodorus, had all no doubt contributed to the development of tactics. Wherever they had learned the art, professionals like those whom Cyrus intended to hire were able to change front rapidly, to refuse a flank when enemy cavalry threatened to turn their line, and to adopt other formations than the phalanx—for instance, companies in column parallel to each other at short intervals, a more suitable formation than a continuous line when troops were advancing across broken ground. They were also trained to handle their shields and weapons smartly in drill movements; to detach parties of younger men against skirmishers who were harassing the column on the march; and to retreat steadily, step by step, with their faces towards the enemy.

These accomplishments seem at first sight to be of small value against archers, who might be expected to shoot down the hoplites at a distance, and, if they missed their mark, to run away before their enemy was close enough to hurt them. But hoplites had shown at Marathon that they could charge through arrows. And even if they did not catch the archers themselves, a small force of light infantry attached to them could give chase at little risk, once the enemy was running. In the same way, though Artaxerxes and his Persian nobles might literally ride rings round the hoplites, they would thereby expose themselves to a charge from Cyrus's own household cavalry (cf. *Cyropaedia* ii. 1.9). Moreover, however great the King's advantage in numbers, Cyrus knew, as the Greeks were to realize later (*Hellenica* vi. 1.12) that the war would be against only one man, to whom the rest were subject. And for that one man he seems to have felt profound contempt. His brother could not even sit his horse in the hunting field,[1] much less his throne in a crisis (Plutarch, *Artaxerxes* 6.3). Whereas Cyrus, even when they were being brought up together as boys, had excelled all their contemporaries—the most modest, the most obedient to his elders, the best horseman, the best archer, the best spearman, the best student. 'And when he reached the proper age, he was the greatest lover of hunting, and at the same time most ready to court danger in pursuit of wild beasts. Once, when a bear charged him, he did not run away, but met it head on, and was clawed down from his horse. He carried the scars of his injuries all his life, though he killed the beast in the end. But he rewarded the first man to come to his help in such a way that many people thought him most fortunate' (*Anabasis* i. 9.2–6) (cf. Plate 8).

Cyrus, then, must have flattered himself in the belief that if once he encountered Artaxerxes face to face, his own personal prowess would settle the matter. The charge of the Greeks, directed against the centre of the army, where the King and the royal standard might be looked for, would, if it achieved nothing else, disorder the enemy and give Cyrus his chance to come at his brother. If the King ran away, or if he refused to take the field in person, the Persian nobles, even those who had hitherto supported him, would recognize that Cyrus was the better man. The normal rules of tactics did not apply; if the King himself was beaten it would not matter if the rest of his army was victorious.

A large army of mercenaries could not, of course, be raised overnight, and it was necessary for Cyrus to conceal his intentions

---

[1] In the conclusion of the *Cyropaedia*, in which he describes the degeneracy of Persian manners and morals since the time of the great Cyrus, Xenophon does not fail to notice Artaxerxes's shortcomings in this respect (*Cyropaedia* viii. 8.12). 'Formerly they used to go out hunting so often that the hunts provided sufficient training for themselves and their horses. But since King Artaxerxes and his court took to drink, they stopped going out themselves or leading others out hunting in the same way. Indeed, if there were any hardy men who went hunting often with their own retainers, the court circle evidently bore a grudge against them and hated them, as better men than themselves.'

as far as possible until the time came for action. Accordingly, he ordered the commanders of his garrisons to recruit as many good Peloponnesians as possible—as a precaution against Tissaphernes, from whom the Greek cities of Asia had revolted to Cyrus. Only at Miletus had Tissaphernes been able to forestall Cyrus's supporters, and for its possession they were now carrying on a private war. Xenophon (*Anabasis* i. 1.8) says that the King did not mind, because he thought that Cyrus was wasting his resources, and Cyrus was careful to pay tribute for the cities that he held.

But a large part of his army was to be held outside the King's dominions until the time came for action (*Anabasis* i. 1.9–11). Clearchus the Spartan—now exiled for attempting to seize Byzantium for himself (Diodorus Siculus xiv. 12.2–9; Xenophon, *Anabasis* ii. 6.1ff., repeats uncritically Clearchus's version of the affair), was given money to raise an army in the Gallipoli Peninsula, whose Greek cities were ready to pay him for protection against the Thracians. Aristippus the Thessalian needed mercenaries to attack his political enemies. Cyrus gave him four times what he asked for—six months' pay for four thousand men—telling him to bring them over when he sent for them (in fact he only sent his young friend Menon with fifteen hundred men). Other commanders, Socrates the Achaean and Sophaenetus of Stymphalus, were instructed to raise and bring forces for the war with Tissaphernes.

Xenophon does not mention himself at this point, but later (*Anabasis* iii. 1.4ff.) tells his own story, which suggests that he himself was anxious to leave Athens, though not permanently. Since he applied to Socrates, and apparently to nobody else, for advice, we might conclude that Xenophon's father was by this time dead, for Xenophon would surely never have been an undutiful son who obeyed Socrates rather than his own parents. There is no evidence to show that he was already married, and he probably had few personal ties at Athens. As he tells it, he had 'accompanied the army neither as a general nor as a captain nor as a private soldier, but Proxenus had sent to invite him from home, because they were bound by ancient ties of hospitality.

And he promised that, if he came, he would make him a friend of Cyrus, whom, he said, he himself valued above his own country. However, when Xenophon had read the letter, he discussed the journey with Socrates the Athenian. And Socrates suspected that friendship with Cyrus might furnish some grounds for a political accusation against him, because Cyrus appeared to have supported the Lacedaemonians eagerly against Athens in the War. So he counselled Xenophon to go to Delphi and take the advice of the god about the journey. But when Xenophon went he enquired of Apollo to which of the gods he should sacrifice and pray, in order to make the voyage that he had in mind best and most honourably, and, after its accomplishment, to come safely through. And Apollo instructed him in the gods to whom he ought to sacrifice. So when he came home again he told Socrates of the oracle. But when Socrates heard he blamed him because instead of asking first whether it would be better for him to go or to stay at home, he had made up his own mind that he ought to go, and only asked how he could best make the journey. But, he said, since he had put the enquiry in this way, he ought to do just as the god commanded. So Xenophon sacrificed as the god had instructed him and sailed away. And at Sardis he found Proxenus and Cyrus on the point of marching up country, and was presented to Cyrus. And since Proxenus urged him to stay with them, Cyrus joined in urging him, and said that as soon as the campaign was over he would send him home. And he said that the expedition was against the Pisidians. So Xenophon joined the army, deceived—but not by Proxenus.'

Xenophon's simplicity in believing that so great an army had been so secretly collected merely for a local punitive expedition is surprising. Tissaphernes at least saw through Cyrus's pretences, and rode in all haste to warn the King, taking five hundred cavalry with him (*Anabasis* i. 2.4–5).

NOTE ON SOURCES

Xenophon was not the only contemporary writer to deal with Cyrus's expedition. On the King's side, there was Ctesias, his

personal physician, who attended him on the battlefield of
Cunaxa, and also gave an account of the fate of the generals whom
Tissaphernes later trapped, in which he tried to justify himself
in the eyes of Greece by describing his own kindness to Clearchus.
Ctesias was used by Xenophon (*Anabasis* i. 8.26–7) for the details
of Cyrus's death, and survives in a Byzantine summary (little
more than chapter-headings). He was also an important source for
Plutarch's *Artaxerxes*.

Plutarch also quotes Dinon, who, probably about 300 B.C.,
wrote a *History of Persia*, using, it would seem, Persian official
records.

Xenophon, in his own *Hellenica*, bridges the gap between the
re-establishment of the Athenian democracy and the outbreak of
war between Persia and Sparta in 399 B.C. with a short account of
how the Spartans had supported Cyrus (*Hellenica* iii. 1.2). He
adds that 'how Cyrus collected his army and marched with it
against his brother, and how the battle took place, and how
Cyrus was killed, and how after this the Greeks escaped to the
sea, has been written by Themistogenes of Syracuse'.

Plutarch (*Moralia* 345E—'On the Glory of Athens') supposed that Xenophon originally published his own *Anabasis* under
the pseudonym Themistogenes, which suggests that no separate
Anabasis by Themistogenes existed in Plutarch's time (late first
century after Christ). However, the *Souda*, a sort of Byzantine
classical dictionary, says that Themistogenes also wrote about
his own country (Syracuse), which seems to give him some
reality, independently of Xenophon. Did some Syracusan use a
pseudonym made famous by Xenophon, in order to hide his
identity from the tyrant Dionysius? Another Byzantine tradition
(Tzetzes, *Chiliades* vii. 937) that Xenophon was the lover of
Themistogenes and published his own book under his name to
please him, is obvious romance.

'Sophaenetus' is quoted four times by Stephanus of Byzantium, a geographer of about A.D. 500, as authority for four names,
three of which, the city of Charmande, the Physcus river, and the
Carduchi, also occur in Xenophon. The fourth, that of the Taoi,
represents Xenophon's Taochi. 'Sophaenetus' is presumably

Sophaenetus of Stymphalus, the oldest of Cyrus's Greek generals (*Anabasis* v. 3.1; vi. 5.13), though it is strange that he is not quoted by any earlier writer, especially since Plutarch seems to have gone into the sources for the battle of Cunaxa with some care. Stephanus tells nothing about his work, except the bare mention of these names. It is often thought that Sophaenetus underlies the account of the retreat given by Diodorus Siculus (xiv. 18–31), and this theory might be supported by the fact that Diodorus omits the action against Tiribazus, during which Sophaenetus was left behind in charge of the camp (Xenophon, *Anabasis* iv. 4.19). Diodorus in fact compresses the story (mentioning for instance, only one snowstorm, where Xenophon tells of two) and has very little to say about the hard fighting that Xenophon describes. He never mentions Xenophon at all, until, in a quite separate section of his history (xiv. 37), he says that 'after the soldiers who had campaigned with Cyrus got safely back to Greece' about five thousand of them chose Xenophon as their general and won victories under him in Thrace. This may be because Diodorus is simplifying his narrative: he says (xiv. 19.7) that Clearchus commanded the Peloponnesians, except the Achaeans under Socrates, Proxenus the Boeotians and Menon the Thessalians; later that Clearchus commanded all the mercenaries in the battle (xiv. 22.5), then after his death 'the Greeks chose a number of generals, but gave the supreme command to one man, Chirisophus the Lacedaemonian' (xiv. 27.1), and Xenophon is not named until he achieved the supreme command in his turn. This is clearly not accurate; for instance, Proxenus's command did not consist entirely of Boeotians; in fact, among the captains, 'one Apollonides, who spoke with a Boeotian accent', appears as an exception among Peloponnesians like Agasias of Stymphalus and Hieronymus of Elis (*Anabasis* iii. 1.26ff.). Moreover, if Diodorus was really using Sophaenetus, why does he never name him? He cites only one source, Ephorus, and him only for the number of the King's army (Diodorus xiv. 22.2), which he gives as four hundred thousand men, the same figure as that quoted from Ctesias. And why does Diodorus (xiv. 29.1) call the Taochi Chaoi, not Taoi? Or is this merely a copyist's mistake?

On the other hand, Diodorus (xiv. 23.6) gives Tissaphernes a special importance in the battle of Cunaxa, and reports at some length (xiv. 25.1–6) on the mission of Phalinus, a Greek professional soldier in the service of Tissaphernes, who went to demand the surrender of the Ten Thousand after the battle. Both Diodorus and Xenophon (*Anabasis* ii. 1.7ff.) make the Greek leaders return individual defiances, and they do not give the same speeches to the same men. In particular, Diodorus gives to Xenophon's friend Proxenus a speech which Xenophon puts into the mouth of an otherwise unknown young Athenian, Theopompus, who is perhaps a disguise for Xenophon himself. 'Spoken like a philosopher, my lad,' replies Phalinus in Xenophon's version. Can he have taken Proxenus's young friend for Proxenus himself? There is no reason to suppose that he was familiar with all the Greek generals. Perhaps Phalinus himself (through Ephorus?) is the ultimate source for some part of Diodorus—though not, of course, for the retreat after Tissaphernes had been shaken off.

Isocrates does not mention Xenophon, or any general except Clearchus, in the two short summaries that he gives of the affair— one (*Panegyricus* 145–8) composed shortly after 380 B.C. to encourage the Greeks to unite against Persia, the other (*Philippicus* 90–2) addressed after 346 B.C. to Philip of Macedon, to urge him to take the lead. Isocrates, who, to magnify the weakness of Persia, speaks slightingly of Cyrus's mercenaries as six thousand ne'er-do-wells, can hardly reflect either Xenophon or Sophaenetus.

We may suppose, then, that Xenophon's *Anabasis* was written to rescue his own achievements from undeserved neglect. Whether that neglect was in part occasioned by Sophaenetus (and if either of them is to be accused of unfairness we may suspect the senior man who had been passed over in favour of a brilliant young colleague) we do not know. There were in all probability two editions of Xenophon's book, the earlier ('Themistogenes', now lost) perhaps covering only the same ground as our *Anabasis* i–iv, if the *Hellenica* is to be taken literally to mean that 'Themistogenes' ended with the Greeks' escape to the sea. But if Xenophon was writing to justify himself why should he have omitted his own period of sole command?

At all events, we should not doubt that Xenophon was brave, skilful and popular with his men merely because he himself is his own chief witness. One thing is certain—that the remnant of Cyrus's veterans did in the end choose him their commander-in-chief. They would not have done so if they had not trusted him. But we must allow also that he writes as a reporter, rather than a historian. What he saw for himself he reported well; when he was told a story by somebody else he accepted it uncritically; and when he was not told he did not make it his business to find out.

CHAPTER SEVEN

Cyrus's March

IN his description of the advance from Sardis to Babylonia, Xenophon does not mention himself by name. He records the number of marches, with the length of each, expressed in Persian parasangs;[1] the towns and cities passed, and their condition, some wealthy and populous, some deserted ruins; the rivers, with their width, and notes on the crossings; the mountains and their passes; the rich lands that could feed an army, and the empty country, down the left bank of the Euphrates, where supplies ran short. 'The best of all guide-books to Mesopotamia, the *Anabasis* and Ammianus Marcellinus,' says Gertrude Bell.[2] The Greeks had no concept of a General Staff, but Xenophon seems to have been discharging the duties of a staff officer, and an efficient one too, to judge from the readiness with which he was later accepted as general.

The King, warned by Tissaphernes, was concentrating his forces. 'A student of the Persian Empire could understand that in extent of territory and in population it is strong, but in length of its communciations and the dispersion of its forces weak, if one were to make war by rapid steps' (*Anabasis* i. 5.9). But Cyrus had

[1] '. . . the parasang, like its representative the modern *farsang* or *farsakh* of Persia, was not a measure of distance very accurately determined, but rather indicated a certain amount of time employed in traversing a given space. . . . That the parasang was the same as the modern hour we find by the distance between Larissa (Nimroud) and Mespila (Kouyunjik) being given as six parasangs, corresponding exactly with the number of hours assigned by the present inhabitants of the country. . . . The six hours in this instance are equal to about eighteen English miles' (Sir Henry Layard, *Nineveh and Babylon* (London, 1853) pp. 59–60).

[2] *Amurath to Amurath* (2nd edition, 1924) p. 200.

not completed his concentration either, and could not move fast. So whatever his duties, Xenophon also had leisure to look about him. Four days out from Sardis there was a week's wait at Colossae for Menon to catch up with his Thessalians, a thousand hoplites and five hundred peltasts (Plate 11), light infantry with wicker shields and javelins (*Anabasis* i. 2.6).

Three days' further march took them to Celaenae on the headwaters of the Meander, but here they had to wait a month, until other generals came in, Sosis of Syracuse, Sophaenetus, and above all Clearchus with a thousand hoplites, eight hundred Thracian peltasts, and two hundred Cretan archers (*Anabasis* i. 2.9—also *Anabasis* i. 5.13) a private bodyguard of 'more than forty cavalry, most of them Thracians'. So Xenophon had plenty of time to see the sights—Cyrus's palace and private hunting park, the palace of Xerxes, the stream beside which Apollo had flayed Marsyas. Cyrus could now number his Greeks 'eleven thousand hoplites and about two thousand peltasts' (*Anabasis* i. 2.9),[1] but the advance was still slow. In addition to the Greeks, there was the Asiatic army—ten myriads, with twenty scythed chariots, according to Xenophon (*Anabasis* i. 7.10); seventy thousand, of whom three thousand were cavalry, says Diodorus (xiv. 19.7). These figures are certainly nowhere near the truth, except those for the cavalry and chariots, but we need not suppose that the 'barbarian' infantry was purely imaginary. Xenophon had a good chance to see the Asiatics when Cyrus gave a review in honour of the Queen of Cilicia, who had come (possibly with her husband's connivance) bringing pay for Cyrus's troops, while her husband made a show of holding the Taurus passes for King Artaxerxes. At the review the 'barbarians' had marched past by squadrons and regiments. Certainly the sequel had confirmed the Greeks, and Cyrus, in their belief in their own superiority if it came to a pitched battle. They had been drawn up in line, four deep, armed for battle, with red tunics, greaves, bronze helmets, and uncovered shields, and, after Cyrus and the Queen had driven along the line, had been ordered to charge.

---

[1] These figures do not agree exactly with those reached by adding up the contingents which Xenophon has listed separately.

'When the trumpet sounded, they threw forward their shields and advanced, and next, as they quickened their pace amid cheering, the soldiers, without orders, broke into a double towards the tents. The barbarians were seized with panic, and the Cilician Queen fled in her coach, and the market-people dropped their wares and ran away. And so the Greeks came laughing to their tents' (*Anabasis* i. 2.14–18).[1]

But the barbarians might be able to defend mountain passes against the more heavily-armed Greeks. And the high Taurus range now lay directly in front. The main pass, says Xenophon (*Anabasis* i. 2.20ff.), was a waggon-road, exceedingly steep, and impassable for an army, in the face of opposition. Syennesis, the Cilician King (his 'name' is more properly to be regarded as a title) had been encamped on the heights above as Cyrus approached, and so the army waited for a day in the plain below. But next day came news that Syennesis had abandoned the position. His flank had been turned by the arrival of Cyrus's warships and the Spartan fleet off his coasts, and by his own wife, whom Cyrus had sent home a week earlier 'by the shortest way', together with Menon and his men. Menon's contingent included five hundred light infantry, from the mountain districts bordering upon Thessaly, which may be why he had been chosen for a task that he seems to have performed well, but Xenophon comments only on the loss of two companies of his hoplites—cut off while plundering, said some; separated from the main body and unable to rejoin it, said others. Xenophon was not on speaking terms with Menon and so did not learn his account of the matter.

At all events, the affair gave the Greeks an excuse for plundering the city and palace of Tarsus. But when the plundering was over, and Syennesis, with his wife's help, had made his peace

---

[1] Compare the climax of the review in Kipling's 'Her Majesty's Servants' (*The Jungle Book*, p. 272 of the 1899 edition). 'The line grew and grew till it was three-quarters of a mile long—one solid wall of men, horses, and guns. Then it came on straight towards the Viceroy and the Amir . . . Unless you have been there you cannot imagine what a frightening effect this steady come-down of troops has on the spectators, even when they know it is only a review.' But here of course 'the advance stopped dead' before the Amir had done more than 'pick up the reins on his horse's neck and look behind him'.

with Cyrus, misgivings arose. The Greeks began to suspect that
they were marching against Artaxerxes, and mutinied.

From this affair Clearchus succeeded in emerging as the chief
Greek leader, gaining the confidence, not only of the mutinous
soldiers, whom he persuaded that he had their true interest at
heart, but of Cyrus, and displacing Xenias, who had served Cyrus
longer and had hitherto been the leading Greek general.[1] Clearchus was usually a harsh disciplinarian: 'He thought that an
undisciplined army was good for nothing, and was reported even
to have said that the soldier should fear his officer more than the
enemy' (*Anabasis* ii. 6.10). But in his handling of the mutiny he
showed that, when harshness failed, he could dissimulate, persuade, and use words as cleverly, though not as elegantly, as any
trained rhetorician.

Xenophon does not express disapproval of the way in which
Clearchus dissembled—'bewildering and grieving' Cyrus as well
as deceiving the Greeks. He refused to lead, but offered to serve
under some other general who would undertake to lead them
home, and so brought the soldiers to see for themselves the im-
possibility of independent action, surrounded as they were by
Cyrus's fleets and armies, and lacking provisions and guides
unless he supplied them.

A fifty-per-cent increase in pay was no doubt what most of the
soldiers really wanted, but they were also given an assurance that
they were only marching against a neighbouring satrap, which
seems to have satisfied Xenophon.

But at Thapsacus on the Euphrates it was necessary to drop all
pretences (*Anabasis* i. 4.11ff.), and now Xenophon makes plain
his disapproval of his enemy Menon's selfish behaviour. The
generals held an assembly, and again the soldiers, after a display
of anger, were persuaded by promises of pay and gratuities. But
meanwhile 'Menon, before the other soldiers had declared their
intentions, assembled his own force separately and spoke as
follows: "Gentlemen, if you will be persuaded by me, without
incurring any greater dangers or labours than the other soldiers,

---

[1] cf. *Anabasis* i. 2.10, where Xenias celebrates the Lycaean games of his native
Arcadia with some magnificence, giving golden strigils as prizes.

you will be preferred above them by Cyrus. What is it that I am urging? Cyrus is now asking the Greeks to follow him against the King. Well then, I say that you must cross the River Euphrates before it is clear what reply the other Greeks will give to Cyrus. If they vote to follow, you, who began the crossing, will seem to be responsible for it, and Cyrus will consider you his most eager supporters, and bear you a debt of gratitude—yes, and pay it too. He knows how to, if anyone does. But if the others vote against crossing, we will all go back together the way we came, but he will regard you, the only ones who obeyed, as best to be trusted with garrison duty and commands of companies, and in everything else that you ask him I know that you will find Cyrus your friend." On hearing this they were persuaded and crossed before the others returned their answer. But when Cyrus saw that they had crossed he was delighted, and sent Glous to them to say, "I praise you now. But I shall see to it that you also praise me, or think me no longer Cyrus." So all the soldiers were in the highest hopes, and uttered prayers for his success, and it was reported too, that he sent magnificent gifts to Menon.'

In his account of the review, and of the mutiny at Tarsus, Xenophon mentions 'the market', which took the place of a regular commissariat. There was a waggon-train, and once when it bogged down 'Cyrus stood watching, with the noblest and best of his retinue, and ordered Glous and Pigres to take part of the barbarian army and heave the waggons out. And, when they seemed to him not to be making a real effort, he ordered, as if in anger, the best of his Persian household troops to lend a hand with the waggons. Then certainly one could see some part of their good discipline. They threw off their purple dolmans, just where each of them happened to be standing, and sprang forward as though competing in a race, down a steep bank too. They were wearing their usual expensive tunics and gaily-coloured trousers, and some of them torques about their necks and bracelets about their arms. But without removing them they jumped straight into the mud, and lifted the waggons right out quicker than one could think' (*Anabasis* i. 5.7–8). But part at least of these waggons carried a reserve of flour and wine which was never used

(*Anabasis* i. 10.18). For daily provisions, the soldiers depended on purchase, and so the army was attended by a crowd of merchants, the 'Lydian market'. They were allowed to sell at famine prices when supplies ran short, on the thirteen days' march through the desert by the Euphrates, where there were neither grass nor trees and many of the baggage-animals died of hunger (*Anabasis* i. 5.5–6). Rather than pay four silver pieces for half a gallon of barley, the soldiers 'survived on meat'—a passage that is sometimes quoted to show that the ancient Greeks were vegetarians by preference. Readers who have eaten starved mule may understand it differently. Artaxerxes himself got into similar difficulties later in his reign, when he made an expedition against the Cadusians, a people whose mountainous and misty land produced no grain, but bred up a warlike race of men on pears, apples and similar fruits. The Persians ran out of supplies, and had to kill their beasts of burden; a donkey's head could scarcely be bought for sixty drachmae (Plutarch, *Artaxerxes* 24).

Rather than use the 'Lydian market' the Greeks preferred buying in the cities that they passed—even if it meant paddling across the Euphrates on the tent covers stuffed with dry hay (*Anabasis* i. 5.10).

The tents were no doubt carried on the baggage-mules that are frequently mentioned. These animals also carried personal property, and the fighting strength of the army was reduced because the soldiers chose some of their messmates to look after the baggage (*Anabasis* iv. 1.13; v. 8.5ff.). There were also slaves, and women. Cyrus himself set the example, by taking with him two Greek mistresses (*Anabasis* i. 10.2–3), which did not prevent him, according to camp gossip, from seducing the Cilician queen (*Anabasis* i. 2.12). The soldiers moved, therefore, at the speed of a great crowd of camp-followers, and not at their own best marching pace, which is the chief reason for the slow progress for which Cyrus has been blamed by modern critics.

The day's routine is not described, but it appears that the army broke camp at first light, and moved off without taking a cooked meal, in order to reach its next encampment in the late morning 'about the hour when the market-place fills' (*Anabasis* i. 8.1). Here the soldiers took their first regular meal, and then presumably rested through the heat of the day, and in the evening prepared dinner, with food purchased locally or from the 'Lydian market' to supplement what was carried with them. This might be followed by supper (cf. *Anabasis* i. 10.17–19).

There were, as has been seen, reviews on special occasions, and once, near the end of the march, Cyrus drew his army up in battle order at midnight, and reviewed it, expecting to be attacked at dawn next day (*Anabasis* i. 7.1). But there seem to have been no regular parades or drills in the evening, though both morning and evening exercises (*gymnasia*) formed part of the discipline of the Spartan camp (*Constitution of the Lacedaemonians* 12.6) in which many of the officers had been trained. So there was time for the officers to amuse themselves in the evening or during the day when hunting parties of horsemen could leave the slow-moving column, and easily overtake it at the next halt. One might compare old descriptions of British regiments marching through India. 'As the regiment moves parties peel off to shoot the small game which abounds and some, mounted on their chargers, to spear the pig.'[1]

Once Xenophon's sport may have got him into trouble; the Chalus river, which the army crossed just before reaching the Euphrates, was 'full of huge tame fish, which the Syrians held to be gods, and they would allow no wrong to be done to them, or to the doves'.[2]

---

[1] Lt-Gen. Sir Francis Tuker, *The Yellow Scarf* (London, 1961) p. 27. Of course on active service there had to be restraints. 'The Indulgence which the Col. has been pleased to Grant to the Gentlemen Cadets of riding their Horses on the line of march was meant for the preservation of their health only. . . . They are on no account to separate themselves, but to keep in a body together as much as possible, in Order to be ready at a moment's notice to dismount and form.' (W. C. Macpherson, *Soldiering in India* (Edinburgh, 1928), p. xxx—an extract from a regimental order of 11 December 1772).

[2] These creatures, though Xenophon apparently did not know it, were sacred to the Great Goddess of Syria. Diodorus Siculus (ii. 4.2–6) says that the goddess Derceto (Atargatis) fell in love with one of her own worshippers and bore him a daughter, Semiramis, who was exposed in the wilderness and reared by doves. The goddess, seeking to cover her shame by suicide, flung herself into a lake near her temple at Ascalon, where she was turned into a fish, and this kind of fish was therefore accounted sacred. She was also worshipped at Bambyce (modern Manbij)—Hierapolis, the 'Holy City' of the later Greeks (cf. Lucian, *De Dea*

Once the Euphrates was crossed, there was good hunting, as the march led through desert lands 'as level as the sea, and full of wormwood. And all the other brush or reeds growing there were aromatic, like perfume. There were no trees, but game of all sorts, very many wild asses, and many ostriches. And there were bustards and gazelles. This game was sometimes chased by the mounted men. The asses, when one gave chase, ran forward and stood still, for they ran much faster than horses. And again, when the horses drew near, they did the same, and it was only possible to take them if the horsemen were stationed at intervals and chased them in relays. The meat of those that were taken was like venison, but more tender. Nobody caught an ostrich, and those of the horsemen who chased one soon gave up, for it greatly out-distanced them when it ran away, using its feet for running, and its wings, which it lifted, as a sail. But one can catch the bustards if one flushes them quickly, for they fly a short distance, like partridges, and soon become exhausted. Their flesh is very good to eat' (*Anabasis* i. 5.1–3).[1]

But Xenophon, as well as amusing himself, was learning lessons which remained with him all his life, and which in his old age he embodied in his *Cyropaedia*. Some of them were purely

---

Syria 14)—a short distance from Cyrus's line of march. The fish outlasted her; Gertrude Bell in 1909 saw 'horses . . . being watered at the sacred pool, amid anxious cries from the muleteers, who had heard rumours of its fabulous depth' (*Amurath to Amurath*, p. 26). But a few years earlier D. G. Hogarth ('Hierapolis Syriae', *BSA* xiv (1907–8) p.189) found holy fishes elsewhere nearby: 'At the village of Sam is a deep walled pool of pellucid spring water full of enormous fish, which to my ignorant eyes seemed a kind of carp. These fish are held sacred and fed by the villagers . . . but why the fish are so sacred they would not, and probably, could not, tell.' F. W. Hasluck ('The Caliph Mamoun and the Prophet Daniel', *JHS* 42 (1922) pp. 99ff.) describes other holy fishes, including that which caused the death of a Caliph, and the holy fishes of Tripoli which went to fight the Russians in the Crimean War.

[1] Bustards and gazelles were still abundant in Mesopotamia in the nineteenth century, when Layard (*Nineveh and Babylon*, pp. 246, 481) and his party amused themselves with shooting and hawking. He particularly notes the bustard's habit of 'sitting very close, frequently not rising until it was nearly trodden under foot', and that 'it is almost always captured on the ground, and defends itself vigorously with wings and beak against its assailant'. He also remarks (p. 270) on the capture of wild asses by the Arabs.

technical—What foods kept best on a long march? What tools should be carried by the waggon-train? How could the indispensable 'market' be encouraged to accompany an army? (cf. *Cyropaedia* vi. 2.25–3.4). But he was also watching the Greek officers to see how they handled their men, and Cyrus himself, in whom he had begun to see a model of kingship. The Athenian aristocratic ideal had failed him; here were new patterns of leadership.

Cyrus had been lucky to ford the Euphrates, with his infantry and baggage. The river was submitting himself to the future King, said the men of Thapsacus. Usually travellers crossed by boat.[1] But Cyrus's enemy Abrocomas was before him, and had destroyed the boats. He seems to have had only a small force—enough to watch the rebels' movements until it was certain that Cyrus was coming down the Euphrates against Babylon, not striking eastwards for Ecbatana, the northern capital. Xenophon did not appreciate the King's strategy, by which the rebels' progress was carefully watched while Cyrus himself seems to have had no idea what his brother was doing. Abrocomas had earlier failed to defend the strong position at the Syrian Gates, and Xenophon (*Anabasis* i. 4.4–5) ascribes this to Cyrus's forethought in arranging to turn it by sea if need be. It seems never to have occurred to him, even after the Greeks found themselves cut off in Babylonia, that the King might have led them into a trap deliberately.

Resentment between Clearchus and Menon may have played its part in a serious incident that occurred on the march down the Euphrates (*Anabasis* 1.5.10–17). When the army halted opposite the city of Charmande, a quarrel broke out among the soldiers who were purchasing supplies, and Clearchus beat one of

---

[1] Gertrude Bell (*Amurath to Amurath*, p. 23) notes that 'the Euphrates can easily be crossed in boats at many places', between Birejik (Zeugma) and Thapsacus, and cites Procopius *De Bello Persico* ii. 20 for the same observation. But (p. 26) boats were dependent on wind and current—'It is the Euphrates! And we were all silenced.' Cyrus might have swum the river with his cavalry, like Ibrahim Pasha, the Kurdish leader (p. 39)—'There he forded, he and eight hundred men with him . . . They swam the river with their horses and rested that night at Serrin.' But infantry and baggage could not have crossed like this.

Menon's men. Later in the day he made the mistake of riding through Menon's camp with only a few attendants, on his way back from supervising the market. 'One of Menon's soldiers, who was chopping wood, saw Clearchus riding past, and threw his hatchet at him. He missed; but another man threw a stone, and another and another, and then many, and an uproar broke out. Clearchus escaped to his own men, and immediately called them to arms. Ordering his hoplites to remain, with their shields placed against their knees,[1] he took his Thracians and the cavalry that he had in his force, more than forty, most of them Thracians too, and rode against Menon's men, so that they were thrown into consternation, as was Menon himself, and ran to their arms. Some of them merely stood wondering what was happening. But Proxenus (who happened to be coming up later, with a regiment of hoplites at his back) immediately led his men between the conflicting parties, grounded arms, and asked Clearchus to stop behaving like that. But Clearchus was angry that, when he had barely escaped being stoned, Proxenus tried to smooth over his injuries, and told him to get out of the way. Meanwhile Cyrus too came up and learned what was happening. And immediately he took his javelins in his hands and with those of his trusted friends who were with him came galloping between them and said: "Clearchus and Proxenus, and the rest of you Greeks here, you do not know what you are doing. If you start fighting each other, you may count on it that I shall be cut down this very day, and you yourselves not much later. For if our affairs go badly, all these barbarians whom you see will be even more our enemies than those who are with the King." When he heard this, Clearchus contained himself. And both sides desisted and grounded their arms where they stood.'

After this Clearchus and Menon were kept as far apart as possible. But Cyrus continued to trust Clearchus, and made him the only Greek member of the court-martial that condemned to death Orontas, a Persian of the blood-royal, who had intended

---

[1] The normal 'stand at ease' position. The heavy shield was rested on the ground, but leaned against the knees, not laid down flat, so that it could be picked up instantly (cf. Diodorus Siculus xv. 32–3).

to desert to Artaxerxes (*Anabasis* i. 6). But the fact that, in Cyrus's eyes and the army's, Clearchus was the chief Greek general, did not mean that he was commander-in-chief. His advice might be taken, but Cyrus was the only man who could give orders to each of his jealously independent commanders.

Cyrus himself, in Xenophon's eyes, stood above the quarrels and intrigues of his officers. In the stories already repeated he appears brave, quick at appreciating a situation, prompt and decisive in his actions. He was also intelligent and (what is perhaps more rare in princes) willing to apply his intelligence, as is shown by the fact that he had evidently learned to speak Greek fluently, unlike Tissaphernes, who used an interpreter (*Anabasis* ii. 3.17). But the quality that impressed Xenophon most in Cyrus was his magnanimity—not merely his generosity with money, though that so dazzled Xenophon that he did not notice a number of awkward facts. 'It was not Cyrus's way to withold payment when he had money' (*Anabasis* i. 2.11). Well and good— but at this point in the story the mercenaries were three months in arrears, and Cyrus was only rescued from his difficulties by a present from another's man's wife. This was probably not, as Xenophon seems to think, an unexpected windfall, but the story does not do any of its main actors much credit, even if we discount the gossip about Epyaxa and Cyrus, and suppose that Syennesis was himself behind the intrigue. Again, it was all very well to promise the soldiers five silver *minae* (more than a year's pay) as a gratuity when they reached Babylon, but the Babylonians would no doubt have preferred a king whose generosity showed itself to his subjects rather than to foreign adventurers.

But, quite apart from his freedom with money, Cyrus did show a genuine desire to deal better with his subordinates than they with him (cf. *Anabasis* i. 4.8). This appears most impressively in the affair of Xenias and Pasion, who, after the army had reached the Syrian coast, 'embarked on a merchant ship, taking aboard their most valuable possessions, and sailed away'. Cyrus publicly declared that he would neither send his warships to bring them back, nor deprive them of their wives and children, who were in Tralles, one of his fortresses, but would restore their families as a reward of their former good service. Similarly,[1] in describing the trial of Orontas, Xenophon makes him admit that he had twice betrayed Cyrus already, and twice been forgiven. 'Cyrus asked him again, "Could you still become my brother's enemy, and faithful to me?" But he answered, "Even if I were to become so, I could never still seem so to you".' His condemnation followed, Clearchus casting the first vote. His execution makes an interesting contrast with that of Theramenes. After his judges, including his kinsmen, had at Cyrus's bidding taken hold of his girdle in sign of condemnation, 'the men whose duty it was led him out. But when those saw him who had formerly done reverence to him, they did reverence even then, though they knew that he was being led to death. But after he was brought into the tent of Artapatus, the most faithful of Cyrus's mace-bearers, from then on nobody ever saw Orontas again, either living or dead. As to the manner of his death, nobody spoke with knowledge, but different people put forward different conjectures. And his grave has never yet been seen' (*Anabasis* i. 6.6–11).

It was less in keeping with the character of a magnanimous prince to burn the palace of Belesys, satrap of Syria, and cut down the trees in the 'great and fair paradise, which held all that the seasons bring forth' (*Anabasis* i. 4.10). Xenophon is however careful to point out that Cyrus did not let magnanimity interfere with duty. 'Certainly nobody could say that he allowed evil doers and wicked men to laugh in his face. On the contrary, he was of all men most unsparing in dealing out justice. One could often see along the public roads men who had been deprived of feet or hands or eyes. So under Cyrus's government a man, be he Greek or barbarian, provided he did no wrong, could travel without fear wherever he wished, taking his wealth with him' (*Anabasis* i. 9.13). It is distressing to find Xenophon applauding such

---

[1] Xenophon heard Clearchus describe the proceedings. Clearchus himself was apparently dependent on Cyrus's translation of Orontas's examination (*Anabasis* i. 6.9–10).

measures, but Cyrus would have won approval in his own part of the world until recently.[1]

But of course it was his generosity, more than his justice, that interested the Greeks. At the conference of commanders that followed the last review of the army, one of his confidants questioned both his willingness and his ability to discharge all his promises after victory, and drew this reply: 'Gentlemen, our ancestral empire extends southward until human habitation is made impossible by the heat, and northward until it is made impossible by the cold. In all the expanse between, my brother's friends rule as viceroys. But if we conquer, we must place our own friends in control of these territories. Accordingly, my fear is not that I may lack the means to reward each of my friends, if all goes well, but that I may lack sufficient friends to reward. As for you Greeks, I shall give each of you a crown of gold' (*Anabasis* i. 2.7ff.).

[1] 'My zaptieh broke in here. "Effendim," said he, "it fell out once that I was in Bombay—yes, I was sent from Basrah with horses for one of the kings of India. And there I saw a poor man whose passport had been stolen from him, and he carried his complaint to the judge. Now the judge was of the English, and he fined the thief and cut off two of his fingers. That is government; in India the poor are protected."

' "Allah!" said one of the coffee-drinkers in undisguised admiration. I knew better than to question the validity of the anecdote' (Gertrude Bell, *Amurath to Amurath*, p. 95).

CHAPTER EIGHT

The Battle of Cunaxa

So it was with expectation of 'crowns imperial, crowns and coronets' that, some six months after leaving Sardis, the Greeks approached the decisive battlefield. Since leaving the desert behind them, they had been aware that a large body of the king's cavalry, reckoned from their tracks and horse-droppings to be about two thousand strong, was going in front of them, keeping them under observation and destroying forage and supplies. Orontas had offered to drive them off with a thousand of Cyrus's cavalry, but, after his intention of deserting to the King was revealed, Cyrus seems, probably for fear of further treachery, to have made no attempt against them. They for their part kept the enemy under observation, and screened their own main army most efficiently.

Xenophon accepted uncritically the report (*Anabasis* i. 7.12–13) that the enemy were one hundred and twenty myriads strong, with two hundred scythed chariots and six thousand Household Cavalry in addition. Each of the four great satraps with the King was supposed to have three hundred thousand men—though Xenophon had already heard (*Anabasis* i. 2.4–5) that one of them, Tissaphernes, had left his province with only five hundred horse! He does allow that, since Abrocomas arrived after the battle, the King had only nine hundred thousand men in the field, but does not question the word of the deserters (deliberately sent to discourage and mislead Cyrus?) and prisoners who provided these figures.

Plutarch follows Xenophon, but (*Artaxerxes* 13.3) notes that Ctesias put the figure at four hundred thousand (ten myriads for each satrap?), and this number is also given by Diodorus (xiv. 22.2), who got it from Ephorus.

Since we have no reliable ancient figures, we can only guess. My own guess is based on the belief that the ancient sources are at least correct in saying that Cyrus had more Asiatics than Greeks, and that his brother had the larger army. Since numbering his men at Celaenae, Cyrus had been joined by seven hundred hoplites under Chirisophus and four hundred who had deserted from Abrocomas, and had lost a hundred of Menon's men (*Anabasis* i. 2.9; 2.25; 4.3). There must also have been some wastage from sickness, and clearly a large number of men were detached as baggage-guards. Ten thousand four hundred hoplites and twenty-five hundred 'peltasts' (among whom, it would seem, are classed the Cretan archers, and light infantry elsewhere called 'unarmoured') were counted at a final review, held on what was expected to be the eve of battle (*Anabasis* i. 7.10).

The three thousand Asiatic cavalry allowed Cyrus by Diodorus (xiv. 19.7) may come close to the true figure. There seem to have been three separate bodies of cavalry in the planned order of battle—about a thousand Paphlagonians on the right wing, Cyrus himself in the centre, immediately to the left of the Greeks, with his household cavalry, about six hundred strong, and on the left 'Ariaeus, Cyrus's lieutenant-general, and the rest of the barbarian host' (*Anabasis* i. 8.5–6). Ariaeus's force will have included, probably, a third body of cavalry, and the barbarian infantry who ran away from the Greeks at the review and failed to heave the waggons out of the mud. They were no use in the battle either; but perhaps that was not altogether their fault. They were, at least, sufficiently numerous to convince the Greeks at Tarsus that they could not break away from Cyrus by force, and one cannot believe that Xenophon imagined a hundred thousand barbarians out of less than three thousand cavalry. It must not be forgotten that the Greeks, and the Asiatics, had had a good look at one another when they were paraded for Queen Epyaxa, and at that time Xenophon, since he was not in the ranks, had a better opportunity than most for a general view of both armies. Perhaps we may allow twenty thousand barbarian infantry, more or less, giving Cyrus something under forty thousand men in all.

Sixty thousand might not be an impossible number (if one thinks of such battles as Plassey and Buxar) for the King's army, and perhaps Xenophon may be somewhere near the mark in giving him six thousand household cavalry and two hundred scythed chariots (*Anabasis* i. 7.12).

Through the desert stages, Cyrus's army must have marched in a single long column, so that men and animals could be watered from the river.[1] At the final review it was drawn up for battle, and on the following day Cyrus continued the march with both parts of the army, Greek and barbarian, in battle order, expecting that Artaxerxes would stand and fight along the line of a ditch that he had dug 'extending through the plain for twelve parasangs as far as the Wall of Media' (*Anabasis* i. 7.14–15). But the ditch was unguarded, and Cyrus's army was able to pass through 'a narrow passage beside the Euphrates, between the river and the ditch, some twenty feet in width'. If the whole army did defile through this passage, as Xenophon says it did, it must again have formed a single column, and perhaps this change of formation accounts for the comparatively short distance—three parasangs, with the ditch in the middle—recorded for this day's march.

In Babylonia, it might have been expected that other sources of water would have been available—village wells, inconvenient and inadequate for great numbers of men and animals, and canals, of which four, flowing from the Tigris to the Euphrates, a parasang apart, are mentioned in the text of *Anabasis* i. 7.15. But this passage, coming as it does between the description of the King's ditch and the account of Cyrus's march past it, may be a misplaced note by a later commentator. The main water supply was still the river. Xenophon does not say that the army deployed again, or even marched in several columns to make rapid deployment

---

[1] 'The water of the Euphrates is much esteemed by the inhabitants of its banks. It is, I think, an acquired taste; the newcomer will be apt to look askance at the turgid liquid that issues from the spout of his teapot and to question whether a decoction of ancient dust can be beneficial to the European constitution' (Gertrude Bell, *Amurath to Amurath*, p. 35).

possible. Cyrus very soon stopped expecting a battle, and the need for water was obvious.[1]

We may suppose, then, that Cyrus's army was still moving in a single column along the river. That column must have been over twenty miles long.[2] The order of battle had been arranged at the time of the final review (*Anabasis* i. 7.1–2), and the army marched by the right—that is, the leading units were those which were to form the right of the line of battle, and the intended left brought up the rear. But, with the rear a long day's march behind the vanguard, at least a day's notice of the enemy's approach was needed to form the line, by halting the van and marching up each successive unit to take post on the left.

The vanguard, accordingly, was formed by the Paphlagonian horse, who had evidently pushed out patrols some way in front—but had been unable to penetrate the King's cavalry screen and so could not report on the movements of his main army. Then came the Greek light infantry; then the hoplites, Clearchus leading, and Menon now bringing up the rear. They were followed by Cyrus himself, his household troops, the waggon train, the Asiatic infantry, and, in all probability, a third body of cavalry forming the rearguard under Ariaeus. Given a day's notice, they could form the line, with Cyrus in the centre, his two bodies of infantry on either side of him, and the rest of the cavalry on the two wings.

Cyrus had expected that his brother would offer battle at the entry to Babylonia—'If he is the son of Darius and Parysatis and my brother, I shall not take this without a battle.' But after the

---

[1] For the inconveniences and delays of village wells, compare Genesis xxiv 10ff. The importance of water-supply, especially for cavalry, in hot, dry climates, is of course emphasized by modern writers; see, for example, on the British campaigns of 1917–18 in Palestine, G. Tylden, *Horses and Saddlery* (London, 1965) pp. 42–4; Cyril Falls, *Armageddon: 1918* (London, 1964) pp. 17. 29, 56. Major Tylden considers it 'possible to water horses of one troop, approximately forty, in an hour' by drawing water by hand from very deep (150 feet or more) wells. The ordinary village well would of course be much shallower, but the delay would be considerable.

[2] Sir F. Maurice, an experienced soldier, writes: 'If the march discipline was reasonably good, a column of 10,000 infantry . . . would be approximately six miles in length' ('The Size of the Army of Xerxes', *JHS* 50 (1930) p. 229), Cyrus's march discipline was bad.

defensive ditch that connected the river with the 'Median Wall'
was past, he began to change his mind. Silanus, the Greek prophet
who had foretold ten days earlier that there would be no battle
within that period, was rewarded with the immense sum of three
thousand darics (Clearchus had raised an army with ten thousand)
and lived to carry most of them home, deserting his comrades at
Heraclea on the Black Sea (*Anabasis* i. 7.18; vi. 4.13). On the next
day discipline relaxed, and by the next 'Cyrus was travelling
seated on his chariot with a few men in order in front of him.
Most of his army was marching in an undisciplined manner, and
many of the soldiers' weapons were being carried for them on
waggons or pack-animals' (*Anabasis* i. 7.20).[1]

'And now,' Xenophon continues (*Anabasis* i. 8), 'it was about
the hour when the market fills' (late morning) 'and the station
where they intended to fall out was near, when Pategyas, a nobleman of Cyrus's household, appeared in front, at full gallop, with
his horse in a lather, and shouted directly to everyone he met,
both in Persian and Greek, that the King with a great army was
approaching, ready for battle. Then there was great confusion.
For the Greeks and everyone else thought that he would fall
upon them when they were in disorder. And Cyrus jumped down
from his chariot, put on his breastplate, mounted his horse and
took his javelins in his hands. And he gave orders to all the rest to
arm themselves and form up, each in his own position. Then
indeed they formed up in all haste, Clearchus having the right
wing, next the Euphrates river, Proxenus next to him, the others
after him. Menon and his force held the left wing of the Greek
contingent. Of the barbarian force, about a thousand Paphlagonian cavalry were stationed beside Clearchus on the right
wing, also the Greek contingent of peltasts; and on the left was
Ariaeus, the lieutenant of Cyrus, and the rest of the barbarian
army; but Cyrus and his horsemen, about six hundred strong, in

---

[1] Xenophon perhaps remembered this scene when in the *Oeconomicus* (8.4) he
made Ischomachus admonish his wife on the need for order as follows: 'And, my
dear, an army, if it is without order, is a thing most full of confusion, and most
easy for the enemy to deal with. But to its friends it is a most inglorious sight, and
utterly useless—donkeys, hoplites, servants, light-armed troops, cavalry, chariots,
all mixed up together.'

the centre, armed with cuirasses and thighpieces and helmets—all except Cyrus who went into battle bareheaded.' This was the order that had been pre-arranged no doubt, but more was needed than commanding the army to form. It would take hours for Menon's men to reach their position on the left of the Greek line,[1] and most of the Asiatics were further back still. So for the right of the line there was a long wait, after they had taken up their positions, with nothing to do but speculate on what they had been told about the King's huge army, and wish they had taken some food from the pack-animals while there was a chance.

'And now,' continues Xenophon, 'it was mid-day, and the enemy were not yet in sight. But in the late afternoon, there appeared a dust like a white cloud, and a short time afterwards as it were a blackness in the plain at a great distance.[2] And when they drew nearer, there was a twinkling as of bronze and spear-points, and the regiments could be distinguished. There were cavalry with white cuirasses on the enemy's left. These were said to be under the command of Tissaphernes.[3] Next, men with wicker shields; next, hoplites with wooden shields coming down to their feet. These were said to be Egyptians. Then more horsemen, more archers. All these were marshalled by nations, and each nation marched in a rectangle full of men. In front of them were

---

[1] It will be remembered that Clearchus and Menon, at the time of the affair of the beaten soldier, brought their contingents into camp far ahead of Proxenus, who was then in the rear of the Greeks. The whole incident ran its course before he came up with his regiment, in the nick of time.

[2] Compare Sir Winston Churchill's description of his first sight of the Dervish army (*My Early Life*, p. 189 of the 1941 edition): 'A friendly subaltern who had been on patrol came along . . . "Enemy in sight," he said, beaming. "Where?" we asked. "There, can't you see? Look at that long brown smear! . . . We had all noticed this dark discoloration of the distant horizon, but had taken it to be a forest of thorn-bushes.' Reporting to the Sirdar shortly afterwards, Churchill estimated that he had between an hour and an hour and a half to make his preparations. But the Dervish army halted until the next day, when (p. 199) 'the masses have defined themselves into swarms of men, in ordered ranks bright with glittering weapons, and above them dance a multitude of gorgeous flags'.

[3] We need not suppose that this was a guess. Tissaphernes and his bodyguards, and their distinctive uniform, will have been familiar to their old enemies in Cyrus's army. White may have been his livery: his 'white-shielded Carians' appear in *Hellenica* iii. 2.15. But cf. Plutarch, *Artaxerxes* 11.9; the King's men wore white surcoats, Cyrus's red.

chariots with wide intervals between them, the scythe-bearers, as
they are called ... It was supposed that they were intended to
drive into the Greek ranks and cut through them. But what Cyrus
told the Greeks, when he summoned them and warned them not
to be alarmed by the clamour of the barbarians, proved false. For
they advanced, not with clamour, but in the deepest possible
silence, quietly, evenly and slowly. Meanwhile Cyrus rode past,
himself, with Pigres the interpreter and three or four others, and
shouted to Clearchus to lead his force against the enemy's centre,
because the King was there. "And if we beat this part," he said,
"our whole business will be finished." Clearchus saw the mass in
the centre and heard Cyrus say that the King was beyond the
Greek left (for the King had such a superiority in numbers that,
though he commanded his own centre he was beyond Cyrus's
left). None the less, Clearchus was unwilling to tear away his
right wing from the river, because he was afraid that he would be
outflanked on both sides, and replied to Cyrus that he would see
to it that all was well.'

   Plutarch contrasts the caution of Clearchus with Cyrus's boldness (*Artaxerxes* 7) and blames Clearchus for all that followed.
But, though Xenophon himself seems to support that view, it is
hard to see what else Clearchus could have done. Cyrus's line
was outflanked, not merely because the King had more men to
start with, but because most of Cyrus's men had not yet reached
the front—and never did. Even the Greeks were not yet all in
line. 'Meanwhile the barbarian army' (i.e. the King's, not the
barbarian part of Cyrus's army) 'came steadily on, but the Greek
army, remaining still on the same ground, was being formed in
order from the men who were still coming up' (*Anabasis* i. 8.14).
Quite apart from the well-known danger of attempting a march
across the front of the advancing enemy, how could Clearchus
move off to the left while new units were constantly being
marched up on the left and halted in line with those already there?
The result could only have been complete confusion. Cyrus, of
course, had ridden up past the infantry and reached the front
before them. His own household troops would also arrive on
time, and Ariaeus came into action somewhere, somehow, and

was wounded. But if the final dispositions were not those that had been planned, the blame lies with Cyrus, not with Clearchus, who even if he had given the order to his own men, could not have ordered the other generals; he could only have discussed the matter with them—and there was no time for discussion.

Here Xenophon first appears in his own narrative. As Cyrus was riding along the line, glancing now at his own army and now at the enemy, Xenophon came out to ask for orders and was told to tell everyone that the omens and sacrifices were favourable. 'As Cyrus said this, he heard a noise passing through the ranks, and asked what it was. Xenophon replied that the watchword was being passed back along the ranks.' (The Greek deployment must have been completed at last.) 'Cyrus wondered who had given the order, and asked what the word was. Xenophon replied, "Saviour Zeus and Victory". When Cyrus heard, "I accept it," he said, "and so let it be". So saying he rode away to his own position.'

The King's army was now only five or six hundred yards away, and the Greeks, apparently spontaneously, raised the paean and advanced. The line bulged; those who were being left behind broke into a double to catch up, and soon they were all running forward, shouting the war-cry and banging their shields with their spear-shafts. To extend the line as far as possible in face of the King's superior numbers, the Greeks were probably drawn up four deep, as at the review for the Cilician queen—only half the normal depth, but they were confident of their superiority.

The barbarians gave way and fled before the Greeks were even in arrow-shot. The charioteers abandoned their vehicles, some of which were carried among the barbarians themselves, while others reached the enemy, but did no harm, as the Greeks opened their ranks to let them through. 'One man was caught, as though he had been knocked down at a horse-race' (*Anabasis* i. 8.20). The peltasts on the right wing (*Anabasis* i. 10.7) used the same tactics against Tissaphernes and his cuirassiers, who alone had not fled at the first onset, but had ridden through the Greek line, doing no harm but being struck at as they went past. For the

Greeks, it was a glorious victory. But it was an empty one, since the King was undefeated.

However Artaxerxes himself now gave Cyrus the chance that the Greeks had failed to make for him. Though elated by the Greek victory, Cyrus had kept his household cavalry in hand, instead of joining in the pursuit, and observed the enemy's centre, where he knew his brother would be in person. Now the King, having no enemy on his own front (as Xenophon expressly states: *Anabasis* i. 8.13) 'began to bend his line round in order to carry out an encircling movement' (*Anabasis* i. 8.23).

At this point in Xenophon's narrative we are faced with a dilemma. If Cyrus's Asiatic infantry were actually drawn up in line on the left of Cyrus and his body-guard, and if Ariaeus with another body of cavalry was still further to the left, and if the King was still outside the left flank of the whole of Cyrus's army, Cyrus's position in the line must have been separated by several thousand yards (just how many would depend on the actual number of his Asiatics and how they were drawn up; the Greek line, drawn up four deep, may have been about a mile and a half long) from the King.[1] This is hardly acceptable, because all the witnesses agree that Cyrus made a personal attack on Artaxerxes and his household troops. So either the two lines of battle were more nearly equal than Xenophon supposed, and his description of the King's turning movement is incorrect, or Cyrus was on the left of his own line, not the centre. This second explanation (adopted here) requires us to suppose that Xenophon said that Cyrus's Asiatic troops were on the left because that was where

[1] For an alternative solution, based on the supposition that Cyrus's army did march in several columns, enabling the Asiatic infantry to reach the field in time (though it is allowed that they did nothing when they got there), see J. Kromayer, *Antike Schlachtfelder* (Berlin, 1924–31) vol. IV, pp. 223ff. This account proposes that the King himself was beyond the left flank of the Greeks, but not the whole of Cyrus's army: his extreme right wing outflanked Cyrus's extreme left, but the 'bending round' of his line observed by Xenophon was a movement by the left part of the King's centre, intended to penetrate the gap left in Cyrus's line after the Greeks had charged, and so attack the rear of the Greeks. Kromayer considers that Cyrus was a skilled and experienced general who would not have demanded impossibilities—but in fact, though he had financed other people's fleets and armies, he had never before handled a large army on the field of battle.

the Greeks had been told they would be and where they should have been. In fact, they never reached their position, because they were too far in the rear to arrive at the battlefield in time.

The King, then, began to bend his line round to encircle Cyrus's left flank. Xenophon explains in the *Cyropaedia* (vii. 1) that the only way to carry out this manoeuvre was to halt the main body while the wing (which was to carry out the encirclement) led off to form a new line, at right angles to the original one, and facing inwards. So most of the King's cavalry halted, and against them Cyrus led his own six hundred at full gallop.

The charge of the Heavy Brigade at Balaclava supplies a good modern parallel to what happened next. 'Scarlett's three hundred' were faced by a far greater number of Russian cavalry, whose main body had halted in order that the wings might 'crush all close comers with an easy and pitiless hug'. The British charge penetrated this stationary mass, and, despite the fact that 'the Russians evinced a degree of steadiness not unworthy of a nation which was famous for the valour of its infantry', broke it up and drove it from the field. 'By the judgment of Lord Lucan—not tested, however, by the hand of the watch—it has been computed that . . . the time was about eight minutes.' During much of that time General Scarlett himself, his aide-de-camp, and the commanding officers of the regiments engaged, were entirely cut off, and fighting single-handed against crowds of enemies.[1]

So it was that Cyrus broke through the ranks of his brother's cavalry, making directly for the royal standard. Xenophon may have seen the charge begin, but of course he had no detailed knowledge of how it ended, until, many years later, he read (as he tells us: *Anabasis* i. 8.26–7) the account of Ctesias, the physician, who had been in personal attendance on the King. Of this, a rather fuller summary is preserved by Plutarch (*Artaxerxes* 9ff.). It seems that Cyrus killed with his own hand Artagerses, the commander of the guard, and broke through to his brother, whom he wounded and unhorsed. But his impetuosity, and his hard-mouthed charger, carried him still deeper into the enemy ranks.

---

[1] See the excessively detailed account in A. W. Kinglake's *Invasion of the Crimea*, vol. II, pp. 426ff. in the New York edition.

He was bare-headed, and had used both his javelins. Many of the King's men submitted to him, but in the confusion and gathering darkness he was first wounded above the temple and then, as he tried to make his way on foot, supported by a few friends who had kept up with him, killed by a common foot-soldier. His household perished with him.

Artaxerxes meanwhile had been brought out of the fight to a small hill. A little muddy water was procured for him from a poor camp-follower, and his troops began to rally to him. He might lack his brother's athletic prowess, but (as he was later to show on his Cadusian expedition; cf. Plutarch *Artaxerxes* 24) he was not without courage and endurance. Artasyras, 'the King's Eye', had already reported the death of Cyrus, and the good news was con-firmed by a patrol ('thirty messengers') sent out for the purpose. By the light of torches, the King descended to view the body: the right hand and head were lopped off and presented to him, and he displayed the head to his followers, grasping it by its long thick hair (Plutarch, *Artaxerxes* 14ff.; the cutting off of the head and hand is also mentioned by Xenophon, *Anabasis* i. 10.1).

According to Xenophon (*Anabasis* i. 10), the King attacked Cyrus's camp—that is, the halted baggage-train. There can have been no regular camp in the circumstances of the battle. Ariaeus and the Asiatics fled to the place where they had spent the previous night. (Most of the infantry must have been a long way in the rear still.) The King and his men plundered the camp, but the Greeks who were with the baggage formed up and beat off the Persian attack, saving not only all that was in their own lines but Cyrus's younger Greek mistress, 'the Milesian', who escaped naked out of the hands of the barbarians.[1]

Meanwhile the Greek army, still in line of battle, had continued the pursuit to a distance of some three miles. The King learned of the Greek victory from Tissaphernes (who also had reached the camp, after breaking through the peltasts at the beginning of the action) and formed up his own men to come up behind the

---

[1] The older, Aspasia the Phocaean, was captured. For her subsequent career, as concubine to Artaxerxes and to the Crown Prince Darius, and finally as priestess of 'Artemis' at Ecbatana, cf. Plutarch, *Artaxerxes* 26–7.

Greeks. But Clearchus had observed the attack on the camp, and consulted with Proxenus, who was next him in the order of battle. The Greek line was faced about, towards its original rear, but the King, instead of meeting it directly, swerved off outside its left flank (that is, the original left, furthest from the river, which had become the right). As he did so, he picked up 'the men who had deserted to the Greeks during the battle' (prisoners that is, who had surrendered but not been properly secured) and Tissaphernes and his men (*Anabasis* i. 10.6; but we have been told in i. 10.5 that the King had already met Tissaphernes in the camp. Actually of course what the Greeks saw was one large body of Persians coming away from the camp and forming up, then moving off round their own flank, being joined on the way by more scattered bodies of the enemy, including 'the deserters' and perhaps some of the white cuirassiers. Neither the men in the camp nor the main body, in all probability, saw the enemy commanders close enough to identify them, and the moment when they met was a guess.)

There was now a danger that the Persian would roll up the Greek line from the flank; so the Greeks resolved 'to bend back their wing and place the river at their backs'. One has the impression that the generals, who could see what was happening behind them and (*Anabasis* i. 10.10) consult about it, had not, as was usual in Greek warfare, taken a place in the ranks, but were outside the phalanx, probably on horseback.

The Persians now formed in battle order and advanced against the Greeks, as they had done at the beginning of the action, but when the Greeks charged, with even higher courage than the first time, the enemy ran away again, from an even greater distance. The Greeks pursued as far as a village (no doubt Cunaxa, after which the battle was called) where they halted, because there was a ridge above the village where the King's men had again turned to meet them, not the infantry any more, but the cavalry. The Greeks could not see what was happening, but some of them claimed to make out the golden eagle on the royal standard. When the Greeks again advanced, the Persian cavalry retired, not in one body, but scattering in all directions. Clearchus halted at the foot of the ridge, and sent a horseman, Lycius of

Syracuse, to the top, who reported that the enemy was in full flight. 'Just at this point the sun set. The Greeks halted, grounded their arms, and rested, and wondered that Cyrus could not be seen anywhere, and that he sent no messenger. For they did not know that he was dead, but thought that he had gone off in pursuit or to seize some point in advance.' So they returned, hungry, to the plundered camp.

Such was the battle, as described by two ancient eye witnesses from their opposite points of view. A different version is supplied by Diodorus (xiv. 23.5–7) according to which, after the brothers had met as though to mimic the rash conflict, so renowned in tragedy, of Eteocles and Polynices, and the wounded King had been carried out of the battle, Tissaphernes took over the command. This implies, presumably, that he had ridden at the King's bridle-hand in the early part of the action, and if it is true it is, to say the least, surprising that Ctesias, who has plenty to say about his conduct after the battle, ignores him during it.

Diodorus continues by describing how Tissaphernes and Cyrus both fought brilliantly and slew numerous enemies, but at last Cyrus, charging too imprudently, was cut off and slain. What is the source of all this? One might claim that there are traces elsewhere in Diodorus's narrative (xiv. 23.1) of some other author, not Xenophon, on the Greek side. According to Xenophon, in the first onset the Persians ran away before the Greeks were within arrow-shot. According to Diodorus, the Greeks advanced slowly until they came into range, and then, upon the orders of Clearchus, broke into a double, so that the enemy would misjudge the range and shoot over their heads. Different parts of the line might have had different experiences, and here we may have the version of Sophaenetus, for instance. Diodorus goes on to say that the barbarians, though they discharged a multitude of missiles, 'fought for only a very short time with javelins, and thereafter joined battle hand-to-hand'. This seems to be pure fiction—based perhaps on the battle of Plataea in 479 B.C.; hence Diodorus speaks of the Greeks as 'the Lacedaemonians with the rest of the mercenaries', though there were only a few Lacedaemonians present. The comparison of Cyrus and Artaxerxes to tragedy heroes strengthens the impression that this is a literary exercise, and for the personal encounter of the brothers we can no longer imagine a source on the Greek side. How could Sophaenetus have known that the King was wounded, that Tissaphernes had taken over command, and that Cyrus was dead? If he did know, why did he leave the rest of the generals to learn the news from Glous next day? It is possible that Sophaenetus stayed with the baggage and organized its defence, and if so he will have given a different picture of the battle from Xenophon's, but of the result of the cavalry charge he knew no more than Xenophon did.

None the less, Tissaphernes may have done more than Xenophon allows. According to Xenophon, the second part of the battle, when the Greeks changed their front and advanced to the village below the ridge on which they saw the King's standard, ended just before sunset. According to Ctesias, the King descended from the hill to which he had been taken by torchlight. It would seem then, that all the time the Greeks and Persians were manoeuvring against each other, the King was on the hill (Xenophon's ridge where they saw the royal standard). He was not, then, in command of the forces below, as Xenophon and the Greeks supposed. We may suppose that the Greeks saw that the attack on the camp was made by large numbers of men from the King's right wing, who had been outside Cyrus's left and untouched by his charge. The Greeks supposed that the King himself had led them, but in fact he was on the ridge (the only place where they saw his standard) the whole time. These men defeated Ariaeus, who had barely reached the battlefield from the rear, but the Greek baggage-guards beat them off—and Tissaphernes too, who had come from the other end of the line. But Tissaphernes pulled them together, collected what other troops he could, including the 'deserters', and made his demonstration against the Greek flank and rear. If so, one can see why the King judged that Tissaphernes, who had charged when everyone else ran away, cut his way through, attacked the camp, and tried to reorganize the broken left wing, deserved the prize for valour that Diodorus (xiv. 26.4) says he later received. One cannot help wondering, once more, whether Phalinus, the Greek professional in the service of Tissaphernes, was not the ultimate source for Diodorus and claimed that his master was the man who really won the battle.

The official Persian communiqué will, of course, have given Artaxerxes himself the credit for the victory, and it would seem, for the death of Cyrus too. Parts of it seem to have been preserved in Dinon's story (also quoted by Plutarch) according to which the King, after being twice unhorsed and remounted by the faithful Tiribazus, rushed, on the third encounter, against Cyrus and killed him with his own hand. This is clearly an official version; the young Persian Mithridates who actually gave Cyrus his first wound, according to Ctesias, was lavishly rewarded, but the statement of his services allowed only that he had picked up and presented to the King the trappings that fell from Cyrus's horse as it ran loose. Later he boasted in his cups of what he had really done, and was punished with a most horrible death—as, by the machinations of the Queen Mother, were all those who had a hand in Cyrus's killing.

It was a saying of the great Prince of Condé that to see defects in war one must serve a campaign with the Spaniards.[1] Xenophon's campaign under Cyrus may have instructed him in the same manner. At the end of his life, in the *Cyropaedia* (vi. 3.5ff.), he makes his hero, the great ancestor after whom the rebel Cyrus was named, fight and win a pitched battle against Croesus of Lydia. He does not let this ideal story-book Cyrus blunder unprepared upon the enemy line of battle. His spies bring him intelligence from the enemy camp; his patrols observe the signs that the enemy is near—'men gathering fodder and wood, and pack-animals carrying loads of the same, and others grazing'; and at a great distance, 'either smoke or dust rising in the air'. So the hero halts his army, in order to carry out the preparations necessary before coming into contact with the enemy, including a meal and a night's rest. Against Artaxerxes, the Greeks had gone into action unfed, and at the end of a day's march. And in the *Cyropaedia* the army is carefully drawn up and wins a brilliant victory, following a prearranged tactical plan. At Cunaxa there was no opportunity to put the prearranged plan into effect.

[1] Lord Mahon, *Life of Condé* (New York, 1845) vol. II, p. 100.

CHAPTER NINE

The Aftermath

THE Greeks were late to learn of the death of Cyrus, and even later to understand that the rebellion had died with him. They first proposed to set Ariaeus on the throne, and, even after he realistically declined this offer, they made it clear that they were not going to surrender their weapons and come to the King's gates to obtain what grace they could find. 'We have now no assets except our weapons and our courage. If we keep our weapons I think that we can make use of our courage too, but if we give them up I think we will be deprived of our bodies also' (*Anabasis* ii. 1.12). They were prepared to offer their services to the King, but Artaxerxes, though later in his reign he employed large numbers of Greek mercenaries for the very purpose that Clearchus suggested—the attempted recovery of Egypt—had at present no use for such expensive auxiliaries. He did not want another battle, nor did he want the Greeks to remain in Babylonia, supplying themselves from his richest province. Ariaeus and the other Persians were to be pardoned. The Persians were greatly outnumbered by their subject peoples, and the King could not afford to reduce their strength unnecessarily. Besides, for all that Xenophon has to say about the enthusiastic support that Cyrus attracted, Cyrus himself had said that he could not trust his Asiatics if things seemed to be going wrong (*Anabasis* i. 5.16). Perhaps the King was ready to believe that they had joined the rebellion unwillingly.

But they must work their passage home, by helping Tissaphernes to get rid of the troublesome Greeks. Tissaphernes was to leave Mesopotamia by marching up the Tigris (supplies along

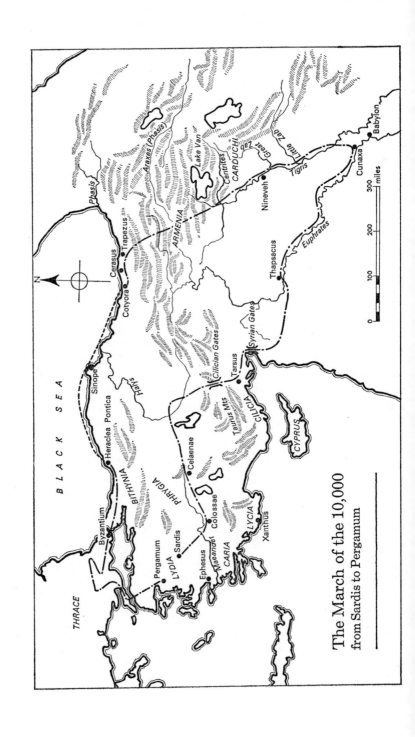

The March of the 10,000
from Sardis to Pergamum

the Euphrates route were exhausted; *Anabasis* ii. 2.11), and then
turn westward, back to his own province. The rebels, once they
had made their peace, would accompany him, and so would
the Greeks, who were of course anxious to return home. When
the right time came, the Greeks could be harassed by the Asiatic
cavalry and light infantry. Perhaps their morale and discipline
would give way and they could be destroyed; if not they could
be shepherded up into the mountains of Kurdistan, where the
hill tribes and the winter snows would make an end of them.

In this critical period, Clearchus established his authority, not
merely by his professional knowledge and stern discipline, but
by force of example. 'Henceforth Clearchus commanded, and the
rest obeyed, not because they had elected him, but because they
saw that he alone understood a commander's duties, and the
others were without experience.'[1] When it was necessary to throw
bridges over the irrigation canals (*Anabasis* ii. 3.10ff.), he showed
his leadership, 'with his spear in his left hand, and a stick in his
right. And, if he thought that any of the men assigned to this
duty was slacking, he would call out the proper man and strike
him, and at the same time he went into the mud and took a hand
in the work. So everyone was ashamed not to try their hardest to
help. The men under thirty had been detailed for this duty. But
when they saw Clearchus joining in the work, the older men too
gave a hand.' (Clearchus himself was 'about fifty': *Anabasis* ii.
6.15.)

Clearchus also had a useful sense of humour, which helped him
to quieten a midnight panic by proclaiming a reward of a talent
(fifteen years' pay!) for whoever laid information against the man
who had turned a donkey loose in the camp (*Anabasis* ii. 2.20).
When Persian plenipotentiaries came to discuss a truce, his
reply of 'No truce before breakfast' obtained both a truce and

[1] Compare the obedience of the Scottish nobles to Alexander Leslie in 1639:
'Such was the wisdom and authority of that old little crooked souldier, that all,
with ane incredible submission, from the beginning to the end, gave over them-
selves to be guided by him, as if he had been Great Solyman' (*The Letters and
Journals of Robert Baillie*, quoted by Thomas Carlyle, *London and Westminster
Review* no. 72 (1841), reprinted in *Scottish and Other Miscellanies* (Everyman's
Library). p. 125).

provisions (*Anabasis* ii. 3.5). When Phalinus offered him truce
if he stayed where he was, war if he advanced or retreated, he
answered that he accepted the King's terms, and when pressed
to say whether he meant war or truce, replied, 'Truce if we
remain; war if we retire or advance', and so concealed his intentions (*Anabasis* ii. 1.27).

But in cunning he proved no match for Tissaphernes, who
persuaded him that he intended to lead the Greeks home, and
hinted that, in return for the service that he was doing them, they
could further his own secret ambitions. 'The King alone can
wear the Tiara upright upon his head; but upon the heart another
man might well wear it, if you stood by him' (*Anabasis* ii. 5.23).

Meanwhile the Greeks had been led across the Tigris and up its
east bank, as far as the Greater Zab and within a few days' march
of tribal territory. It was time to strike. Clearchus, Proxenus,
Menon and two other generals were invited to a conference, and
suddenly arrested. A red flag was hoisted over the satrap's tent;
and at once his soldiers cut down the captains who had accompanied the generals, and the soldiers who had entered the Persian
camp to buy provisions. Parties of cavalry galloped across the
plain to cut off foragers, to the bewilderment of the Greeks, who
were at a loss to understand this sudden activity until a fugitive,
Nicarchus the Arcadian, came in, horribly wounded, with the
news. They were now plunged into despair, and the disintegra-
tion of their army seemed imminent.

Xenophon concludes this section of his story (*Anabasis* ii. 6)
with character sketches of the generals, who were conveyed to
the King at Babylon and later put to death. The character of
Menon may perhaps be supposed to have been written under the
influence of some personal injury, which Xenophon does not
describe. General accusations of ambition and treachery do not
tell us much, and he only hints that Menon was ready to join his
friend Ariaeus in betraying the Greeks (cf. *Anabasis* ii. 4.15).
Perhaps the repeated observation that Menon used to mock his
friends is revealing. Had Xenophon laid him under some obligation (for instance, by hospitality at Athens) which Menon
rewarded by making him appear ridiculous in the eyes of Cyrus?

The contrasted figures of Clearchus and Proxenus have already been mentioned. The harsh discipline of Clearchus produced good soldiers, and was accepted in time of danger as the salvation of his men, though they often left him when the danger was past. The character of Proxenus is worth giving in full. 'From his first youth he wished to become a man capable of great achievements. This desire led him to pay fees to Gorgias of Leontini.[1] After studying under him, he thought that he was also capable of command, and that, though befriended by men of the highest rank, he was not inferior to his benefactors. So he entered his career with Cyrus, from which he expected a great name, great power, and great wealth. But though he had these grandiose ambitions, he also had this very evident characteristic, that he wished to achieve none of them with injustice, but thought that he must gain them with justice and honour, and not otherwise. He could command gentlemen, but he was incapable of inspiring either reverence or fear for himself, and actually respected his soldiers more than his subordinates respected him. And he was evidently more afraid of making himself disliked by the soldiers than the soldiers were of disobeying him. He thought that it was enough, for the reality and appearance of leadership, to praise the man who did well, and not to praise the man who did wrong. And so those of his associates who were honourable and good liked him, but wrongdoers schemed against him, thinking that it was easy to get round him. He was about thirty years old at his death.'

Such a commander must have needed support, and the readiness with which Proxenus's captains accepted Xenophon when he summoned them on the night following the arrest of the generals (*Anabasis* iii. 1.26ff.), suggests that Xenophon had given it, efficiently and tactfully.

Whatever their characters, the deaths of the generals plunged the army into despair. 'Few tasted their evening meal; few kindled fires. Many did not come to their posts that night, but rested where each happened to be, being unable to sleep for sorrow and

[1] The great teacher of rhetoric, criticized, not unkindly, by Plato in the dialogue that is named after him.

longing for their countries, parents, wives, children, whom they thought they would never see again.' Xenophon 'grieved with the rest and was unable to sleep. But when he obtained a little sleep he saw a dream. He thought that there was a thunderstorm and a bolt fell upon his father's house, and set it all in a blaze. He woke at once in terror, and judged that the dream was in part good, because when he was in troubles and dangers he had seemed to see a great light from Zeus. But in part, too, he was afraid, because the dream seemed to come to him from Zeus the King, and the fire seemed to blaze all around him. So he was afraid that he would not be able to escape from the King's country, but would be beset on all sides by insurmountable difficulties' (*Anabasis* iii. 1.3; 11–12).

However he roused himself with the reflection that it was no use waiting to grow older if he handed himself over to the enemy that very day, called Proxenus's captains, and with very little opposition was accepted, despite his youth, in place of his dead friend. Xenophon was not, and does not pretend that he was, in sole command. In its retreat up the Tigris, harassed by Tissaphernes, its winter march across Kurdistan and Armenia to the Greek colony of Trapezus on the Black Sea, and its continued march westwards to Sinope, the army was directed by the majority vote of the generals (*Anabasis* vi. 1.18). After this a single supreme commander was at last chosen, but it was Chirisophus the Lacedaemonian—obviously more to please his friend, the Spartan admiral Anaxibius, than because the soldiers really wanted him; within a week his command was dissolved.

During the spring and summer of 400 B.C., while the 'Cyreans' were making their way towards Byzantium, Sparta and Persia were maintaining a precarious peace. Artaxerxes, with other troubles on his hands, would overlook Sparta's past support for Cyrus if the Spartans would recognize his suzerainty over the Greek cities of Asia, once allied to Athens. But the former partisans of Cyrus in those cities were afraid of Tissaphernes and had appealed to Sparta. Until the Spartans committed themselves to a war of liberation, the appearance of a large and well-trained army which nobody wished to employ or could afford to keep, in the sensitive area at the mouth of the Black Sea, was a most unwelcome complication—worse, if the army was led by an Athenian.

A sudden quarrel between Anaxibius and the Persian satrap Pharnabazus, early in the winter of 400–399 B.C., caused Anaxibius to release Xenophon, whom he was bringing back to Greece under semi-arrest, and send him to take full command of the Cyreans. Sparta's official attitude, as expressed by Anaxibius's successor, was still hostile, and the army maintained itself through the winter in the service of the Thracian prince Seuthes. But early in 399 B.C. Sparta and Tissaphernes were at war, and messengers came to summon the army to Thibron, the Spartan general, and later to retain Xenophon himself in the Spartan service.

CHAPTER TEN

Xenophon's Leadership

It has often been observed that one reason that the loss of its chief generals was not immediately fatal to the Greek army was that its soldiers were not, as the Greeks put it, 'servants of one man', but citizens of free states, accustomed to reach decisions for themselves by open discussion and vote. Even before the death of Cyrus, the soldiers had shown at Tarsus and at Thapsacus that they must be persuaded, not compelled, and would follow the officers whom they trusted, not those who were set over them. Since Cyrus showed his hand as a rebel, they had not been subject to any lawfully constituted authority. When, therefore, the whole army was summoned to an assembly (as it was on the morrow of the generals' murder), the soldiers were not merely informed of the situation—'put in the picture', in the modern phrase—but asked to approve the generals' decisions and (*Anabasis* iii. 2.37–8) invited to make proposals of their own. The basic procedures—the introduction of motions by official speakers, the formal putting of the vote, the show of hands— were familiar. That the officers, including the captains, should hold a preliminary meeting, as they now did (*Anabasis* iii. 1.32ff.) before the assembly was called, suggests analogies with the Council, at Athens as elsewhere. Moreover, the new generals, including Xenophon, were approved by popular vote (*Anabasis* iii. 1.46–7), not merely appointed by their fellow officers. Like the elected officials of Greek city states, they had to justify their conduct in office—not at the end of their period of command, but when they had brought the army through its most pressing dangers to the Black Sea coast. Here again the captains performed the formal functions of a council, and acted as the court before whom the soldiers brought their complaints (*Anabasis* v. 7.34–8.26).

Like a state, the army also had its treasury—a 'common stock', maintained apparently out of an agreed proportion of the general spoil. From this the guide who brought the Greeks within sight of the sea was rewarded (*Anabasis* iv. 7.27). From this too tithes were set apart and entrusted to the generals for eventual dedication to Apollo and Ephesian Artemis. It was many years before Xenophon paid his dues, but he did it handsomely in the end (*Anabasis* v. 3.4ff.).

But the comparison with a city state must not be pressed too far.[1] Those of the soldiers who survived to enter the Spartan service in 399 B.C. eventually developed an *esprit de corps* as 'Cyreans', but they were Arcadians, Achaeans or Lacedaemonians first. It was all very well for Clearchus to tell the mutineers at Tarsus (*Anabasis* i. 3.6) that they were 'his country, his friends and his allies'—but he was in exile and his sincerity is not above suspicion. Most of the soldiers had countries and friends of their own, to which they were anxious to return. They had not embarked on mercenary service because they were destitute, but had laid out their own money in order to make fortunes under Cyrus, 'whose virtue they had heard', and to bring those fortunes back to Greece, where they had left parents, wives and children (*Anabasis* vi. 4.8). So the mere suggestion that Xenophon had plans to settle their 'moving republic' on some suitable site, as a new Greek colony in the Black Sea region, brought him instant unpopularity (*Anabasis* v. 6.15ff.; vi. 4.1–8). Moreover the different contingents of Cyrus's army had been separately raised, in different parts of Greece, and the Arcadians and Achaeans were eventually to reject the unification of the army under a Spartan commander-in-chief—did this mean they must choose a Spartan

---

[1] It is interesting that besides this picture drawn from life of an army organized as a city state, Xenophon also gives us, in *Cyropaedia* viii.1, a picture of a state organized like an army, with the civil administration modelled on the military chain of command. How closely he supposed the actual Persian Empire to conform to this model is not easy to decide. It would in any case be a mistake to suppose that Xenophon's notion of the ideal state was a gigantic autocracy, even if it were as well administered as the empire described in the *Cyropaedia*.

toast-master every time they had a drinking-party?—and set off
to make their own fortunes by plunder. Only a near disaster, from
which they were rescued by Xenophon, re-united the army
(*Anabasis* vi. 2.9ff.).

If these divisions were not apparent when the Greeks were cut
off in the heart of Persia, it was because they were temporarily
united by the common danger, and by the common purpose.
With this purpose and this danger in mind, the soldiers might
approve when the generals called for the sacrifice of private
property—tents and waggons at once (*Anabasis* iii. 3.1); later,
after they had entered the mountains of Kurdistan, all but 'the
most essential and strongest' baggage animals, and all recently-
captured prisoners. (Sale of prisoners as slaves was one of the
most hoped-for sources of profit.) 'The large numbers of pack-
animals and prisoners were delaying the march, and the many
men who guarded them were taken off the fighting strength'; the
need was obvious, and so, though the matter had not been
approved by general vote, 'the soldiers obeyed, except a few who
conveyed some possession by stealth, such as a handsome boy or
a pretty woman they were fond of' (*Anabasis* iv. 1.13–14).

But this did not establish a precedent. The first complaint
against Xenophon, when the generals were brought before the
court of enquiry (*Anabasis* v. 8.1ff.), was from a muleteer whose
load had been distributed among the soldiers to provide for an
invalid. 'A man was being left behind because he could march no
longer. I knew no more of him than that he was one of us, but I
made this man carry him, to save his life. Furthermore, as I think,
the enemy were close behind us. The fellow agreed. "Well," said
Xenophon, "after I had sent you on, I overtook you again when
I came up with the rearguard, digging a pit to bury the man, and
when I learned what you were doing I praised you. Then, as we
stood by, the man bent his leg, and the bystanders called out that
he was alive. And you said, "Let him live as much as he wants,
but I shan't carry him". "Then I did strike you; quite true. It
seemed to me that you knew that he was alive." "So what?" said
he. "Did he die any the less, as I showed him to you?" "We will
all die some day," said Xenophon, "but is that a reason for you

to bury us alive?" Then everyone shouted that he had not been beaten enough.'

Xenophon confessed that he had struck other soldiers, to keep them moving, so that they should not perish in the snow. He had acted, not out of insolence, but in the spirit of a father[1] or teacher or a physician, who cuts and cauterizes in order to cure. If he had acted from mere insolence, why did he strike nobody now that he was in better health and had more wine to drink? The truth was that they had now reached calm waters; in a storm a ship's officers were angry at their men for so much as nodding, for a small mistake could cause disaster. If they had thought at the time that he was acting unjustly, why had they not intervened, with swords for votes?

This makes evident the real difference between the generals and magistrates of a free commonwealth. Xenophon was not concerned with maintaining the laws; there were no laws; it was his business to give orders, and see that they were obeyed. To enforce discipline, he could use measures that no citizen—no Athenian citizen at least—would have tolerated from his magistrates. He must punish arbitrarily and on the spur of the moment —though corporal punishment was clearly a last resort; he had used it, and so had Clearchus, but he shows elsewhere (*Hellenica* vi. 2.19) that he well knew that it could demoralize rather than discipline. If a general lost his men's trust there was no law behind which an unpopular officer could shelter.

So a general must constantly establish himself in his soldiers' eyes. He must set an example in facing hardship. When a snow-storm came on the army as it lay in the open, and the men were reluctant to stir under their covering of snow, Xenophon himself rose naked to split firewood. 'Then someone else got up and took the cleaver from him and began to split. After him others got up and lit a fire and rubbed themselves with oil' (*Anabasis*

---

[1] Captain V. S. Littaeur (*Russian Hussar* (London, 1965) p. 235) describes how, as an officer in the Russian Imperial army, he struck one of his N.C.O.s rather than bring him before a court martial for serious offences committed on active service. After the Bolshevik revolution, when the man could have taken his revenge, he made a point of thanking Captain Littaeur for his 'fatherly punishment'.

iv. 4.11–12). The general must not be selfish, like the soldiers, who, when the blizzard heaped the snow in six-foot drifts and the men survived the night by lighting fires, refused to allow the rearguard to approach except in exchange for part of their rations (*Anabasis* iv. 5.5).

The private soldiers constantly looked to their officers, who must show, by high morale and good discipline, that they deserved their extra pay and special privileges (*Anabasis* iii. 1.36–7; is there a conscious reminiscence of *Iliad* xii. 310ff.?). The general must present an impressive appearance, as in the first assembly, when Xenophon 'stood up, armed for war as splendidly as he was able, thinking that, if the gods granted victory, the fairest display befitted the conquest, and if he was marked to die, it was right to have counted himself worthy of the finest adornments, and in them to meet his end' (*Anabasis* iii. 2.7).

A good officer would even pretend a confidence that he did not feel. Xenophon, as a former cavalryman, was no doubt impressed by the thousands of Persian horsemen, but he heartened the Greek infantry by telling them that 'ten thousand cavalry are nothing more than ten thousand men. Nobody has ever been killed in action by the bite or kick of a horse, but it is men who inflict casualties in battles. We are on a far safer footing than cavalry; they hang on to their horses, afraid of us and afraid of falling off. But we have our feet on the ground and will strike more strongly, if anyone approaches us, and will find it much easier to hit our targets (Plate 10). The one and only advantage that cavalry have is that they can run away more safely than we can' (*Anabasis* iii. 2.18–19). Xenophon's real thoughts on this subject are no doubt those that he puts into the mouths of the first Cyrus and his faithful Chrysantas, when the fictitious Persians of the *Cyropaedia* (iv. 3.4–23) are being reorganized as cavalry. Apart from practical military advantages, riding is as good as flying, and the horseman is even luckier than the Centaur, in that he has an extra pair of eyes and can get rid of his horse-body whenever it is likely to prove an embarrassment.

Nor could the general act with complete frankness when he saw that some course of action would be necessary but the men were not yet ready to follow it. At Trapezus on the Black Sea, the men would 'soldier no more; you may say what you like', and demanded ships so that they could be wafted home like Ulysses. But Xenophon 'when he saw their folly, put nothing to the vote, but persuaded the cities to build a road, which they willingly did, when he said that they would be quicker rid of them if the roads were passable' (*Anabasis* vi. 2.14).

Special privileges were not to be abused. Xenophon makes a virtue of his poverty at the end of the expedition (*Anabasis* vii. 3.20; vii. 8.1–2), though he does not expressly blame his colleague Timasion for acquiring Persian carpets and silver cups. Nor must the officer take advantage of his position to make his duties easier—or even appear to do so. Early in the retreat, Xenophon had to race Tissaphernes for a height overlooking the road (*Anabasis* iii. 9.37–49). Xenophon's own men were in the rear, and Chirisophus the Lacedaemonian, the commander of the vanguard, lent Xenophon a detachment, to whom he was a comparative stranger. 'There was a great noise from the Greek army cheering on their own men, and a great noise from the troops of Tissaphernes cheering on theirs. And Xenophon rode on horseback beside his men, and encouraged them: "Soldiers, think that you are now racing for Greece, for your wives and children! A little effort now, and we will make the rest of our march without fighting!" But Soteridas of Sicyon said, "It's an unfair match, Xenophon. There you sit on your horse, and I struggle along carrying my shield." When Xenophon heard this, he jumped down from his horse, pushed him out of the ranks, took his shield from him, and went as fast as he could carrying it. But he was wearing his cavalry cuirass, and so was overloaded. So he told the front ranks to lead on, and the rear ranks to pass him, as he followed with difficulty. But the other soldiers hit Soteridas and threw stones at him, and cursed him, until they made him take his shield and go on. But Xenophon remounted and led on horseback, as far as the ground allowed, and when it was no longer rideable he did his best on foot. And they reached the height before the enemy. Then the barbarians turned and fled, each where he could, but the Greeks held the height.'

Xenophon seems to have learned a lesson from this affair. When leading his men to the attack in Thrace, he dismounted, explaining to the surprised Seuthes that 'the hoplites will run faster and more cheerfully if I lead on foot' (*Anabasis* vii. 3.45).

The good general was not only to set an example to his men; he was to make himself accessible to them at all times. (Xenophon emphasizes this point in connection with other generals whom he admired—Hermocrates (*Hellenica* i. 1.30) and Teleutias (*Hellenica* v. 1.14). Once Xenophon's accessibility was the saving of the army. The Greeks had fought their way through Kurdistan, suffering in seven days more losses than the total inflicted by the King and Tissaphernes (*Anabasis* iv. 3.2). They had reached the Centrites river, the boundary of Armenia. But the ford was deep, and on the far bank were the forces of the satraps Orontas and Artuchas. The Carduchi were massing in the mountains, and the Greeks were again desperate. 'For that day and night they remained at a loss how to proceed. But Xenophon saw a dream' (just as he had after the murder of the generals). 'He seemed to be bound in fetters, which burst of their own accord, so that he was freed and passed as far as he wished to go. At the point of day he went to Chirisophus and said that he had hopes that all would be well, and told him the dream. Chirisophus was glad, and the moment dawn appeared the whole number of generals assembled and sacrificed, obtaining good omens at the first attempt. So the generals and captains came away from the sacrifices and ordered the army to make breakfast.'

While Xenophon was breakfasting two young men ran up to him. 'For all men knew that he could be approached both at breakfast and at dinner, and that even if he was sleeping one could wake him and speak to him on matters of military importance.' These young men said that they had been collecting brushwood for a fire, when they saw an old man, a woman and some girls on the far bank, spreading out clothes at a point where rocks ran down to the very river bank, which would prevent the approach of the enemy's cavalry. They had stripped to swim over and steal the clothes, but found they were able to cross without the water reaching their waists. 'So Xenophon immediately poured a libation, and told the young men to do likewise, and pray to the gods who had made plain the accomplishment of the dreams and the crossing and all other good things.'

The general was himself to know his officers and their individual quality. Xenophon insists on this in the *Cyropaedia* (v. 3.46–50): 'Cyrus thought it most remarkable that when workmen all know the names of the tools of their particular crafts, and doctors know the names of all their instruments and medicines, a general could be so negligent as not to know the names of his subordinate officers, whom he has to use as his tools ... For it seemed to him that men who think their officer recognizes them are keener to be seen doing something honourable and more desirous of avoiding blame.'

So one of the most attractive features of the *Anabasis* is the generosity with which Xenophon praises his subordinates by name. Democrates the Temenite 'seemed often . . . to have provided true information, reporting fact as fact and falsehood as falsehood'. Aristeas of Chios 'was in many places of great value to the army' (*Anabasis* iv. 1.28; 4.15). Stratocles, captain of the Cretan archers, did good service against the longbowmen of the Carduchi (*Anabasis* iv. 2.28), whose clothyard shafts could pierce a man clean through his head, or through his shield and corslet into his lungs. When the Carduchi were rolling boulders down on to the rearguard and had broken one man's leg, and Xenophon's shieldbearer had deserted him, Eurylochus of Lusii ran up to him and threw his shield in front of both. This Eurylochus was the friend of Agasias of Stymphalus, who had earned Xenophon's particular good will by driving out Apollonides the Boeotian, the only one of Proxenus's captains who had wished to surrender after the generals' murder—a disgrace to Greece, said Xenophon; but Agasias said he was no Greek but a Lydian, as his pierced ears proved (*Anabasis* iii. 1.31; iv. 2.21; iv. 7.11–12).

Agasias was one of a group of captains whose rivalry in valour often attracted Xenophon's attention. For a dangerous operation, the generals called the captains, 'to explain the situation and ask if any of them was willing to be a brave man and volunteer to go. From the hoplites, Aristonymus of Methydrium volunteered,

and Agasias of Stymphalus; and in rivalry with them Callimachus of Parrhasia said that he was willing to go, taking with
him volunteers from the whole army. "For I know," said he,
"that many of the young men will follow where I lead" ' (*Anabasis* iv. 1.26–8).

On another occasion, when the Greeks were trying to storm
the hill fort of the Taochi, and the defenders were rolling down
stones upon them, ten waggon-loads at a time, Xenophon proposed to exhaust the enemy's ammunition by deliberately drawing their fire. The Greeks were sheltering in a small wood;
Callimachus set the example by running out and regaining the
shelter of the trees before the stones struck him. 'But Agasias,
when he saw what Callimachus was doing, with the eyes of the
whole army upon him, was afraid that he would not pass him and
be first into the fort. So, without calling on Aristonymus, who
was near him, or on Eurylochus of Lusii, though they were his
comrades, or on anyone else, he ran himself, and passed everyone.
When Callimachus saw him passing, he seized the rim of his
shield (Plate 6*b*). Thereupon Aristonymus of Methydrium ran
past them, and after him Eurylochus of Lusii. For all these men
were rivals in valour and competed against each other. And so in
rivalry they took the fort' (*Anabasis* iv. 7.1–12).

It is sad that the last we hear of Agasias, at the very end of the
expedition, is that he was wounded in a raid specially intended to
enrich him and some others of Xenophon's favourites by captur-
ing a Persian noble and his household (*Anabasis* vii. 8.8ff.).

Though Xenophon is generous to his subordinates, he is often
accused of being unjust to his colleagues, the other generals. We
may reject Diodorus's statement (xiv. 27.1) that the Greeks chose
Chirisophus commander-in-chief immediately after the death of
Clearchus. (Xenophon himself makes it clear that Chirisophus
presided and put the vote at the assembly: *Anabasis* iii. 2.1ff.)
But Chirisophus commanded the vanguard, which must have
had more hard fighting than Xenophon describes, and even if we
allow that the rearguard had the worst part, it included the
division of Timasion, another young general, as well as Xenophon's (*Anabasis* iii. 1.47; 2.37).

But Timasion's exploits were probably inferior to Xenophon's. During the first part of the retreat along the Tigris, the army marched in hollow square, with one side protected by the river. The Persian attacks will not have fallen equally upon both divisions of the rearguard, but mostly upon that further from the river—Xenophon's. When the Greeks entered the mountains, the army formed one long column. 'Chirisophus led the army, taking his own contingent and all the light-armed, and Xenophon followed with the hoplites of the rearguard, having no light-armed troops ... Chirisophus reached the crest before seeing any of the enemy. Then he led downwards, and each part of the army as it crossed the ridge continuously followed onward to the villages in the glens and recesses of the mountains' (*Anabasis* iv. 1.6–7). From now on, Timasion's division evidently no longer helped bring up the rear.

Even if we grant that a reporter who had had the chance to interview all the generals might have given us more of their actions, we need not accuse Xenophon of lying in order to magnify his own achievements. He writes frankly as an eyewitness, not as an enquirer. And those who question his superior talents should remember that in the end he was the soldiers' choice—and Timasion's too (*Anabasis* vii. 5.10; of course we have only Xenophon's own word here).

Nor should it be doubted that from the first Xenophon showed superior professional skill in tactics and handling men in formation; to imagine that the gift of oratory that he displayed (*Anabasis* iii. 2.7ff.) was enough in itself to establish him as leader is to miss the point of Socrates's lesson to Glaucon (*Memorabilia* iii. 6). But though Xenophon was a skilled tactician he did not change the army overnight from a 'Spartan' to an 'Athenian' system of tactics; the hollow square formation that he proposed, no doubt with his colleagues' previous agreement, had been used by the Spartan Brasidas in Thrace (Thucydides iv. 125) before the Athenians used it in Sicily (Thucydides vi. 67.1). Nor did he himself, but 'the generals', find the remedy when this formation fell into confusion when defiling through passes or over bridges (*Anabasis* iii. 4.19ff). His own tactics against the Persian cavalry and slingers—using parties of infantry unsupported by cavalry to chase them off—were faulty, and he acknowledges the justice of the older general's reproofs (*Anabasis* iii. 3.1ff.). But he also found the remedy; to improvise a small cavalry troop, mounted on such horses as were available, and to raise a volunteer force of Rhodian slingers, whose leaden bolts would outrange the stones of the Persians (expert technical knowledge again).

Xenophon also gives examples of his skill and imagination in adapting tactical formations to the ground and to the enemy's position—a branch of generalship in which, as has been seen, he judged the professional drillmasters to be deficient (*Memorabilia* iii. 1.11). A notable instance was the action against the Colchians, who were drawn up on a long ridge. The Greeks first deployed in the usual phalanx, but Xenophon pointed out the disadvantages of a continuous line on rough ground, and suggested more suitable tactics, which gained an easy victory (*Anabasis* iv. 8.9ff.). We may imagine Chirisophus, the competent, highly-trained, perhaps unimaginative Lacedaemonian, in command of the vanguard, sighting the enemy and applying the normal textbook solution to the problem. Xenophon, arriving from the rear when the deployment was almost complete, found a better answer, which he incorporates in his book, not just to draw attention to his own cleverness, but as a valuable practical lesson to his readers. Similarly he describes the Greek tactics on a night march—the slow-moving hoplites in advance, the cavalry in the rear, so that the army should not become separated in the darkness (*Anabasis* vii. 3.37–8)—not merely because they proved effective on the occasion that he is describing, and won the approval of Seuthes of Thrace, but for his reader's practical instruction.

Xenophon seems to have kept Chirisophus's friendship throughout. They had one quarrel, he says, when Chirisophus first beat, and then allowed to escape, a village headman who was guiding them through Armenia (*Anabasis* iv. 6.3). Generally they were the best of friends, congratulating each other when there were good things to share, and exchanging good-humoured teasing when it was necessary to 'steal a march'—a proper job for Spartans, who were taught to steal as children, said Xenophon,

to which Chirisophus replied that Athenians were clever at steal-
ing the state revenues (*Anabasis* iv. 5.33; 6.14–16).

There is no reason to doubt that Xenophon favoured the eventual choice of Chirisophus as sole commander—though not so
much from friendship as from fear that the Spartans would dis-
approve of his own candidacy; regretted the dissolution of his
supreme command 'on the sixth or seventh day after his election'
(*Anabasis* vi. 2.12); and was truly sorry when he fell into despon-
dency, and shortly afterwards died, after drinking a medicine for
fever (*Anabasis* vi. 4.11).

Tactics was not the only branch of military science in which
the general had to be competent. 'Without provisions, both
general and private are good for nothing', Clearchus had reminded the Greeks at Tarsus (*Anabasis* i. 3.11). The nature of the
campaign was such that Xenophon's main duty in the matter of
supply was to find plunder—so obtaining 'not only provisions
but glory in the eyes of the world', as the Spartan Teleutias was
later to say (*Hellenica* v. 1.17). Later there were 'hospitable gifts'
to be extracted from the Greek cities on the Black Sea, and finally
Seuthes of Thrace had to be kept up to his promises in the matter
of pay and provisions—his agent should have sold the cloak off
his back rather than let the soldiers go short, said Xenophon;
so earning a reputation, which eventually stood him in good
stead, of being 'not a bad fellow in most respects, but the soldiers'
friend' (*Anabasis* vii. 5.5; 6.4). At least, if Xenophon never had a
chance to organize a regular supply train, like that which later
he found to be an admirable feature of the Spartan military
system (*Constitution of the Lacedaemonians* 11.2; cf. *Cyropaedia*
vi. 2.25–3.4), he learned how much food a large body of men
required. He could smile at Coeratidas the Theban (a former
colleague of Clearchus; cf. *Hellenica* i. 3.15ff.), who, 'though not
an exile, was going round Greece playing the general and offering
himself if any city or nation needed a general'. This man proposed to take over the command of the Cyreans at Byzantium, and
lead them to profitable adventures in Thrace (*Anabasis* vii. 1.33ff.).
But it was first necessary to make good his promise to supply
all the food and drink that they wanted. 'Next day Coeratidas

came with the sacrificial victims and the prophet. He was followed by twenty men carrying barley-meal and another twenty with wine, and three carrying olives, and one man with the biggest load of garlic that he could possibly manage, and another with a load of onions.' Needless to say, the amount was inadequate to satisfy appetites which at Heraclea had found 'three thousand measures of meal, two thousand jars of wine, twenty oxen and a hundred sheep' insufficient for three days' supply (*Anabasis* vi. 2.3–4). 'On the first day Coeratidas failed to obtain good omens and distributed nothing to the soldiers. On the next, the victims were standing by the altar, and Coeratidas was garlanded as though to offer sacrifice. But Timasion and Neon and Cleanor came up and told Coeratidas not to sacrifice, because he was not to lead the army if he did not give them provisions. He told them to make the distribution. When he had not nearly enough to give a day's ration to each soldier, he took up his sacrifices, and went off, resigning the command.'

For all the somewhat malicious turn that Xenophon gives the story, his purpose in telling it is serious. In *Memorabilia* iii. 4 he reports a conversation between Socrates and Nicomachides, a veteran regimental commander, with the scars of honourable wounds, who complains that the people have passed him over for the generalship and elected a mere businessman, who understands nothing but how to collect money. Socrates in his reply shows how valuable this ability, and the qualities of a 'good economist', are to a general.

Finally, the good general had to remember that, as Socrates had said (*Memorabilia* i. 4.15) the gods sent their counsellors to mankind. A sneeze, which interrupted Xenophon just when he was discussing hopes of safety, was an omen from Zeus the Saviour (*Anabasis* iii. 2.9); Zeus the King sent dreams at moments of crisis, and a portent at Xenophon's first departure from Ephesus—an eagle screaming on the right hand, a favourable sign, but also an indication that troubles were coming and he would gain little wealth; the bird was sitting, and eagles are mobbed by small birds when sitting and gather their food flying (*Anabasis* vi. 1.23). But Gracious Zeus relented, when propitiated with proper sacrifices (*Anabasis* vii. 8.4–6). So the general had to consult the prophets; to learn the gods' will by sacrifice before undertaking any operation; to forestall their anger by purifying the camp when the soldiers had committed sacrilege (*Anabasis* v. 7.35); and even to still the North Wind when the soldiers were freezing in the blizzard (*Anabasis* iv. 5.4).

CHAPTER ELEVEN

The Barbarians

XENOPHON travelled the route of the Ten Thousand once only, under conditions most unfavourable for historical, geographical or anthropological enquiry. Of ancient history, he gives only (*Anabasis* iii. 4.7–12) a note on the ruins of 'Larisa and Mespila,[1] inhabited long ago by the Medes' and destroyed by the anger of Zeus. It is curious that he knew nothing of Nineveh as such; Ninus and King Sardanapalus (Assurbanipal) were later to become part of Greek folk lore.

Xenophon's geographical indications are not sufficiently precise for his exact route to be traced. It must have been at the gorge of Finik (the Pinaka of Strabo xvi. 1.24), where the Tigris breaks out of the mountains of Kurdistan, that the Greeks found themselves enclosed between the heights and a river so deep that they could not sound it with their spears, and, having rejected as impractical a proposal to put the army across four thousand at a time on inflated skins, made the desperate decision to force their way through northward to Armenia (*Anabasis* iii. 5.7ff.). The crossing of the Centrites was (in Layard's opinion at least)[2] at the ford of Tilleh, 'where the united waters of Bitlis, Sert, and the upper districts of Bohtan, join the western branch of the Tigris ... We crossed the lower or eastern (stream)[3] which we found wide and exceedingly rapid, the water, however, not reaching above the saddle-girths. The villagers raised the lug-

---

[1] For the names—'Capital city' and 'Lower town'—cf. R. D. Barnett, 'Xenophon and the Wall of Media', *JHS* 83 (1963) pp. 25–6.

[2] *Nineveh and Babylon*, p. 49.

[3] In September 1848; the Greek crossing was probably about two months later in the year.

gage and supported the horses against the current, which, rushing over loose and slippery stones, affording an uncertain footing, threatened to sweep the animals down the stream.' Xenophon (*Anabasis* iv. 3.6) describes how, when the Greeks first tried to cross, the water came over their breasts, 'and the river-bed was rough with large and slippery stones, and it was impossible for them to hold their shields in the water. If they did, the river dragged them down, and those who carried their shields over their heads were exposed to missiles.' Later (*Anabasis* iv. 3.30), when they actually managed to cross, many of the soldiers who had been told off to cover the operation went to look after the baggage, which was evidently meeting the same difficulties as Layard's.

It is not known exactly where the Greeks crossed the Tigris, the Euphrates and the Araxes, which Xenophon (*Anabasis* iv. 6.4) calls the Phasis, perhaps supposing that he was fording the headwaters of the river, more familiar to the Greeks, that flowed through the land of Colchis into the east end of the Black Sea (cf. *Anabasis* v. 6.36; v. 7.1ff.). The great city of Gymnias must have stood somewhere near modern Bayburt, but we do not know where, nor the exact position of the 'mountain named Theche' to which, on the fifth day as promised, the guide provided by the governor of Gymnias conducted them. 'When the vanguard reached the top of the mountain and caught sight of the sea, a great clamour arose. Xenophon and the rearguard heard it, and thought that more enemies were attacking from in front ... But when the shouting grew louder and came nearer, and still the men who were coming up kept running to those who were still shouting, and the shouting became much greater as the number of men increased, Xenophon thought it was something more serious. So he mounted his horse, took Lycius and the cavalry, and went to the rescue. Very soon they heard the soldiers shouting 'The Sea! The Sea!' and passing the word along. Then everyone began to run, including the rearguard, and the baggage-animals and horses broke into a gallop. When they reached the crest, the men embraced each other, and their generals and captains, in tears. Suddenly someone gave the word, and the soldiers brought stones and made a great cairn. There they set up a quantity of raw-hides and staves and captured bucklers, and the guide himself hacked the bucklers and told the others to do so. Then the Greeks dismissed the guide, presenting him from the common stock with a horse, a silver cup, a Persian dress, and ten gold pieces. And he asked specially for sealstones, and received many from the soldiers. He showed them a village where they could bivouac, and the road by which they were to go on to the Macrones, and when evening came departed under cover of night' (*Anabasis* iv. 7.19–27).

As for the manners and customs of the different peoples, Xenophon of course noted their weapons and tactics. The Carduchi were mighty archers, and the strength of their mountain fastnesses enabled them to 'pay no heed to the King'.[1] They had once been invaded by a royal army, twelve myriads strong, 'but not a man returned, owing to the difficulty of the country' (*Anabasis* iii. 5.16). The Chaldaei too were free and warlike, though they served the Persian satraps as mercenaries, armed with long wicker shields and spears (*Anabasis* iv. 3.4). The Chalybes, who descended from their mountain fastnesses to harry the rear of the Greeks, were the most valiant of the tribes through whom they passed, and the only ones who fought them hand-to-hand. They were equipped with linen corselets, greaves, helmets, and pikes fifteen cubits long. At their belts they carried curved falchions, with which they butchered those who fell into their hands, and cut off their heads. They carried the severed heads with them, and sang and danced in sight of the Greeks (*Anabasis* iv. 7.15ff.; there is perhaps a mistake in Xenophon's notes here).[2]

The Macrones too had wicker shields, spears, and corslets made of hair, but when they were about to bar the Greeks'

---

[1] As their descendants the Kurds, in 1909, 'feared not God nor the Sultan' (Gertrude Bell, *Amurath to Amurath*, p. 285).

[2] Strabo (xii. 3.19) mentions 'Chalybes' in the same area, but adds that their 'modern' name was 'Chaldaei'. Xenophon, at *Anabasis* v. 5.17, lists the independent nations whom the Greeks had had to plunder for subsistence as Carduchi Taochi and Chaldaei, but in his narrative mentions the Chaldaei only (as already noted) among the Persian mercenaries. (But 'Chalybes and Taochi' are named as mercenaries at iv. 4.18, suggesting that Xenophon was confused.) Perhaps, then

passage through thick woods 'there came up to Xenophon a man of the peltasts, who stated that he had been a slave at Athens, and said that he recognized the men's speech. "And I think," he said, "that this is my own country." ' Through his good offices, the Macrones were persuaded to give the Greeks free passage, after exchanging spears in token of good faith, and even to clear the road and provide what provisions they could for sale (*Anabasis* iv. 8.1–8).

Of the way of life of the 'barbarians', Xenophon saw what an invader might. The houses of the Carduchi were full of bronze vessels, which the Greeks spared, hoping to reach an agreement with their owners (*Anabasis* iv. 1.8). In Armenia the Greeks stayed longer, recovering, among a people too weak to resist them, from the hardships of their march across the snowbound plateau, and Xenophon describes more fully the village where he was quartered, and its inhabitants (*Anabasis* iv. 5.24–36). The headman—he whose escape later caused the quarrel between Xenophon and Chirisophus—proved very co-operative, for his family's sake. His daughter had been only eight days married; her husband, however, was not with her, being out hare-hunting when the Greeks took the village.

The houses were underground, with mouths like wells, through which the people went by ladders, but spacious below. Goats, sheep, oxen, poultry and their young were all wintering on hay inside the houses; there were separate passages dug out for their entry. (Layard in 1848 noted that the villages were still the same: 'The low hovels, mere holes in the hillside, and the common refuge of man, poultry and cattle, cannot be seen from any distance, and they are purposely built away from the road to escape the unwelcome visits of travelling government officers and

---

this warlike people was the Chaldaei, not the Chalybes, of whom one branch lived as iron-workers, subject to the Mossynoeci, on the Black Sea near the Paphlagonians (*Anabasis* v. 5.1; compare the 'Alybe' of *Iliad* ii. 857 and the naked Chalybes who send iron in Virgil, *Georgics* i. 58).

'Chaldaei' may be connected with Haldi, the god of Urartu—biblical Ararat. They are not the people of 'Ur of the Chaldees', or 'the astrologers, the Chaldeans and the soothsayers' who failed to interpret the writing on the wall for Belshazzar (Daniel 5.7).

marching troops. It is not uncommon for a traveller to receive the first intimation of his approach to a village by finding his horse's fore feet down a chimney, and himself taking his place unexpectedly in the family circle through the roof' (*Nineveh and Babylon*, p. 14).)

The Greeks found wheat, barley, vegetables, and beer ('barley wine') in great bowls—very strong, unless mixed with water, but most pleasant when one got used to it. It was sucked through reeds, to avoid the barley grains that floated level with the lips of the vessels. Xenophon made the headman dine with him, and told him to take heart, because they would not take away his children, and would repay the provisions that they consumed from his house, if in return he guided them to the next tribe. This he promised to do, and even disclosed his buried store of wine, so the soldiers passed a cheerful night, keeping a good watch on the headman and his family none the less. Next day Xenophon took the headman to Chirisophus, visiting the soldiers in the different villages on the way, who were celebrating in good spirits, and all insisted on offering them breakfast before they left. 'On every table were set mutton, kid, pork, veal, poultry, with many sorts of bread, both of barley and of wheat-flour. Whenever anyone wanted to drink a man's health, he dragged him to the bowl, where he had to stoop down and drink like an ox.

'The soldiers allowed the headman to take whatever he liked. But he accepted nothing, except that wherever he saw one of his kinsmen, he always drew him to him. When they came to Chirisophus, they found his men too in their billets, crowned with wreaths of dry hay, and with Armenian boys in their barbarian clothes waiting upon them. They showed the boys what to do in dumb show. After Xenophon and Chirisophus had greeted one another, they questioned the headman jointly through the Persian-speaking interpreter on the name of the country. He replied "Armenia". They asked again for whom the horses were being kept.' (Xenophon had taken seventeen young horses in his village.) 'He replied that they were tribute for the King. And he said that the neighbouring land was the country of the Chalybes, and explained which way the road lay. Then Xenophon took him back to his own household, and gave the headman a horse that he had captured some time previously so that he could fatten it for sacrifice, because he had heard that it was sacred to the Sun and was afraid that it would die as a result of its sufferings on the march. He himself took one of the young horses, and gave one to each of the other generals and captains. These horses were smaller than the Persian breed but much more spirited. Then the head-man instructed them to bind sacks about the feet of the horses and baggage-animals when they led them through the snow. Without the sacks they sank up to their bellies.'

In the following winter (400/399 B.C.) Xenophon again learned something about life in cold climates. 'There was much snow, and it was so cold that the water they brought for dinner froze, and the wine in the jars, and many of the Greeks had frost-bitten ears and noses. Then it was obvious why the Thracians wear fox-skin caps over their heads and ears, and tunics not just about their bodies but about their thighs, and, on horseback, mantles that come down to their feet, not short cloaks' (*Anabasis* vii. 4.3–4) (Plate 11).

Of all the nations through whom the Greeks passed, the most barbarous, by common consent of the soldiers, were the Mossy-noeci, or 'turret-dwellers', so called from their wooden towers (cf. Strabo vii. 3.18). They lived on the south coast of the Black Sea, and part of them offered to give the Greeks free passage in return for help against the other part. Xenophon's first notes on them, as usual, deal with military equipment including the three-men dugout canoes in which they arrived (*Anabasis* v. 4.11ff.).

The fighting men formed in groups of a hundred, 'exactly like choruses setting to each other, all with thick bucklers of white bulls' hide, shaped like an ivy-leaf; in their right hands a six-cubit throwing-spear, with a point in front, and at the back a ball formed out of the wood of the shaft. They wore tunics which came above their knees, as thick as blanket-weave linen; on their heads, leather helmets of Paphlagonian type, with a knob in the middle, very close to the tiara in form. And they had iron scimi-tars.' Then one of them took command, and all the others went, singing in rhythm, right through the Greek army against their

enemies. They were routed, and many of them were killed, along
with some of the Greeks who had accompanied them. Like the
Chalybes, the victorious barbarians cut off the heads of the fallen,
and displayed them to the Greeks and their enemies from their
own people, and danced, singing in measure. But next day the
Greeks took their Metropolis and another town from which all
fled, except their kings, who never stirred from the wooden
turrets in which they were kept, and even then would not come
down, but 'were burned on the spot, turrets and all'.

As the Greeks, after their victory, advanced through the tribe's
territory, Xenophon observed their outlandish food—bread
baked the previous year and kept in store; chestnuts; slices of
dolphin-flesh pickled in jars; the dolphin-blubber that they used
as the Greeks used olive-oil; their wine, vinegary until mixed with
water, when it became sweet; the children in rich men's houses,
fattened on boiled nuts until they were almost as wide as they
were tall, white and soft and brilliantly tattooed, front and back.
Their customs were furthest removed from those of the Greeks;
they talked and laughed to themselves; jumped up and danced,
as though to show off, wherever they happened to be; and did in
secret what other men do openly, and openly what other men do
in secret, even demanding to lie in public with the women of the
Greek camp. All were white-skinned, men and women alike—
unlike the sunburned Greeks.

The attitude of Xenophon and his comrades towards 'the
barbarians' in general is not easy to analyse. They classed as 'barbarians' all of mankind that was not 'Hellene'—that is, all who did
not speak some intelligible form of Greek—from King Artaxerxes
in Babylon to the king of the Mossynoeci in his turret; from
Cyrus, administering justice and planting orchards, to the wild
Carduchi. Obviously they could not have a single consistent
attitude to the whole of 'barbary'. But they were very conscious
of their own identity as Hellenes, and anxious not merely to
return to Hellas but to avoid the reproach of having done, while
in barbarian service, anything prejudicial to their fellow-Hellenes.
'Nobody will ever say that I led Hellenes to the barbarians, but
betrayed the Hellenes and chose the friendship of the barbarians,'

said Clearchus (*Anabasis* i. 3.5; he was in fact deceiving both sides at the time. Later he reminded Phalinus, the Greek who had come from Tissaphernes to persuade the Cyreans to surrender after Cunaxa, that whatever advice he gave would certainly be reported in Hellas: *Anabasis* ii. 1.17.)

Yet against 'the barbarians' Xenophon displays neither social nor racial prejudice. Guest-friendship, with all its sacred obligations on both sides, was perfectly possible between Greek and barbarian—not merely as a device by which Cyrus could attach his Greek captains to him (*Anabasis* i. 1.10–11) or as a bond between the traitors Menon and Ariaeus (*Anabasis* ii. 4.15), but between Agesilaus of Sparta and the son of Pharnabazus (*Hellenica* iv. 1.39).

As for social contacts, the officers of the Cyreans entertained Paphlagonian ambassadors at dinner, followed by a cabaret-performance by soldiers of the army, which is worth describing for its own sake. First came Thracians, who mimed a duel to the death, then Aenianians and Magnesians, who 'danced the so-called harvest dance, under arms. The manner of the dance was this: One, laying aside his arms, sows and drives his team, often turning round as though afraid, and a robber approaches. When the first dancer catches sight of him, he snatches up his weapons and meets him, and fights for his team. They did this measure to the flute. At last the robber bound the husbandman and led the team away. But sometimes the ploughman overcame the robber. Then he yoked him beside his oxen and drove him with his hands bound behind his back.'[1] 'Shield-dances' by a Mysian, and by Arcadian hoplites, impressed the Paphlagonians, and the final turn was the production of a dancing-girl, beautifully arrayed and equipped with a light shield, who nimbly danced the Pyrrhic dance, amid much applause. The Paphlagonians asked if even women served as the Greeks' auxiliaries, and were told that these were the girls who had driven the Great King from the camp (*Anabasis* vi. 1.1–13).

[1] For similar mimings, obviously intended to secure a good harvest, within the present century, cf. R. M. Dawkins, 'The Modern Carnival in Thrace', *JHS* 26 (1906) pp. 191ff.

In their turn, the Cyrean officers were entertained next winter by Seuthes of Thrace, and Xenophon escaped the social dilemma in which he was placed by the lack of a suitable present for his host by 'standing up boldly (being by now somewhat in liquor)' and offering himself and his companions as faithful and willing friends in time of danger (*Anabasis* vii. 3.15ff.).

Nor was marriage between Greeks and barbarians unthinkable. Admittedly Xenophon was more than half joking when he suggested (*Anabasis* iii. 2.25) that the Greeks, like the lotus-eaters, might forget their journey home, if once they learned to converse with the tall and beautiful wives and daughters of the Medes and Persians. But Seuthes was quite serious when he offered Xenophon his daughter's hand (*Anabasis* vii. 2.38), and if Xenophon had accepted he would have done no more than other Athenian generals, including the great Miltiades. The password, on the first night that the Cyreans served with Seuthes was 'Athena, according to our kinship' (*Anabasis* vii. 3.39), in memory of similar unions, going back to the time of the mythical Tereus and the daughters of King Pandion.

But Xenophon makes little suggestion that barbarians had 'human rights'. 'The place must be taken. There are no provisions for the army if we do not take it,' said Chirisophus to Xenophon when they came to the fort of the Taochi. Xenophon admits that it was 'a dreadful sight' when, after the place was captured, the women threw their children over the cliffs, and then themselves, and the men likewise. But his compassion seems to be balanced by his regret that 'very few human captives were taken, though many oxen, donkeys and sheep', and he spares less pity for the barbarians than for Aeneas of Stymphalus, a captain, who 'saw a man dressed in a beautiful garment running to hurl himself over, and laid hold of him to stop him. But the man clutched at him, and both were carried over the rocks and perished' (*Anabasis* iv. 7.3; 13–14).

Similarly in Armenia, when the Greeks first quartered themselves in the villages, then concentrated in the open for fear of an attack by Tiribazus, then were driven by stress of weather to return to their former billets, Xenophon notes that 'those who at their former departure had wantonly burned the houses were punished by being poorly quartered' (*Anabasis* iv. 4.14), but says nothing about the rightful proprietors. Nor, in describing how the soldiers feasted in the next group of villages (*Anabasis* iv. 5.24ff.), does he spare a thought for the 'barbarians' who starved in consequence. Yet he evidently felt a liking for the village headman and was moved when, instead of availing himself of the opportunity to plunder his neighbours at the soldiers' invitation, 'he accepted nothing else; only, where he saw one of his kinsfolk he always drew him to himself.'

Agreements made with barbarians were to be observed. The Greeks bargained for a passage through the lands of the Macrones and Mossynoeci, and would have been glad to come to an agreement with the Carduchi, who were also enemies of the Persian King. As it was, they refrained from burning their villages, and gave up prisoners whom they had taken, in exchange for the bodies of their own dead, 'for whom they did as far as possible all that is customary for good men' (*Anabasis* iv. 2.23).

Even defenceless barbarians were to be spared, if the gods so directed. The generals 'had thoughts of invading the territory of the Tibareni and making some profit for the army, and rejected the offerings of hospitality that came from the Tibareni, but, telling them to wait while they took counsel, began to sacrifice. But after they had made many sacrifices, at last the prophets all declared their opinion that the gods would in no way consent to the war. Then they received their hospitality and treated their country as friendly when marching through' (*Anabasis* v. 5.2–3).

The rights of fellow-Hellenes, after the army had reached the sea and the limits of the Greek world, were to be respected. This was in accordance with the thought of the time; Plato, in his *Republic* (v. 469B–471C) lays down rules to be observed by his Guardians when making war, and emphasizes that Hellenes should not enslave each other, waste each other's land, or strip each other's dead, except of weapons. War of Hellenes against barbarians or barbarians against Hellenes is natural, and rightly so called; between Hellenes, war is a sickness of Hellas and properly to be regarded as civil strife.

But in the actual world Greeks did of course make war on each other, and the willingness of the Cyreans to respect the integrity of Trapezus, Cerasus or Cotyora was conditional upon the appearance of supplies—'hospitable gifts' whose cost to the 'hosts' might be in part offset by the selling of further provisions in a market where the soldiers were perhaps ready to let their plunder go at bargain prices. But, on suspicion of cheating, they had recourse to violence instead of lawful redress; Zelarchus the provant-master was hunted with stones, 'as though he had been a wild boar or a stag', but made his escape—'and if he cheated you, he has sailed away without paying the penalty. And if he was innocent, he has fled from the army in fear of being unjustly put to death without trial' (*Anabasis* v. 7.24ff.).

Contact with the Greek cities brought a further complication; many of the neighbouring barbarians lived on good terms with the Greeks—even the Mossynoeci had their Trapezuntine consul —and the army had to respect the difference between the 'friendly' Colchians near Trapezus, and the more distant hill tribes, like the Drilae, whose strongholds could be attacked in search of provisions. Xenophon could flatter himself that by raiding these enemies he was also helping his fellow-Greeks, but the Greeks themselves were only too anxious to get rid of their 'guests'— justifiably, for not all the soldiers shared the scruples of the generals, and the generals could not always hold their men. Chirisophus and Xenophon strongly resisted the Arcadians who would have levied blackmail upon Heraclea; 'it seemed improper to both of them to compel a Greek, and friendly, city to give what its people did not want to give.' But Heraclea would have been plundered if it had not shut its gates in time (*Anabasis* vi. 2.4–8). Earlier one of the captains, Clearetus, would have plundered a little native village, friendly to the Greek city of Cerasus and so off its guard, and deserted the army with his loot, if he and his friends had not been killed in the attempt. When the villagers sent ambassadors to protest, they were stoned to death (*Anabasis* v. 7.13ff.). Nobody was punished for this outrage, though the camp was ritually purified. Finally, at Byzantium the soldiers did indeed seize the city, imperilling both Cleander the Spartan governor and Anaxibius the admiral, and offered it to Xenophon, who refused, moved, as he told them, not only by fear of the Spartans but by the knowledge that their own friends and kinsfolk would rightly have joined in making war upon men who, after beating the barbarians, had not occupied one of their cities, but had seized a Greek city at the first opportunity (*Anabasis* vii. 1.18ff.).

The Spartans, for their part, when once they had got the army outside the walls, shut the gates against it, and by selling into slavery the sick and the stragglers who were left behind, showed their unwillingness to treat the Cyreans as civilized fellow-Hellenes.

It was not until the following spring that the Spartans started their own war of liberation against 'the barbarian', and Xenophon and his veterans came into favour.

CHAPTER TWELVE

Xenophon and Agesilaus — in Asia

THE Spartan agents who returned Xenophon's horse to him and refused to accept any of the fifty gold pieces that he had received for it (*Anabasis* vii. 8.6) were in fact advancing him a year's pay at a general's rate, and no doubt intended to get their money's worth. Whether from discretion or from modesty, he never names himself in the *Hellenica*, but he indicates that the Cyreans were kept together as a distinct corps in the mixed army of enfranchised helots, mercenaries and allies with which the Spartans were waging war. He seems to have commanded the corps under Thibron, and under Dercylidas, who succeeded to the chief command late in 399 B.C. and retained it until the arrival of Agesilaus in 396. 'The commander of the Cyreans', when a Spartan board of inspectors noted the improved conduct of the soldiers in 398 B.C., replied that the soldiers were the same that they had always been; it was the commander in chief who had changed (*Hellenica* iii. 2.7). Xenophon is doubtless concealing himself here, and his narrative of these campaigns in Asia often seems to be that of an eye-witness; for example, this account of an incident in the campaign of 397. Tissaphernes and Pharnabazus had joined forces and crossed to the north bank of the Meander, threatening the main Spartan base at Ephesus. Dercylidas therefore abandoned a projected march southwards into Caria and re-crossed the Meander himself. He and Pharax the admiral were marching 'with their army in no regular order, supposing that the enemy had gone forward into the territory of Ephesus, when suddenly they saw right in front of them sentries on the monuments' (grave-tumuli, overlooking the plain on either side of the river). 'They on their part sent up men on to the monuments and towers on their own side, and saw drawn up in the way that they were taking white-shielded Carians, and all the Persian army that was there, and all the Greek troops that either of the satraps commanded, and their cavalry, very many, that of Tissaphernes on the right wing, that of Pharnabazus on the left. When Dercylidas saw this, he ordered his regimental and company commanders to deploy as quickly as possible, eight deep, and the peltasts to form up on either flank, also the cavalry, such and as many as he happened to have. He himself began to sacrifice. As much of the army as came from the Peloponnese kept still, and prepared for battle. But as for those who were from Priene and Achilleum and from the islands and the Ionian cities, some left their weapons in the corn and ran away (for the corn was deep in the plain of the Meander). And those who did stay obviously had no intention of staying for long' (*Hellenica* iii. 2.14–17). But Tissaphernes had no wish to fight, remembering his actions against the Cyreans and thinking that all the Greeks were the same. So a truce was made, and envoys were sent to Sparta and the King to negotiate for a peace which would leave the Greek cities free.

It must be emphasized that in transferring the Cyreans to the Spartan service, and in entering it himself, Xenophon was not acting as a traitor to his own city. Athens was officially allied with Sparta against the barbarian enemy, and had indeed sent a contingent of cavalry to Asia at Thibron's request, though the democratic leaders used the request for their own ends, when 'they sent some of those who had served in the cavalry under the Thirty, thinking that it would be the better for the people if they went abroad and died there' (*Hellenica* iii. 1.4). Xenophon's comment reflects the resentment of these men, which he seems to have shared as he shared their background, though he does not go so far as to charge the democracy with violating its oaths.

But the democratic party perhaps found a way far more damaging to himself of expressing its true feelings towards the war, and to Sparta. Before he was retained in the Spartan service,

Xenophon had intended to return home 'for the decree of banishment had not yet been carried against him at Athens' (*Anabasis*
vii. 7.57). This seems to imply that he was banished shortly afterwards, and recalls the fears of Socrates that service under Cyrus
might lead to a political prosecution (*Anabasis* iii. 1.5) and Xenophon's own obvious anxiety to clear the memory of his master
from any imputation that he had encouraged Xenophon to enter
that service. Moreover, Pausanias (v. 6.5), writing in the second
century after Christ, says that Xenophon was exiled for joining
Cyrus, the deadly enemy of the Athenian democracy. We may
suppose that the fame that Xenophon had been anxious to win
(*Anabasis* vi. 1.20) had had ironic consequences; nobody had
noticed his departure from Athens, but he had returned famous,
another dangerous young man trained by the notorious Socrates,
and the more able he had shown himself the greater the danger
to the democracy.

But there is another possibility. After the events recorded in the
Anabasis, Xenophon, according to Diogenes Laertius (ii. 51–2),
'came to Asia, to Agesilaus, the King of the Lacedaemonians,
conveying to him Cyrus's soldiers as mercenaries. He enjoyed
his friendship to an extraordinary degree. At this time he was
sentenced to banishment by the Athenians on a charge of supporting Sparta.' This version is clearly not merely compressed but
distorted. Xenophon did not convey the Cyreans directly to
Agesilaus, who only arrived in Asia in 396 B.C. But we cannot
exclude the possibility that supporting Sparta was the charge on
which Xenophon was exiled, and that the decree was passed after
he had become one of the King's friends. If this were so, it would
be much to Xenophon's discredit. Agesilaus arrived at the seat of
war in 396 B.C. In 395 the discontent against Spartan domination
of European Greece was brought to a head by Persian agents,
who managed to bring on a war, in which Athens very soon
openly joined the enemies of Sparta. If Xenophon had hitherto
been in good standing at home, and now deliberately chose the
Spartan side against his own city, for the sake of the King's
friendship and the profits that went with it, it is hard to excuse
him.

But Diogenes (ii. 52) cites as one of his chief sources (though not, certainly, for the actual decree of exile) 'Dinarchus, in his speech against Xenophon for high treason'. This makes his evidence suspect. Dinarchus, the last of the 'canon' of classic orators, was born about 360 B.C., and, being a resident alien, not an Athenian citizen, could not have prosecuted in a treason trial in any case (see the brief account of his life by Dionysius of Halicarnassus and (pseudo-) Plutarch, *Lives of the Ten Orators*, 850). His speech must have been an academic exercise, in which no doubt Xenophon was (posthumously) attacked for supporting Sparta rather than his own country. It is, incidentally, a tribute to Xenophon's fame that, like Hannibal and 'Swedish Charles', he had become a subject of declamation, 'to point a moral and adorn a tale'.

We may suppose, then, that Xenophon was actually exiled in 399 B.C., as a dangerous 'Socratic' who had fought for Cyrus, the enemy of Athens. At the same time, the hidden Athenian opposition to Sparta made itself felt in the banishment of a general who was already beginning to distinguish himself in the Spartan service. 'Laconism' may have seemed to many people to have been Xenophon's real offence, though the charge was 'Service under Cyrus'.[1]

This unfair treatment (as it must have seemed), and the execution of Socrates, must have gone far to justify, in Xenophon's own eyes, his eventual choice of the Spartan side. Moreover (again in Xenophon's eyes), Agesilaus and the Spartans were leading a war of liberation against the barbarian; the traitors were those who, suborned by Persian gold, were attacking the common cause of Greece.

Of what was actually going on in European Greece between 401 and 395 B.C. Xenophon shows little knowledge. His narrative (*Hellenica* iii. 2.21ff.) harks back to the chastisement of Elis by King Agis of Sparta in 400–398 B.C., and to the death of Agis, in order to explain how Agesilaus became King. Agis seems to have been clever but mistrusted. At the critical battle of Mantinea in

---

[1] For a fuller discussion, see Delebecque's *Essai sur la vie de Xénophon*, pp. 117–123.

418 B.C., his officers had refused to obey his orders, and though they were punished for discipline's sake the King was thereafter only allowed to command with the help of an advisory committee (Thucydides v. 64ff.). But Agesilaus, his much younger half-brother, was, to the Spartiate peers, 'one of us'. Plutarch says (*Agesilaus* 1–2) that he had passed through the regular course of Spartan education, from whose severities heirs-apparent to the throne were excused. He was a little man (his father Archidamus had been fined for marrying a little wife who would bear a race of kinglets). One of his legs was shorter than the other, but in his youth he was so handsome that this defect passed unnoticed. Moreover, he had learned to make a joke of it himself—perhaps to escape the bullying to which it exposed him—and he had also learned how to make himself obliging to his friends.

At the time of his brother's death he had reached his late forties, not without credit, but apparently without distinction. But he had attracted the notice, and gained the friendship, of Lysander.

Accordingly, when Agis died, his son, who was still a boy, was by Lysander's efforts rejected, and Agesilaus was chosen King. The reason given was that the boy was a bastard, begotten by Alcibiades when he was assisting the Spartans at the time of his exile from Athens. He had seduced the queen, moved, Plutarch says (*Agesilaus* 3.1–2), not by passionate desire, but by the hope that his descendants would be Spartan kings. So when the boy's supporters urged that an oracle of Apollo warned the Spartans to 'beware of the lame reign', Lysander turned the argument round by saying that the god's true meaning was that they should beware lest the royal house should be crippled by the failure of the true line of descent from Heracles (*Hellenica* iii. 3.3).

Xenophon no doubt learned the story of Agesilaus's accession, and of the revolutionary conspiracy that threatened the beginning of his reign (*Hellenica* iii. 3.4ff.), from the King himself or his advisers. Meanwhile Tissaphernes was keeping up peace negotiations merely in order to win time until his army was reinforced, and by sea too the Persians were preparing a counter-offensive. 'A certain Herodas of Syracuse was in Phoenicia with a ship's owner. He saw Phoenician triremes, some sailing in from other ports, some being manned on the spot, some already fitted out, and he heard in addition that there were to be three hundred of them. So he embarked on the first ship sailing for Greece and told the Spartans that the Persian King and Tissaphernes were preparing this expeditionary force, but with what objective in mind, he said, he did not know' (*Hellenica* iii. 4.1). The Spartan answer was to reinforce their army and send King Agesilaus to command in person, accompanied by a staff of thirty Spartiate peers, of whom Lysander was one. Lysander evidently expected to be the real commander, as he had been in the last year of the war against Athens. He looked forward to managing Agesilaus and restoring the system of government by boards of ten, acting in the Spartan interest, which he had formerly established in the Ionian cities.

What visions of Eastern conquest the Spartans may have had we do not know. They continued to negotiate for the freedom of the Greek cities, but Agesilaus suggested that he had something more in mind, by sailing to Aulis to offer sacrifice as Agamemnon had done before the Trojan War. The Boeotians, when they heard of this, 'sent cavalry and bade him sacrifice no more, and scattered from the altars the victims that they found already sacrificed. And he, calling the gods to witness, and enraged, embarked on his trireme and sailed off' (*Hellenica* iii. 4.3–4). This affair foreshadowed the outcome of his expedition two years later.

Lysander suffered a more rapid disappointment. At first he was surrounded by crowds of courtiers 'so that Agesilaus seemed like a private citizen and Lysander like a King'. But Agesilaus, by constantly thwarting all petitioners whom Lysander supported, made his displeasure clear. Plutarch (*Lysander* 23.7–8) describes a further humiliation, which Xenophon omits: Agesilaus appointed his other officers commanders and governors, but made Lysander carve at his table, saying that the Ionians might now go and pay court to his carver. At all events, Lysander, after reproaching the King with knowing how to humiliate his friends, was despatched to the Hellespont, where he did good service before returning to Greece next year (*Hellenica* iii. 4.7–10). His further ambitions—having failed to rule Sparta through the King whom he had made, he had schemes of making the monarchy elective—were cut short by his death next year, fighting the Thebans. Xenophon has been blamed because, though his writings are largely concerned with patterns of leadership, he fails to do justice to the greatest leaders of his time—Lysander and the Theban Epaminondas. But Agesilaus, though his 'lame reign' brought disaster in the end, was also among the great.

Xenophon's friendship with Agesilaus must have begun in military service under the King. He may have continued to command the Cyreans in the campaign of 396 B.C., but his command was certainly ended in 395, when a new staff of thirty Spartiates arrived, and one of them, Herippidas, took over the Cyreans (*Hellenica* iii. 4.20). But there were other duties in which Xenophon's background of theoretical knowledge and unique practical experience would be invaluable. Citizens of Greek states received in youth military training appropriate to their social rank and economic standing, but the men whom Agesilaus had brought from home, apart from his thirty Spartiate 'peers', were helots whose duty until now had been to till the soil for their Spartan masters, and who had been kept most carefully disarmed (cf. *Hellenica* iii. 4.2; the Spartans voted to give Agesilaus thirty Spartiates, two thousand 'newly enfranchised' and a levy of six thousand allies. These figures do not include the Cyreans and other mercenaries, and it is not clear whether they include the one thousand 'newly enfranchised'—*Hellenica* iii. 1.4—who had served with Thibron and Dercylidas). These peasants had no doubt been selected for approved loyalty to their masters as well as for physical strength, but they had still to be turned into soldiers.

In the second book of the *Cyropaedia*, written nearly forty years later,[1] Xenophon gives an imaginary picture of how Cyrus the

---

[1] The *Cyropaedia* must have been finished after 362/1 B.C., since, in the final chapter, discussing the degeneracy of present-day Persians, Xenophon alludes to the traitorous rebel satraps who in that year delivered their nearest relatives as hostages to the Egyptians and then betrayed their associates to the Persian King (*Cyropaedia* viii. 8.4; cf. Diodorus Siculus xv. 92). The affair was sufficiently outrageous to be held up as an example some years later; on the other hand, Xenophon might have begun the *Cyropaedia* at an earlier date. There seems, however, no sufficient reason to associate the book's beginning with Agesilaus's departure to Asia in 365 B.C., to lead a mercenary army in the 'Satraps' War', or to suppose that it was written discontinuously over a period of years.

Great and his 'Persian peers' made their commoners into an army, which may be drawn from the training that Agesilaus gave his recuits. He shows the men being taught to follow their officers unquestioningly, to form column and line by filing into their mess-tents and deploying as they leave them, and to have confidence in their own equipment by fighting mock battles in which those who are equipped for 'hand-to-hand' battle with fennel stalks give harder knocks than those who are armed with clods of earth to serve as missiles (*Cyropaedia* ii. 3.17–20). He also gives a picture of rough but cheerful good-fellowship between 'peers' and 'commoners'. Cyrus himself invites to his own mess for dinner, not only the officers, but sometimes whole companies at a time, as a reward for good conduct and ingenuity in training, and sets the same food before all, regardless of rank (*Cyropaedia* ii. 1.30). However, one greedy recruit, who complains that he sits half-way down the table and so never has first choice, from whichever end the dish is handed round, is properly paid out. His commander calls him to his own table, where he grabs a large piece of meat, then puts it down in order to take an even bigger one, but the mess-waiter thinks that he has had enough, and takes the dish on past him. Of course this is not the behaviour that one expects of educated gentlemen (*Cyropaedia* ii. 2.1ff.), but in fact the humour of Cyrus's camp, with its exchange of heavy personal remarks, is not so different from that of Xenophon's *Symposium*, written expressly to show how gentlemen relax in their lighter moments, and the table manners are not so unlike those of Cyrean officers. When Seuthes of Thrace invited Xenophon and his officers to dinner, those before whom the food was set—cauldrons full of meat skewered to loaves—were expected to follow their host's example and toss portions to their fellow-guests, leaving themselves a mere taste. But 'a certain Arcadian, Arystas, a great eater, left the distribution to look after itself, laid hold of a three-pound loaf and a lump of meat, set them on his knees and began his dinner. When the butler brought him the drinking-horn, he saw Xenophon not yet eating his dinner and said; "Give it to him. He's free to take it already, and I'm not yet"' (*Anabasis* vii. 3.21–5).

Whether or no the Spartiates did behave to the 'newly-enfranchised' as Xenophon makes his Persians treat their commoners, the fact that a king of Sparta and a few of his 'peers' were ready to entrust themselves, not only in this war but repeatedly thereafter, to a large number of recently-freed and armed helots, does suggest that the relationship between helots and masters was not, as is sometimes suggested, entirely a matter of hatred kept from open rebellion by terrorism and midnight murder.

Besides being trained, the army of Agesilaus had to be fitted out. Xenophon (*Hellenica* iii. 4.16–19) gives a picture of the army in winter quarters at Ephesus, preparing for greater things after the campaign of 396 B.C., which had been largely frustrated by the superior Persian cavalry. By offering prizes for skill at arms, Agesilius encouraged his men in their training, 'so that one could see the gymnasia full of men exercising, the riding ground full of men occupied in horsemanship, and the javelin-men and archers practising their skills. He made the whole city a remarkable sight. For the market-place was full of horses and armour for sale, and the copper-smiths and carpenters and bronze-founders and leather-workers and painters were all preparing warlike weapons, so that one might indeed think that the city was a workshop of war. One might have been heartened too by the spectacle of Agesilaus leading, and his soldiers after him, going from the gymnasia with wreaths on their heads and offering the wreaths to Artemis. For wherever men honour the gods, practise warlike arts, and study discipline, in all probability every circumstance will be filled with good hope.

'And he considered that contempt for the enemy invigorates men for warfare. Accordingly he proclaimed by the heralds that the barbarians who had been captured by the foragers would be sold naked. So when the soldiers saw them, pale because they never stripped, soft and unexercised through always travelling in vehicles, they thought that the war was just like having to fight women.'

The cavalry, whose inadequacy had frustrated the campaign of 396 B.C. (*Hellenica* iii. 4.11–15), were placed under the command of Xenocles, one of the new staff of thirty Spartiates who had arrived with Herippidas, and 'another' (*Hellenica* iii. 4.20). It is tempting to suppose once more that the anonymous figure is Xenophon himself, but if so he is writing very carelessly, because his text implies that the 'other' was also one of the Spartiates. At all events, a new professional cavalry was raised, by proclaiming that 'whoever provided a horse, arms and men fit to pass muster would be excused personal service'—better a good mare than a bad man, as Agamemnon had said (cf. Plutarch, *Moralia* 209 B–C).

The experiment succeeded. Many years later Xenophon advised the Athenians to add mercenaries to their cavalry because 'the Lacedaemonian cavalry began to enjoy a good reputation when they recruited mercenary troopers' (*Hipparchicus* 9.3). In the campaign of 395 B.C. Agesilaus won his greatest victory, and, according to Xenophon, the cavalry played a decisive part.

But Xenophon's story differs completely from that given by the fragmentary *Hellenica Oxyrhynchia* (published in 1908 from a papyrus found in Egypt), whose version is followed by Diodorus Siculus. It is not just a matter of disagreement in detail; the stories are so unlike that one or other must be complete fiction. To write a fictitious account of a battle in a history book seems totally irresponsible, but before damning either Xenophon or the Oxyrhynchus historian we should consider that we accept the convention established by Thucydides (i. 22.1) that an ancient historian may, if he is unable to discover the actual words used in a speech, report what the historian himself believes to be appropriate to the situation—in fact, make up a speech as a vehicle for his own ideas. A similar convention might allow historians to compose a battle-piece designed to show, not what actually happened, but how, in the author's opinion, such a battle ought to be fought; not how Agesilaus actually defeated Tissaphernes, but how, in the author's opinion, Greeks might defeat Persians.

In Xenophon's story (*Hellenica* iii. 4.21–4), Agesilaus opened the campaign of 395 B.C. by telling his allies to prepare to march directly into the heart of the enemy's country. In the previous year he had deceived Tissaphernes by advertising a march into Caria, against the satrap's own home, and then striking at

Phrygia; and this year Tissaphernes was again deceived when Agesilaus did as he had said he would. While the enemy forces were concentrated on the Meander to defend Caria, Agesilaus marched directly on Sardis, and had reached the Pactolus valley before the enemy's cavalry overtook him on the fourth day. The Persians ordered their baggage-train to cross the Pactolus and encamp, while they themselves started out to cut off the scattered Greek foragers. Agesilaus sent his cavalry to the rescue; the Persians concentrated to meet them, and Agesilaus, who knew that the enemy's infantry had not yet come up, led out his whole army to support the cavalry, sending the younger hoplites and peltasts first. The Persians gave way before the combination of all arms; some fell in the river, some escaped, but the Greeks followed them up and took their camp, where Agesilaus secured the booty from the plundering peltasts, and 'many goods were taken which sold for more than seventy talents. In addition, it was there that the camels were captured, which Agesilaus carried off to Greece.'

Xenophon's story has been thought to contradict itself. How could the Persian baggage-train have reached the battlefield before the infantry? But the luxurious Persian horsemen, who 'had more coverlets on their horses than on their beds, because they cared more for being softly seated than for horsemanship' (*Cyropaedia* viii. 8.19), would not have marched without their tents, carpets and silver cups (cf. *Anabasis* iv. 4.21), and by loading these 'necessities' on camel-back had created a baggage-train that could outmarch their infantry.

The other version (*Hellenica Oxyrhynchia* xi(vi); Diodorus Siculus xiv. 80) says that Agesilaus ravaged the Caystrian plain and the territory at the foot of Mount Sipylus. Tissaphernes pursued him with a great army—ten thousand cavalry and fifty thousand infantry according to Diodorus: the figures in the *Hellenica Oxyrhynchia* are too damaged for restoration. Agesilaus marched with his army in a hollow square along the foothills, until he came to Sardis, where he laid waste the 'paradise'. Then, turning back, he sent Xenocles with fourteen hundred men (again Diodorus's figure) under cover of night, to lay an ambush

in a thickly wooded place.[1] Next day, Agesilaus trapped the barbarians between his main army and the ambush, and won a
glorious victory, killing six hundred of the enemy (*Hellenica
Oxyrhynchia*; Diodorus multiplies the figure to six thousand).

If we allow that neither version of the battle is impossible in
itself, we still have to decide which represents what really happened. Many modern historians[2] prefer the *Hellenica Oxyrhynchia* because of the greater wealth of detail in this account.
Xenophon, it is argued, had been left behind at Ephesus after his
supersession by Herippidas; he was not present at the battle and,
by the time he had a chance to question those who were, memories were indistinct. He could learn nothing certain about the
battle, but could not leave Agesilaus's greatest victory out of his
history completely. So he dashed off an imaginary sketch, sup-
plementing his invention, perhaps, with memories of his
experiences with the Cyreans—for instance, making Agesilaus
drive the Persians into the Pactolus just as the improvised cavalry
of the Ten Thousand, supported by peltasts and hoplites, had
driven the Persians who were harassing them under Mithradates
into a watercourse (*Anabasis* iii. 4.4–5; Mithradates had archers
and slingers with him as well as cavalry).

This would be plausible if we did not know for certain that
Xenophon was again with Agesilaus by 394 B.C. at the very

---

[1] The manoeuvre would certainly be dangerous, but modern critics who argue
that this large force could not have been detached without being detected perhaps
do not allow sufficiently for the Persian practice of breaking off contact at night,
to safeguard their cavalry. For fear of being caught unarmed and with unsaddled
horses, Tissaphernes had always encamped 'not less than sixty stades'—six or
seven miles—away from the Greeks during the retreat up the Tigris (*Anabasis*
iii. 4.34–5). And (*Cyropaedia* iii. 3.26–7) Xenophon explains that Asiatics fortify
their camps because they depend on their cavalry, and 'a cavalry army is easily
thrown into confusion at night, and hard to handle, especially a barbarian one.
For their horses are hobbled at their mangers, and, if they are attacked, it is hard
to loose the horses in the dark and bridle and saddle them, and arm themselves;
and to mount and ride through the camp is impossible.'

[2] The reader should in fairness be warned that this is the prevalent view. See
especially Ch. Dugas, *Bulletin de correspondence hellenique*, 1910, pp. 58–95, and
I. A. F. Bruce, *Historical Commentary on the Hellenica Oxyrhynchia* (Cambridge,
1967) pp. 150ff. For a defence of Xenophon, see W. Kaupert, in J. Kromayer
and G. Veith, *Antike Schlachtfelder in Griechenland* iv, p. 268.

latest, or if we could believe that no eyewitnesses carried the news of the battle to Ephesus immediately after it was fought. If Xenophon had given a sketchy version of the Oxyrhynchus historian's story we might indeed suppose that the latter had access to better and more immediate information (from what source may be questioned; Diodorus Siculus seems most inadequately informed on the previous year's campaign (xiv. 79), though it must be allowed that he may not reflect his sources faithfully, and also that (xiv. 36) he gives information that Xenophon does not report on Thibron's operations before the Cyreans joined him). But that Xenophon never learned anything about the battle at all seems impossible.

Xenophon was of course perfectly capable of writing fictitious battlepieces, as he does in the *Cyropaedia* (cf. especially vi. 4–7–vii. 1). But these are always filled with the sort of elaborate detail whose absence has been made a ground for criticising his version of the Battle of Sardis. Elsewhere in the *Hellenica* (notably in his account of the Battle of Leuctra: *Hellenica* vi. 4.4ff.) when his information is inadequate, he does not supplement it out of his imagination in order to present a seemingly complete story.

Moreover, a fictitious story might have been expected to increase Agesilaus's glory by multiplying the forces opposed to him, not to say that he defeated the enemy's cavalry alone when in fact he had routed sixty-thousand horse and foot. It seems most probable that Xenophon's story is a sketch because, like Sir Jacob Astley, he was 'very busy that day'; and that the Oxyrhynchus historian, who was certainly very much better informed that Xenophon about what was happening in Europe, knew much less about events in Asia. Agesilaus had won a great victory over Tissaphernes; six hundred of the barbarians had been killed; the Spartiate Xenocles had been 'mentioned in dispatches'. From these facts the historian constructed an elaborate set piece, to illustrate how, in his opinion, a Greek general might conduct a campaign against a Persian army.

However the battle was won, both versions agree that it led to the downfall and execution of Tissaphernes. Agesilaus could have had peace from his successor, Tithraustes, on the basis of home rule for the Asiatic Greeks, subject to payment of tribute to Persia, but preferred to continue the war. Tithraustes was at least successful in buying the Spartans off from his own territory and sending them to plunder that of Pharnabazus. Agesilaus was now entrusted by the Spartans with an unprecedented supreme command by land and sea—the latter executed through the lieutenancy of Pisander, his brother-in-law. But he seems to have thought that the best way to use his forces was to ravage the Persians' territory, especially the estates of the great satraps. Sooner or later they would become tired of seeing their homes devastated and make peace on his terms; in the meantime he was supporting his army and enriching his friends.

Xenophon seems to have had his share. He notes appreciatively the way in which Agesilaus enriched his friends by allowing them to buy on credit from the prize-agents (*Agesilaus* i. 17–19), and it was remembered against him long afterwards that 'Phylopidas the Spartiate sent him as a present slaves captured at Dardanus, and he disposed of them as he wished' (Diogenes Laertius ii. 53; the point of the reproach is presumably that the slaves were Greek. We cannot date the incident, which Diogenes actually mentions after Xenophon's establishment at Scillus.) But Xenophon seems to have developed doubts as to both the justice and the effectiveness of Agesilaus's strategy. Too strict an insistence by Herippidas on confiscating plunder for the common stock alienated Spithridates, the great Persian noble whom Lysander had won to the Spartan side—a heavy blow to Agesilaus for personal as well as public reasons, since he had become enamoured of Megabates, the son of Spithradates (*Hellenica* iv. 1.20–8; *Agesilaus* 5.4–5). Perhaps even worse to bear were the reproaches of Pharnabazus, at whose meeting with Agesilaus in the winter of 395–394 B.C. Xenophon seems to have been himself present (*Hellenica* iv. 1.29ff.). At the appointed spot, 'Agesilaus and his thirty officers were waiting, lying on the ground in some hay, when Pharnabazus arrived, wearing a costly dress. When his servants spread for him carpets, on which the Persians sit softly, he was ashamed of his luxury, and lay down himself, just as he was.' His courtesy seems more to be commended than the Spartan

austerity, and his speech reduced the Spartiate officers, as Xenophon acknowledges, to a shamefaced silence. 'Agesilaus, and all
you Lacedaemonians who are present, I, when you were at war
with the Athenians, was your friend and ally. I strengthened your
fleet with subsidies. On land I fought in person on horseback by
your side, and pursued your enemies into the sea. Not once did
you have reason to accuse me of double dealing towards you, like
Tissaphernes, either in my actions or in my speech. Such has been
my character, and now I am so dealt with by you that I have not
so much as a meal in my own country, unless I scavenge among
your refuse, like the beasts of the field. My father left me fair
dwelling-houses and parks full of trees and animals, in which I
took delight, and I see them all cut down or burned. If, then, I do
not understand piety and justice, do you teach me what they are,
among men who understand gratitude.'

Agesilaus, when at length he replied, acknowledged Sparta's
debt to Pharnabazus, but said that when Greek cities were at war
the personal obligations of citizens to individuals were set aside
by patriotic duty. Guest-friends sometimes killed each other; the
Spartans were now making war, not on their former friend but on
a Persian subject. He invited Pharnabazus to join Sparta, not as
a subject but as an ally. Pharnabazus nobly replied that if the
King his master superseded him he would join the Spartans, but
otherwise he would fight the Spartans with all his might. Agesilaus clasped his hand, with a wish that such a friend might be his
own, and a promise to withdraw from the satrap's territory. So
the meeting ended. As Pharnabazus was riding away, his son, a
boy still in the flower of youth, waited for a moment, then ran up
to Agesilaus saying, 'I make you my guest'. The King accepted,
and the boy gave him his beautiful javelin, telling him not to
forget. Agesilaus, unprepared for this gesture, took the trappings
off the horse of his secretary, Idaeus, and gave them in return.
Many years later when the boy was driven out by his brother
during his father's absence, Agesilaus befriended him, even to the
extent of influencing the judges of the boys' foot-race at Olympia
to admit his beloved, who was suspected of being over age.

Both Agesilaus and Pharnabazus did as they had promised.

Agesilaus withdrew at once from the satrap's territory, and within a year was back in Greece to meet the enemies whom the Persians had raised at home. Pharnabazus, by this time, was preparing to descend upon the Peloponnesian coast with the victorious Persian fleet, whose command he shared with Conon the Athenian.

Agesilaus's strategy has been blamed: it has been argued that he ought to have carried on a naval war about Cilicia and Cyprus, as the Athenians had done in the mid-fifth century, or if the main effort was to be made by land, as the traditions of Sparta suggested, it should have been directed to securing the great cities of Caria, as Alexander the Great later did, and so preventing the Persians from using them as naval bases. But Alexander had a siege train, which enabled him to reduce Miletus and Halicarnassus. Agesilaus, though he overran Anatolia as far as the ancient Phrygian capital of Gordium, never took a single major fortress. Xenophon seems to be looking back on these campaigns when, in the *Cyropaedia*, he makes his hero, who has advanced victoriously to Bablyon but been compelled to retire without permanently occupying the enemy's territory, compare his progress to that of sailors, who sail on and on, and the waters that they have passed over are no more their own than those that lie ahead (*Cyropaedia* vi. 1.16).

CHAPTER THIRTEEN

Xenophon and Agesilaus – in Europe

By laying aside his own ambitions and obeying the order that recalled him to Europe in 394 B.C., Agesilaus, in Xenophon's eyes, played the part of a true patriot. Though ruler of cities and islands, commander by land and sea, and full of hopes for the successful prosecution of a just war, he 'obeyed his city, not otherwise than if he had been standing in the Office of the Ephors, alone in front of the Five' (*Agesilaus* 1.36). Xenophon himself accompanied him on his march (*Anabasis* v. 3.6; for the narrative of the march, *Hellenica* iv. 3, *Agesilaus* 2.1–16)—certainly not as a refugee; there can have been no place for refugees on this forced march, which traversed in less than a month the territories that Xerxes had taken a year to pass through (*Agesilaus* 2.1; cf. *Hellenica* iv. 2.8). Besides, Agesilaus had left what seemed an adequate guard for the Asiatic cities, was in hopes of settling the business in Europe quickly, and had promised to return. His fleet, under Pisander, still controlled the entrance to the Aegean, and if Xenophon had been anxious to escape to Europe before the Persian counter-offensive developed he could have done so by sea, and taken with him his wife, Philesia, whom he seems to have married some time after 399 B.C., and their sons Gryllus and Diodorus—apparently twins, as comparisons with Castor and Pollux, the twin sons of Zeus, indicate (Diogenes Laertius ii. 52; cf. Pausanias i. 22.4, who seriously doubts whether statues of the actual 'Dioscuri', dedicated on the Athenian Acropolis in honour of the Athenian cavalry some time before Xenophon's birth, may not represent Xenophon's sons!).

Since Diogenes Laertius calls Philesia Xenophon's 'little

woman', rather than 'the General's lady', it has been suspected that she was some conquest of his campaigns—after all, what opportunity had he of obtaining the hand of an Athenian lady of fashion at this time? But his sons had no difficulty in eventually being recognized as Athenian citizens, and the circumstances of his marriage must be left doubtful.

Xenophon, then, must have accompanied the army officially, and presumably as a senior commander, not as a war-historian. Agesilaus does not seem to have been the sort to seek immortality through the arts (indeed, Plutarch tells us—*Agesilaus* 2.2—that he expressly forbade, on his death bed, that any portrait or statue should be made of him.) No poet sang the praises of the kings of Lacedaemon (Pausanias iii. 8.2), and a prose history, published many years afterwards, would have had, in any case, far less propaganda value than poetry (Lysander had shown himself aware of the poets' value in this respect, if his kings had not (Plutarch, *Lysander* 18.3ff.), though his lavish rewards to those who sang his praises were distributed with poor taste).

It seems unlikely that, if Xenophon had been dropped from the Spartan service when Herippidas took over the Cyreans in 395 B.C., he would now have been re-employed, and this makes it more probable that he had been with Agesilaus continuously.

At all events, he was now close to the King. At Amphipolis, on the Macedonian border, he must have heard Dercylidas give the news of the great victory of the Nemea, and marked Agesilaus's reaction to the report that eight only of the Spartans but nearly ten thousand other Greeks had fallen: 'Alas for Greece! Those who have now fallen were enough, had they lived, to overcome all the barbarians in battle!' (*Agesilaus* 7.5; the comment is omitted from *Hellenica* iv. 3.1).

At Narthacium in Thessaly, Xenophon will have shared Agesilaus's pleasure in the defeat of 'the men who most prided themselves in horsemanship' by the cavalry whom the King had raised himself. When, on the borders of Boeotia, the sun was partially eclipsed and the news came that the fleet had been defeated at Cnidus by Pharnabazus and the Athenian Conon,

Xenophon observed how the King, to preserve his soldiers' morale, hid his distress and pretended to celebrate a victory. At Coronea, where the enemy had gathered to block the army's passage, Xenophon joined in the desperate struggle, 'like no other in our time', when the Thebans, not without great loss, cut their way right through Agesilaus's army and escaped to the mountains.

Xenophon blames Agesilaus for choosing the path of valour rather than safety, by opposing the Thebans' retreat directly instead of falling upon their rear. But, with professional instinct, he praises him (*Agesilaus* 2.7–8) for meeting a coalition of half Greece on equal terms, not for playing the hero in the face of impossible odds:[1] 'If I were to say that, I think I would show that Agesilaus was senseless, and I myself a fool for praising a man who risked the most important issues at hazard. But I praise him rather for preparing a force no less than the enemy's, arming it so that it appeared all bronze and scarlet, seeing that his men could endure hardship, and filling their souls with self-esteem, so that they were capable of fighting any opponent at need.' He saw the ground red with blood, the bodies lying, friend and foe heaped together, the pierced shields, shivered spears, and unsheathed swords, some on the ground, some embedded in bodies, some still in the hands of the slain (*Agesilaus* 2.14). He took special note, both in his History and in his Life of Agesilaus, of the wounded King's piety and humanity in granting a free retreat to eighty Thebans who, cut off from their main body, had taken refuge in a temple (*Hellenica* iv. 3.20; *Agesilaus* 2.13). He probably went with Agesilaus to Delphi, where Agesilaus dedicated to the god the tithe of the booty from Asia, worth not less than a hundred talents, and Xenophon himself may have taken the opportunity to discharge his own debt to Apollo by making an offering in the

[1] Major Bellenden's comments on 'the Grand Cyrus' and similar 'nonsensical romances' of the seventeenth century (for which of course Xenophon cannot wholly escape responsibility) seem apt. 'Why, how the devil can you believe that Artamines, or what d'ye call him, fought single-handed with a whole battalion? One to three is as great odds as ever fought and won, and I never knew anybody that cared to take that, except old Corporal Raddlebanes' (Sir Walter Scott, *Old Mortality*, ch. xi).

Treasury of the Athenians, inscribed with his own name and that of Proxenus (*Anabasis* v. 3.5).[1]

Diogenes Laertius (ii. 51–2) and Plutarch (*Agesilaus* 20) indicate that Xenophon accompanied Agesilaus to Sparta, where he was honoured with the ancient equivalent of the freedom of the city, but that shortly afterwards he left, to settle upon an estate which the Spartans had granted him at Scillus. This village, lying to the south of the Alpheus river (cf. Pausanias v. 6.7), was in territory which had been annexed by the city of Elis early in the fifth century B.C., and which the Spartans under King Agis had 'liberated' a few years previously. By settling their distinguished mercenary general here, the Spartans may have intended not merely to reward him but to establish an outpost upon the frontier of a dangerously insubordinate ally. At the same time, by inviting Xenophon to send his sons to be educated at Sparta, they provided themselves with hostages for his good behaviour.

By about 393 B.C., then, we can imagine Xenophon established at Scillus with Philesia. This does not mean that he was no longer in the Spartan service; his reports of Agesilaus's campaigns round Corinth and in north-west Greece still often read like those of an eye-witness—for example, this account (*Hellenica* iv. 5.6–8) of how Agesilaus received the news of the destruction of a detached regiment of the Spartan army at the very moment when he was surveying the spoils of his own victory, and had refused to receive ambassadors who wished to treat for peace:

'While Agesilaus was still sitting, apparently delighted at his achievement, a horseman galloped up with his horse in a lather of sweat. Though many asked him what news he brought, he answered nobody, but when he was near to Agesilaus, leaped from his horse and, running up to him with a face full of gloom, reported the disaster to the regiment at Lechaeum. When the King heard, he immediately leaped from his seat and seized his spear and ordered the herald to summon the commanding officers. They came running together and he ordered the others (for the

---

[1] It has been objected that the Athenians would not have allowed a political exile to make an offering in their treasury. But the treasury belonged to the god, not to the city of Athens.

troops had not yet breakfasted) to take what food they could and
come as quickly as possible, but he himself, with his staff, led off
without eating. And the body guards, fully armed, followed at
speed, the King in front and the rest coming after. But when he
had already gone past the hot springs to the plain of Lechaeum,
three horsemen galloped up and reported that the dead had been
taken up.[1] When he heard this, he gave the order to ground arms,
and after a short rest led his army back to the Heraeum.'

By 387 B.C. the Greeks on both sides were exhausted, and the
war ended with a peace dictated by Persia (*Hellenica* v. 1.31).
'Artaxerxes the King thinks it right that the cities in Asia should
be his own, and, of the islands, Clazomenae and Cyprus, and that
the other Greek cities, both great and small, should be granted
independence, except Lemnos, Imbros and Skyros, which are to
belong to Athens, as of old. If either party does not accept this
peace, I will make war on it with those who approve, by land and
by sea, with ships and money.' It was true that this peace left
most of European Greece in the Spartan sphere of influence, as
the Spartans could break up combinations led by such cities as
Thebes and Olynthus, on the grounds that they were safeguarding the independence of the smaller towns. But the Persians had
not merely recovered control of Asia; their right to intervene in
Europe was acknowledged. Tissaphernes himself was dead and
disgraced, but his policy was triumphantly justified.

Xenophon does not blame Agesilaus for this humiliation to
Greece, though he could have had peace years earlier on better
terms. Nor does he blame him directly for causing the downfall
of Sparta, by pursuing his feud with the Thebans over the next
sixteen years, until the Theban victory at Leuctra in 371 B.C.
showed the Greeks once and for all that the Spartans were not
invincible. The end of their domination incidentally cost Xenophon himself his home at Scillus, and ruined many of his friends,
oligarchs in the allied cities whose power had been maintained by
Spartan arms. But Agesilaus, now grown old, was not in command at Leuctra; the blame for defeat, in Xenophon's eyes, lay

---

[1] Under a truce granted by the victors. This meant that the battle was over and
defeat had been acknowledged.

with Cleombrotus, the king representing the other Spartan royal house, who had never supported Agesilaus's policies adequately, and now ruined all by mismanaging the decisive battle. Agesilaus's early victories were shared between the city and himself; 'as for the defeats that followed, nobody could say that they were incurred under Agesilaus's leadership' (*Agesilaus* 2.23). Xenophon often gives examples of his military skill, not only when important successes followed, but also (e.g. *Hellenica* vi. 5.18–19) when the affair was in itself without major consequences, but could provide an object-lesson to the student of tactics.

Modern critics blame Xenophon for a hero-worship that blinds him totally to the King's faults, and it cannot be denied that friendship and gratitude obviously influence his accounts, not only of Agesilaus's own actions, but of those of his half-brother Teleutias and son Archidamus. But a comparison between the *Hellenica* and the Life of Agesilaus shows that in fact he disapproved of much of the King's conduct. The latter work, composed apparently just after the death of Agesilaus in 360 B.C., is the earliest surviving example of a moralizing biography, intended to display the virtues of a noble character through his actions. In form it clearly resembles a funeral oration, opening with praise of the hero's ancestry, his country, his kingship, and the proofs that he gave of fitness to rule; continuing with a sketch of his career; and ending with the enumeration of particular virtues, justice, valour, wisdom, patriotism, charm, and so forth, with anecdotes to illustrate each.

Thus the King's humanity is shown by his concern that children abandoned when his army shifted camp should not be sold into slavery, or devoured by dogs and wolves; his continence, by the manner in which he overcame his passion for the beautiful Persian boy Megabates; his good faith, by the readiness of his enemies to trust his word (*Agesilaus* 1.21–2; 3.5; 5.4–5). 'He did not blame those who were deceived by their friends, but utterly condemned those who were tricked by their enemies. To deceive those who distrusted him he accounted wise, but to deceive trusting men impious' (*Agesilaus* 11.5). Knowingly to reject virtue he counted a greater fault than ignorance. The gods, he believed, rejoiced no less in pious deeds than in pure sacrifices (*Agesilaus* 11.9; 11.2).

If Xenophon's Agesilaus has some of the qualities of his Socrates, there is no need to suppose that both characters are imaginary, compounded out of Xenophon's own ideals. Agesilaus and Xenophon had no doubt been brought up to respect the same moral values. Both would have judged virtue by the same traditional standards; and, if these standards are examined more critically in Plato's Socratic dialogues than in Xenophon's, it may well be that Socrates did in fact prefer, in Xenophon's case, to confirm his beliefs rather than to dissect them.

In the *Agesilaus*, Xenophon represents the King as setting an example of all virtues. But he was clearly aware of failings which he felt it his duty, as a biographer, to suppress. The facts of the King's career are drawn from the *Hellenica*, indeed the very language is often the same, with minor variations intended to give the *Agesilaus* a more archaic and stately ring. But—far more significant than the addition of incidents too trifling for history but illustrative of character—are the omissions. Agesilaus's meeting with Pharnabazus is mentioned (*Agesilaus* 3.5), to show how the satrap trusted him not to violate his oath of safe-conduct, but the dignified speech of reproach that Xenophon reports in the *Hellenica* is omitted. Evidently Xenophon felt, and was prepared to acknowledge in his history, that Agesilaus had behaved badly to the benefactor of Sparta.

More significant still is his complete silence, in the *Agesilaus*, on the affair of Sphodrias (*Hellenica* v. 4.15ff.). This man, while in command of the Spartan garrison at Thespiae in 377 B.C., had attempted to surprise the Piraeus by a night march, and so driven Athens to join the Thebans in their war of liberation. He was to be tried for his life by the ephors—perhaps more for his failure than his treachery; when Phoebidas had treacherously seized the Cadmea, the citadel of Thebes, in 382 B.C., Agesilaus had ruled that if his conduct had been harmful to Lacedaemon he should justly be punished, but if beneficial, the ancient laws granted freedom of discretionary action in such matters (*Hellenica* v. 2.34— another affair on which Xenophon preserves a discreet silence in the *Agesilaus*). In Sphodrias's case the matter seemed clear—but Archidamus, son of Agesilaus, was in love with Cleonymus, son of Sphodrias—and so Sphodrias escaped; it was impossible to find him innocent, but 'it was hard to put to death a man who from his earliest youth had passed through all the stages of honour. Sparta had need of such soldiers.' Xenophon does not say (as Plutarch does: *Agesilaus* 13.3; see also 23.3–25.1 for his comments on the affairs of Sphodrias and Phoebidas) that Agesilaus, though exact and law-abiding in all else, in his friends' affairs thought that excess of justice was a mere pretext. Nor does he draw attention (as, again, Plutarch does: *Agesilaus* 26.1–3) to the way in which Agesilaus, by frequently making war on the Thebans, 'schooled' them to be the equals of the Spartans.

But his account of the liberation of Thebes in 378 B.C. begins (*Hellenica* v. 4.1) with the reflection that 'one could give many examples, both from Greek history and from that of the barbarians, to prove that the gods do not overlook impiety and sin. But now I shall speak of the present instance. The Lacedaemonians, the very people who had sworn to leave the cities independent, seized the acropolis of Thebes. And they were punished by none other than the victims of their injustice, they who had never yet been beaten by any one of mankind.' Obviously this represents a revision of Xenophon's material after the great Theban victory of Leuctra in 371 B.C., and equally obviously it is not the remark of a writer who is deliberately falsifying history in the Spartan interest and at the expense of the Thebans.

Did Xenophon—disillusioned by Spartan treachery[1]—lay his history aside in 382 B.C., and return to it some time after Leuctra, in order to show how that treachery was punished? More probably

---

[1] Xenophon's anger and disillusionment are also shown in the *Constitution of the Lacedaemonians*, an incomplete but interesting account of Spartan institutions written, as its description of military organization shows, some time before the Battle of Leuctra. A chapter (14) describing the failure of contemporary Spartans to live in accordance with the traditional standards of their state has been thought by many scholars to have been added years afterwards, when Xenophon, shocked by Spartan treachery, wanted to recant his earlier praise. But it is not necessary to suppose this; see A. Momigliano, 'Per l'unità logica della *Lakedaimonion Politeia* di Senofonte', *Rivista di Filologia e d'Istruzione Classica* N.5 14 fasc. 2 (1936) pp. 170–3 (reprinted in *Storia e Letteratura* 108 (1966) pp. 341–5).

he had been continually noting down information that came his way, but only wrote it up for publication years afterwards. Similarly, though the *Hellenica* end with the battle of Mantinea in 362 B.C., the last books, at least, must have been given their final revision not earlier than 358, the year of the murder of Alexander of Pherae, which is described in a digression (*Hellenica* vi. 4.33–7).

But even if the later books of the *Hellenica* were revised at leisure, they still bear the character of a chronicle of such information as came the author's way, rather than a history, the result of active inquiry or systematic investigation of such problems as the nature of the Spartan domination of Greece, and the stages of its overthrow. Xenophon himself probably ceased to take an active part in events after the King's Peace of 387 B.C. Scillus no doubt attracted distinguished visitors (especially every fourth year, at the time of the Olympic festival). But Xenophon's friends would be prominent Spartans, or leaders in the allied cities, especially in the Peloponnese—men like the humane Stasippus of Tegea, whose impious murder by his political opponents was one of the consequences of the breaking of the Spartan power (*Hellenica* vi. 5.6ff.). Even if Xenophon occasionally left his comfortable backwater—for instance, to visit his sons when they were being educated in Sparta—he will still have met men of the same type. His friends will have had little to say about such important matters as the formation of the second Athenian naval league in 377 B.C., or (after Leuctra) the liberation of Messenia from the Spartans. He says nothing because no information came his way, not because he is deliberately suppressing matters painful to the Spartans.

On the other hand, he often carefully reports details of lesser affairs that have come to his notice, when they may furnish practical examples to his reader. He praises (*Hellenica* vi. 2.27ff.) the way in which Iphicrates trained his seamen on the actual voyage to the theatre of war in 372 B.C., and the adroitness (vi. 2.39) with which he secured political support at home. But Xenophon is also quick to point out the way in which this light-infantry expert mishandled his cavalry when he was sent to help the Spartans in

369 B.C. (*Hellenica* vi. 5.49–52)—'I have no fault to find with his well-conducted generalship on other occasions.[1] But his actions at that time, I find have been altogether either useless or in-expedient'—with particular faults carefully detailed. Xenophon does not in fact give us an adequate picture of Iphicrates either as a man or as a soldier. Still more regrettable is his similar treatment of the great Theban Epaminondas, whom he does not even men-tion in connection with his decisive victory at Leuctra (*Hellenica* vi. 4.4ff. gives reasons for the Spartan defeat, rather than an adequate account of the battle). Xenophon draws practical lessons from the conduct of Epaminondas in his last campaign of 362 B.C.: 'I would not pretend that his strategy turned out fortunately. But, for what can be achieved by forethought and boldness, the man was, I consider, in no way wanting' (*Hellenica* vii. 5.8). But Xenophon gives us no character sketch, like those he gives of the murdered generals in the *Anabasis*. The fact was of course that he had never met Epaminondas or any of his friends. He did not know what he was like as a man, and only learned something of his quality as a general from his conduct during his last cam-paigns, as seen from the side of his enemies, Xenophon's own side. But this does not mean that Xenophon deliberately distorts the facts. He is ready, as has been seen, to blame the Spartans, for their ingratitude to their friend Pharnabazus as well as for their treachery against Thebes and Athens. His historical writing is not impartial, not because he is deliberately writing propaganda, but because his circumstances, both when he was living at Scillus and after he had been forced to leave, allowed him to collect informa-tion from one side, not to make general and impartial inquiries.

[1] Especially his victory at Lechaeum in 390 (*Hellenica* iv. 5.11ff.)

CHAPTER FOURTEEN

Domestic Life

XENOPHON'S personal life does not, of course, enter into his
historical writings. But some details are carefully described in the
Anabasis (v. 3.6–13), in order to explain how he paid his debt to
Artemis. 'When he left Asia with Agesilaus on the march against
the Boeotians, he deposited the money with Megabyzus, the
temple-guardian of Artemis, because he himself seemed to be
running into danger. And he charged him to repay the money to
himself, if he came safely through; but if anything happened to
him, to make whatever offering to Artemis he thought would be
pleasing to the goddess. And when Xenophon was in exile, and
was now living in Scillus, where he had been established by the
Lacedaemonians, near to Olympia, Megabyzus arrived at Olympia
to see the games, and repaid the deposit to him. Xenophon
received it and bought an estate for the goddess where the god'
(presumably her brother Apollo, through his oracle) 'directed.
There happens to flow through the estate a River Selinus. And in
Ephesus, past the temple of Artemis, a River Selinus flows. There
are fish in both, and shellfish.[1] In the estate at Scillus there is also
hunting of all sorts of beasts of the chase. And he built an altar
and temple with the sacred money, and thereafter he always set
aside a tithe of the produce of the land in its season, and made a
sacrifice to the goddess, and all the citizens and neighbours and
their wives took part in the festival. The goddess provided for

---

[1] Professor L. A. Mackay reminds me that 'there is a river in Macedon and
there is also moreover a river at Monmouth ... and there is salmons in both'.
Had Captain Fluellen, that authority on the 'true and aunchient prerogatifes and
laws of the wars', read his Xenophon?

the feasters barley-meal, wheat-flour, wine, fruits, and a share of the sacrificial victims from the holy pasture, and of the spoils of the chase too. For a hunt was held on the festival by Xenophon's sons[1] and those of the other citizens, and those who wished to of the grown men also joined in the hunt. And some game was taken from the holy ground itself, and some from Pholoe, boar and fallow-deer and red deer.

'The place lies on the road from Lacedaemon to Olympia, some twenty stades' (rather over two miles) 'from the sanctuary of Zeus in Olympia. And within the sacred ground is a meadow, and wooded hills, suitable for the pasture of swine, goats and oxen, and horses too, so that the draught-animals of the visitors to the festival enjoyed a feast. Round about the temple itself is planted a grove of orchard trees, as many as bear fruit in season. And the temple, allowing for the difference in size, is patterned after the one in Ephesus, and the cult-statue is like the one at Ephesus, allowing for the difference between cypress-wood and gold. And an upright stone is set beside the temple, bearing the inscription:

LAND SACRED TO THE GODDESS.
LET THE TENANT AND POSSESSOR OF THE USUFRUCT
MAKE OFFERING OF EACH YEAR'S TITHE.
FROM THE SURPLUS, LET HIM MAINTAIN THE TEMPLE.
IF THESE DUTIES ARE NEGLECTED,
THE GODDESS WILL SEE TO IT.

It is to be noted that, though the ladies shared in the 'festival'— a cheerful open-air picnic on a large scale, like those with which Greek villages still often celebrate the feasts of their patron saints—they left the hunting to the boys and those men who wanted to join in. It is unlikely that Philesia, Xenophon's wife, is being delicately complimented when the *Treatise on Hunting* (*Cynegeticus* 13.18) ends with the remark that 'not only did those men who were passionate lovers of the chase become good, but so

---

[1] The *Anabasis* in its final form (whatever the date of 'Themistogenes') must then have been written after Xenophon's sons were old enough to organize hunting-parties: not before 380 B.C. at the earliest? If Xenophon's description be taken to suggest that these 'festivals' were things of the past, after 371 B.C.

did the women to whom the goddess granted this favour, Atalanta and Procris and whoever else there may have been' (Plate 9).

Philesia is far more likely to have resembled Ischomachus's wife in the *Oeconomicus*, though, as has been suggested already, this work also seems to contain memories of Xenophon's childhood and youth.[1] It seems to have grown as he wrote it. Its abrupt opening—'I once heard him discussing household management, too, along the following lines'—suggests that it began, not as an independent work, but as a continuation of something else, presumably the *Memorabilia*. Xenophon says he 'heard' Socrates, but, as has been noted, he puts into his mouth remarks about the younger Cyrus which refer to the period after Xenophon had left Athens. But, even if he is inventing, we may allow something 'Socratic' to his inventions.

The work begins (chs. 1–5) with advice from Socrates to his young friend Critobulus, on how to manage his estate and live within his income, culminating in the praise of country life that has already been quoted. At this point Xenophon may have thought that he was writing out of character: Socrates, after all, was a lover of the town, though perhaps we need not take too seriously Plato's remarks on this subject in the *Phaedrus* (230D), preceded as they are by one of the most appreciative descriptions of the beauties of nature in Greek literature. At all events, Socrates was clearly not the right man to describe the management of a country estate, or even a rich man's establishment in town, and Xenophon accordingly had the excellent idea of making him interrogate a 'perfect gentleman', just as he interrogated craftsmen of different sorts (*Oeconomicus* 6.13), and even

---

[1] It may be that, in taking the wife of Ischomachus as a model, Xenophon is being prompted to an unfortunate choice by memories of a society marriage whose eventual consequences he never heard. Andocides the orator, prosecuted for impiety towards the Eleusinian Mysteries, attacked the morals of the Torchbearer Callias; this rich nobleman, married to the daughter of *an* Ischomachus, had been seduced by his widowed mother-in-law, who drove her own daughter from the house—can this really have been Xenophon's young innocent in her riper age? (cf. Andocides, *De Mysteriis*, 124ff.). For that matter, both Atalanta and Procris seem curious choices as patterns of female virtue; the one was turned into a lioness for lying with her lover in the sanctuary of Artemis; the other's jealousy led to her accidental death at her husband's hands.

(*Memorabilia* iii. 11) 'a beautiful woman residing in the city, named Theodote: the sort to associate with whoever persuaded her'. The second,[1] and longer part of *Oeconomicus*, therefore, consists of the account which the noble Ischomachus—delighted at the compliment paid him by his selection as a model of gentility (ch. 7.2)—gives of his own way of life. His own time, he explains (ch. 7.3) is spent out-of-doors: his wife is well capable of managing the home herself. Ischomachus's house, it has already been suggested, may be modelled in part on Xenophon's boyhood home, but the house at Scillus, whether Xenophon built it himself or not, probably was similar in construction and arrangement, and, even if the first home to which he brought Philesia was a temporary one at Ephesus, it may have shared the same essential features. (It is perhaps strange that Xenophon does not specifically mention books among the house's contents, or a study among its rooms.)

The description of Ischomachus's domestic arrangements opens with his young wife biting her lips and blushing with vexation when she has mislaid something her husband gave her to look after, and her training begins with an insistence on good order, which confers a sort of beauty even on pots and pans when they are properly drawn up for inspection. This surely is a soldier's home; and, if what follows is not merely a generalized description of what young upper-class Athenians were brought up to expect of their wives, we may suppose that it reflects the early years of Xenophon's own marriage rather than what Gryllus his father told him about Diodora his mother. To the question whether he educated his wife himself or whether she understood her duties when he received her from her father and mother, Ischomachus replies that she was not yet fifteen years old when she came to him, and had hitherto been most carefully chaperoned, 'to ensure that she saw as little as possible, heard as

---

[1] It is disputed whether Xenophon laid the work aside for some time between the first and second parts. I see no necessity to suppose so. The date of composition is also doubtful. If the *Oeconomicus* followed the completion of the *Memorabilia*, it must have been written after Xenophon had left Scillus, since, as has been noted, *Memorabilia* iii. 5 seems to be written with reference to the situation after the battle of Leuctra.

little as possible, and spoke as little as possible. Do you not think
it a matter of congratulation, if she came knowing only how to
receive wool and show up a cloak in return, and having seen only
how to assign their tasks of weaving to the servant-girls? At all
events, Socrates, she came very well trained in control of her
bodily appetites, which seems to me the most important lesson,
both for men and women.' Ischomachus then describes how he
took her education in hand, beginning with prayer and sacrifice,
in which she took part, with obvious eagerness to learn, and how
he next (ch. 7.10ff.) explained to her the nature of their partnership: 'Tell me, dear wife, whether you have already considered
for what reason I took you, and your parents gave you to me?
For that we could easily have found other bedfellows is, I know,
obvious to you also. But I took thought for myself, and your
parents for you, whom we could best take as partner in household
and children, and I selected you, and your parents, it seems, out
of the possible choices, selected me. For children, if God ever
grants them to be born to us, we will then deliberate, with a view
to how best we may educate them. For this too will be one of our
joint assets, to gain the best possible allies and supporters of our
old age. But at present this household is ours in common. I
declare that I put the whole of my possessions into the joint
stock, and you have deposited in it all that you brought with you.
And we must not reckon up which of us has contributed most in
quantity, but we must know very well, that whichever of us is
the better partner makes the most valuable contribution. To this,
Socrates, my wife returned the following answer: "What assistance could I give you? What ability do I have? Surely everything
rests in you. Mother told me that my duty was to be prudent."
"Good heavens, yes, my dear," said I; "my father said the same to
me. But prudence, in men or women, consists in so acting that
one's existing possessions will be maintained in the best possible
condition, and others added to them, as far as is consistent with
justice and honour."' Ischomachus continues by explaining to his
wife 'the natural abilities that God implanted in you, and to which
the law contributes its praise'. The partnership of male and
female has been designed by the gods for the perpetuation of the

race, and, for mankind at least, to provide supporters for the parents' old age. Men, unlike the beasts of the field, need shelter; but they also need provisions brought in from the open air. So the woman is naturally fitted for indoor activities; the man to bear cold and heat, long journeys and military service, in outdoor labour. God has so prescribed, and human law approves. For a woman, it is more honourable to stay at home than to go out-of-doors; for a man, the contrary. If a man acts contrary to what has been designed for him by the gods, they will not forget, and he will be punished for neglecting his own duties, or performing those of his wife.

As Xenophon accepts the natural differences between man and woman, so he takes slavery for granted. The queen bee[1] remains in the hive and keeps the bees busy at their tasks; so the lady of the house is to stay at home, send out the servants whose work takes them out-of-doors, and oversee those who work at home. She is to watch receipts and expenses, and must 'take forethought and be on her guard, so that what had been laid aside for a year's expenditure is not spent in a month' (*Oeconomicus* 7.36). (The inexperienced girl is provided (9.11) with a housekeeper to help her in her tasks, chosen from among the domestics as most continent in eating, drinking, sleep and sexual pleasures; chosen too for her superior memory, forethought to avoid loss by neglect, and appreciation of the respect that her masters will pay her if she obeys them.) The lady of the house must also look after the sick slaves: an unpleasant task, perhaps, her husband suggests; but she answers: 'Most pleasant indeed, if those who are well cared for are going to bear gratitude and be more well-disposed than they were before.' It will be a pleasure to her, too, to take a slave who is ignorant of wool-working, and train her so as to double her worth; to favour prudent and helpful servants, and punish the bad (later—9.14—Ischomachus compares her duty to that of a magistrate in a well-ordered city). The greatest pleasure of all will come if she shows herself better than her husband and so makes him her servant.

[1] Xenophon, unlike Virgil, who talks of the 'king', knows her true sex (cf. especially Virgil, *Georgics* iv. 149ff., on the labours of the hive).

The young wife need not fear that advancing age will diminish her honour; on the contrary, as partner with her husband and children and guardian of their home, she will advance in honour as in years. Honour and goodness wax in human life, not through the bloom of youthful beauty, but through the virtues (*Oeconomicus* 7.37–43).

For all that, Ischomachus says, his wife did once try to supplement the bloom of youthful beauty (*Oeconomicus* 10). Socrates's remark that he would far rather learn the virtue of a living woman than be shown a likeness by the famous painter Zeuxis[1] leads Ischomachus to describe how he caught his wife rubbing in white lead, so as to seem fairer than she really was, and putting on rouge, so as to seem redder, and wearing high shoes, so as to seem taller than she was by nature. He first asked her what her feelings would be if he tried to deceive her with false coins and similar cheats, as to the value of their joint property. 'She interrupted at once, "Don't say such things! Don't you become like that! If you were like that, I could not love you with all my soul!" "Well then," I said; "did we not agree that we were partners with one another in our bodies too?" "So at least people say," she replied.' Ischomachus then asks whether she would rather that he tried to keep his own body in good condition, so as to be able to present it to her with a truly fine complexion, or that he should rub it with crimson, and smear his eyes with cosmetics for men. Of course she replies that she would rather have his own natural complexion, and he says that he feels the same about her: 'As the gods have made horses most pleasant to horses, oxen to oxen, sheep to sheep, so mankind finds most pleasure in the pure human body.' Nor can paint deceive for long; it will be detected when the wearer gets up in the morning, or revealed by perspiration, tears, or the bath. (In the 'Choice of Hercules', Virtue appears pure and in white raiment, Vice painted and bedizened (*Memorabilia* ii. 1.22). Yet Xenophon approves of these tricks when they are used by a king to impress his subjects. His ideal Cyrus adopts Median robes for himself and his court, because this form of dress hides

---

[1] Had Xenophon actually heard Socrates criticise Art as a mere imitation of the truth, as Plato makes him do in Book x of the *Republic?*

any bodily defects and makes the wearers appear most handsome
and tall; uses high shoes to increase his height; paints his eyes and
heightens his complexion with rouge (*Cyropaedia* viii. 1.40–2).
A ruler, seen from a distance, is not of course subject to the
intimate betrayals that disclose a wife's deceits to her husband.
Xenophon does not add that no man is a hero to his own valet.)

Ischomachus next advises his wife how she may appear truly
beautiful, not merely seem to be so. She is to take exercise—but
not by riding to hounds like 'Atalanta and Procris and whoever
else there may have been'. 'I advised her not always to sit about
slavishly, but with God's help to try to stand up to the loom like
a mistress and to instruct, where her knowledge was superior, and
where it was not so good, to receive instruction, and to oversee
the breadmaker, and to stand by the housekeeper when she was
giving out supplies, and to go round seeing that everything was
in its proper place. This seemed to me to be looking after her
job and taking a walk at the same time.

'And I said that it was good exercise to moisten and knead the
bread, and to shake out and fold the cloaks and blankets. If she
took exercise like this, I said, she would eat with a better appetite,
enjoy better health, and appear with a truly better-coloured
complexion ... And now, Socrates,' he concludes, 'you may be
assured that my wife lives her life after the pattern that I have
taught her, as I have just explained to you' (Plate 12).

Of course, Athens, as well as Scillus, had its religious festivals
(to say nothing of weddings and funerals) which gave the women
the chance for an outing. And, even without leaving the house,
they could enjoy fresh air in the courtyard (compare [Demos-
thenes] xlvii. 52ff., an alfresco luncheon that ended disastrously
when creditors broke in to seize the furniture). They would not,
however, accompany their husbands out to dinner parties; at
the end of Xenophon's *Symposium* (9.6–7), after the entertainers
had mimed the wedded bliss of Dionysus and Ariadne, 'the
unmarried guests swore to marry, but the married mounted
their horses and galloped off to their own wives, to enjoy their
favours'.

Socrates at one point (*Oeconomicus* 10.1) praises Ischomachus's

wife for the 'masculine intelligence' with which she had declared
her pleasure in safeguarding her possessions rather than neglecting them. But Xenophon certainly had no notion that women,
like the female Guardians of Plato's *Republic*, should be relieved
of family cares in order to share the men's duties. Somewhat
strangely, however, he gave his approval, in the *Constitution of
the Lacedaemonians* (1.3ff.) to the upbringing of the Spartan girls,
while expressly noting the points in which it was directly opposed
to all that he praised in the *Oeconomicus*. Leaving wool-weaving
to the servants, they trained their bodies in outdoor competition,
so that they might develop into strong and healthy mothers. It is
a pity that Xenophon did not, besides describing these two
directly opposed systems, leave us in the *Cyropaedia* his own ideal
pattern of women's education. At least, what he does say about
women in that book suggests that his own marriage was happy.

Two incidents especially convey a truly romantic picture of
married love. Cyrus chastises the King of Armenia for with-
holding tribute due to his uncle Cyaxares. He captures the King
himself and all his family, except his son Tigranes, Cyrus's boyhood friend, who (like the headman's son-in-law of *Anabasis* iv.
5.24) happens to be away from home, but arrives in time to hear
judgment passed on his father. The King of Armenia takes refuge
on a hill, but is persuaded to come down and stand trial, in the
presence of the ladies in their coaches (is this a reminiscence of
Cyrus the Younger's dealings with Syennesis and Epyaxa;
Anabasis i. 2.24–6?) Tigranes pleads for his father, and Cyrus,
after inquiry into the financial and military resources of Armenia,
asks the King what ransom he would give for his wife and children. 'As much as I could,' is the reply. But Tigranes, newly-wed
and deeply in love with his wife, declares his readiness to ransom
her 'with his very soul'. Cyrus then freely releases his prisoners,
who, after their return home, praise his character, good looks,
and stature. 'Then Tigranes questioned his wife: "And did you
think Cyrus handsome?" "Good heavens," she said, "I wasn't
looking at him." "At whom were you looking?" said Tigranes.
"At the man who said he would give his own soul to ransom me
from slavery" ' (*Cyropaedia* iii. 1; especially 31–7 and 41).

The romance of another captive princess, Panthea, wife of Abradatas of Susa, 'said to be the most beautiful lady in Asia' ends tragically. She virtuously resists the advances of her captor Araspas, helps to gain her husband to Cyrus's cause, and arms him with golden armour and a purple surcoat, which she has made 'without her husband's knowledge, taking the measure from his armour'. Finally, after his heroic death in battle, she kills herself over his body (*Cyropaedia* iv. 6.11; v. 1.2ff.; vi. 4.2; vii. 3.2ff.).

We may suppose that Xenophon's own marriage had proved something more than a convenient business arrangement. But, to return to Ischomachus and his partnership, the man's duties (*Oeconomicus* 11ff.) lie out-of-doors, and Ischomachus instructs Socrates in the management of a farm—using, by a pleasant touch, Socrates's own methods upon himself, to bring out by question and answer the hidden knowledge that he has possessed all along. Of course Socrates has noticed that the soil is baked hard in summer and turns to mud in winter, so that spring is the favourable season to plough; that the grass on the fallows must be ploughed in before it has seeded itself, to manure the soil; that the seed should be sown evenly (an art that comes by practice); that the thresher should turn the harvest on the threshing-floor and keep it even; that winnowing should begin from the downwind side of the grain-heap, so that the chaff may be blown clear; that trees should be planted more deeply in dry soil than in wet (*Oeconomicus* 16–19). It is all common sense: if some men fail at farming where others succeed, the fault must be want of diligence rather than want of knowledge, just as on active service everybody knows that march discipline must be maintained and sentries properly posted, but not everybody does what he knows is right.[1] Xenophon certainly makes agriculture seem simple, but, comparing his *Oeconomicus* with Hesiod's *Works and Days*, of perhaps four centuries earlier, or with the detailed treatises of the Romans Cato and Columella, one has the impression that Xenophon's knowledge was superficial. He does not explain how to make a plough: he probably did not know; the important

---

[1] 'Our own negligence has undone us', as David Leslie said after 'Dunbar Drove'. Xenophon may again be thinking of Cyrus's march to Cunaxa.

thing was to know how to handle ploughmen. Once again we hear the voice of the retired general officer. 'The man who intends to farm well must train his workers to be eager and willing to obey. And the officer who leads men against the enemy must contrive the same results, by rewarding those who do their duty as good men and punishing the undisciplined' (*Oeconomicus* 5.15). Some ships' officers can accomplish a voyage in half the time, and bring their men in dripping with sweat but well contented, while others arrive hours later with their men cool but grumbling. Some generals cannot train their men to face hardship and danger willingly, or to obey orders except under compulsion; or even to feel shame after a disgraceful reverse; others can take over the same men and turn them into good soldiers. So in private affairs; that master is little to be congratulated whose appearance at the scene of labour does not produce a stir among the workmen, though he can punish the idle and reward the industrious. But the master at sight of whom the workmen are filled with a competitive spirit has 'something of kingly nature' (*Oeconomicus* 21). One can imagine the labourers at Scillus stirring themselves on the General's approach, touching their forelocks respectfully when he found fault with their planting or sowing or haymaking, and then going on with exactly what they were doing before, as soon as his back was turned.

CHAPTER FIFTEEN

Hunting and Horsemanship

IF Xenophon was not really an expert farmer, he was certainly an authority on hunting and horsemanship. It is a pleasing suggestion that his handbooks on these subjects may contain the substance of lessons given at Scillus to his sons. The dates at which they were actually written—no doubt with a wider public in mind—are uncertain. That on hunting (the *Cynegeticus*) is sometimes supposed to be a youthful work, and the opening, overloaded with mythological references, does look like the work of a young man anxious to display his accomplishments.[1] The final chapters, in which the products of the sophists' false educational system are contrasted with the fine characters developed by hunting, also seem immature. But the sensible and judicious advice on the care of hounds; the types of nets used in taking different sorts of game; scent; and tracking hares in snow, seems to be drawn from long and well-digested experience. The book describes hare-hunting, then the hunting of fallow-deer and red-deer (ch. 9), then boar-hunting (ch. 10), with a brief notice of the 'lions, pards, lynxes, panthers, bears and all other similar beasts of the chase' which are to be found in foreign parts. The hunters are in all cases on foot, and use hounds and nets; against

---

[1] Some readers may recall the 'rather *serious* infliction' by which Mr Romeo Simpkins, 'a pert but simple-looking, pink-and-white, yellow-haired youth', intended to recommend hunting to the public of Handley Cross. 'Nothing like hunting . . . *Sacred history*—Nimrod of Babylon—Venus took the field—Adonis killed in chase—Persians fond of hunting—Athenians ditto—Solon restrained ardour—Lacedaemonians and their breed of speedy dogs—Xenophon—Olympic Games—Romans—Aristotle—Oppian—Adrian—Ascanius—Somerville—Beckford—Meynell—Colonel Cook—Nimrod of Calais.'

the boar the hunters also use boar-spears. The stance and grip recommended, with the body balanced on both legs as in wrestling, the left hand forward to guide the spear, and the right held back to impel the thrust, are often illustrated on Greek vases (Plate 9). The hunter is to watch the beast's eye in order to anticipate its movements (10.11–12). How to escape if one falls before a charging boar, and how to rescue one's friends in like case, are also described, but one must not abandon one's spear, because (10.4–5) 'Safety is honourable only to the victor'—a sentiment that finds echoes elsewhere in Xenophon's writing: e.g. *Anabasis* v. 2.20. But it is surprising to find an author of the first half of the fourth century B.C. advising the use of 'Indian hounds' (9.1; 10.1), and this may indicate that Xenophon's work was edited by a later author, who may have been wholly responsible for chs. 1 and 12–13.

The *Art of Horsemanship*, in its present form, is certainly a work of Xenophon's old age, since its final paragraph refers to the *Hipparchicus*. This pamphlet, addressed ostensibly to an Athenian officer and giving advice on the reform of the Athenian cavalry, clearly must have been written after Xenophon's recall from exile (369 B.C.?). But we do not know its precise date. The cavalry's part in guarding against invasion is stressed, but it is dangerous to see an allusion to any particular campaign; the frontier was in fact in danger from the moment that Athens decided, in 369 B.C., to join Sparta against Thebes, even if the Thebans did in fact direct their efforts against the Peloponnese instead of Attica.

The *Art of Horsemanship* refers to the *Hipparchicus*, but is an entirely separate work, and probably written some years later. Had the two been planned to complement each other, the training of the individual would logically have come first. The book opens: 'Since it has been our fortune to practise horsemanship for a long time, we think that we are experienced in this art. Accordingly we wish to show our younger friends too the most correct way, in our opinion, to deal with horses.' The work is professedly a sketch, addressed to the amateur. Xenophon (like Socrates: *Memorabilia* iv. 7) was 'familiar with the more abstruse branches' of a science, which he wished to impart only 'to the extent to which a properly-educated man should be familiar' with it. Moreover he assumes a certain previous knowledge on his reader's part, including an acquaintance with the work of Simon, an earlier Athenian authority (*c.* 424 B.C.? The opening of his work, which is still extant, suggests that it too was a sketch for amateurs).

Obviously, the amateur should know how to avoid being cheated in buying a horse, especially an unbroken colt; so Xenophon devotes his first chapter to the points of the horse, beginning with the feet. A war-horse,[1] however excellent the rest of him might be, would, if he had poor feet, be as useless as a fine house on bad foundations. The horse that Xenophon admires is a good solid weight-carrier, rather heavy in the body; Shakespeare's description of the horse of Adonis (*Venus and Adonis*, lines 295ff.) is sometimes compared:

> 'Round-hoof'd, short-jointed, fetlocks shag and long,
> Broad breast, full eye, small head, and nostril wide,
> High crest, short ears, straight legs and passing strong,
> Thin mane, thick tail, broad buttock, tender hide.'

'How one must break in colts,' says Xenophon (ch. 2.1), 'seems not to form part of our subject.' Cavalry service is the duty of the rich; the young cavalryman should develop his own skill in riding; the older should give his time to his estate, his friends, and his political and military duties. Both should employ a professional for the business of breaking-in. But the amateur, and his groom, should know how to win the confidence of the colt, by seeing that he 'associates hunger and thirst and the attacks of insects with solitude, but food and drink and freedom from things that hurt him with men'. He should be accustomed to crowds, and strange sights and noises, and when frightened should not be roughly handled, but taught by gentle coaxing that there is no danger.

---

[1] Throughout the book, Xenophon has an eye to the horse's use either in battle or as an officer's charger on parade. The suggestion that ch. 12, on cavalry armour and weapons, was added later, when the 'younger friends' grew up and went to the wars, seems not to be warranted.

The master is advised how to instruct his groom in stable management (ch. 4), grooming (chs. 5–6), leading and bridling the horse. These duties are to be carried out by a servant, but the master will keep a strict watch on his conduct, and will especially see that the stall is so arranged that it is no more possible to steal the horse's food from the manger than the master's from the larder. ('The master's eye fattens the horse soonest', as the King of Persia was told: *Oeconomicus* 12.20.) A man who neglects his horse neglects his own safety, and the close watch is necessary not only to prevent thieving but to see if the horse is 'off his oats' through tiredness or the onset of sickness. Xenophon's brief advice to the amateur owner contrasts with the detailed descriptions of symptoms and recommendations for treatment given by the professional veterinarians whose writings have survived from later antiquity.

The grown horse, like the colt, is to be won to give his confidence to his master, not subdued by violence (6.13–15). Never to handle the horse in anger is the essential precept; anger is without foresight and often leads to repentance.[1] When the horse suspects some object he must be brought up to it gently and shown that it is not dangerous, not compelled by blows, which the horse will associate with the distrusted object and so become confirmed in his fear. Association of ideas plays an important part in the horse's education: 'It is merely conventional to calm a horse by smacking the lips and excite him by clicking the tongue, and if from the beginning you were to combine gentle actions with clicking and rough ones with smacking the lips, the horse would learn to become excited with smacking and calm with clicking' (9.10). Again (8.13–14), 'for men to instruct their fellow-men, the gods have granted the power of speech. But a horse can obviously learn nothing from mere words. But if when he behaves according to your wishes you show him some kindness in return, and when he is disobedient you punish him, in this way he will most readily learn to serve you as he ought. It does not take long to state this principle, but it is an essential accompani-

---

[1] In larger matters too: anger drove Teleutias to commit his men to action without judgment, and so cost him the battle and his life (*Hellenica* v. 3.3ff.).

ment of the whole art of horsemanship.' It is interesting to find similar principles laid down, quite independently, by the great modern masters. Thus the Duke of Newcastle writes that 'there are but two things that can make an accomplished horse, *viz.* the hope of reward or the fear of punishment ... When he has been rewarded or punished, he thinks of it, and retains it in his memory (for memory is thought) ... But these are things so well known to complete horsemen that it is needless to say more on this subject ... It is true, the horse cannot express his reasoning by a proposition, not knowing the marks A, B, C; whence he has at least this advantage, that he never errs as men do.'[1]

Since Xenophon's principles are so just, and so universal in their application, the modern reader is constantly tempted to read exact and detailed descriptions of present-day practices into everything that he writes. Xenophon's advice on bitting, for example (ch. 10), is based on the assumption that the reader is familiar with the types of bits in use in the author's day. Of course modern bits are different; even by the Roman period Xenophon was not wholly intelligible, as appears from the curious extracts given by the lexicographer Pollux from a work supposedly interpreting the *Art of Horsemanship*.[2] The advice that 'you must have not fewer than two bits' has nowadays been seen as a reference to the modern double bridle. But the essential principle of the curb was quite unknown to Xenophon (though he used a metal cavesson, the *psalion*: 7.1), and the combination of (curb) bit and

---

[1] Newcastle—exiled from England after his defeat at Marston Moor—originally published his book in French (Antwerp, 1658). An English translation, *A General System of Horsemanship*, appeared in London in 1743, and is now readily available in the facsimile edition issued in 1970 by Messrs J. A. Allen and Co. Ltd. My quotation is from p. 12. Compare also George Borrow's description (*The Romany Rye*, sixth edition (London, 1900) pp. 265–6) of how the 'Fairy Smith' of *Lavengro* charmed the Irish cob. 'You should ask me ... whether I have horses that can be aggravated or soothed by particular words. No words have any particular power over horses or other animals who have never heard them before —how should they? But certain animals connect ideas of misery or enjoyment with particular words which they are acquainted with ...', etc.

[2] These extracts from Pollux should be recognized for what they are, and not substituted for Xenophon's own text.

bridoon is no older than the eighteenth century. Xenophon in fact intends that the horse should be schooled in a 'rough' bit, whose mouthpiece is to be furnished with sharp-edged discs and revolving spiky 'hedgehogs', 'so that when the horse takes hold of it he may be repulsed by its roughness and let it go' (Plate 13*b*). Later the made horse is to be ridden in a smooth bit, 'so that he may be pleased by its smoothness and perform in it too the lessons taught by the rough one'. He is not however 'to despise its smoothness:' 'for this reason we add large discs to the smooth bit, to compel him to open his mouth and let go of the mouth-piece' (10.7).

Obviously Xenophon has no notion of contact between the horseman's hands and the horse's mouth; indeed the rider is repeatedly told to ride with a slack rein (it is a mistranslation to talk of 'light hands') except when actually using the bit to indicate or enforce his will (e.g. 9.9; 10.13; 10.16). The severity of the ancient bit is well illustrated by the horses of the Parthenon frieze, whose lower jaws, instead of being naturally relaxed, are forced stiffly backward; at the same time the horse may seek to take the pressure off the bars of its mouth by throwing its head up and poking its nose in the air. Other horses on the frieze are 'overbent', with the chins brought down to their breasts (Plate 13*a*). This severity was necessary because the rider had neither a saddle to afford him a secure seat nor stirrups to give him a purchase for his feet when pulling his horse up. (Saddlecloths, padded to save the horse's spine and the rider's seat, were used, and also served to protect the horse in action: 12.8–9.) Yet the cavalry tactics of the day made it essential for the rider to be able to pull his horse up and turn it instantly. He was not to charge home—especially not against unbroken infantry—but to gallop up, throw a javelin, wheel about and retire (8.12; 12.12–13; *Hellenica* iv. 3.5; v. 4.39–40; vii. 1.20–2).

Whether for riding bareback or upon a saddlecloth, Xenophon recommends (7.5–6) a seat 'like a man riding upright with his legs apart', not riding short 'as though on a chair' with his thighs horizontal. 'For so the thighs will have a better grip on the horse', enabling the rider to use his weapons better. The lower leg should hang slack from the knee, to reduce the risk of injury from an accidental blow, and also, no doubt, though Xenophon does not say so, to afford free use of the spurs (mentioned at ch. 8.5, and also by comic poets slightly earlier than Xenophon's time quoted by Pollux (x. 53–4)—'goads at the heels' and 'a whip round the ankle bones': perhaps a recent invention).

Xenophon gives (chs. 7–8) instructions for mounting, for riding on the flat, and for riding across country. The horse should be trained to stand quiet after the rider has mounted, to allow him to adjust his dress, his reins and his spear. He should move off at a walk, to avoid undue excitement, and so proceed to a trot and a gallop. The rider should not dismount among other horses, or in a group of men. The horse should be led over jumps before being asked to jump with a rider on his back. The spur should be used to make him collect his hindquarters under him and jump off his hocks (Xenophon is not of course thinking of large fences taken at steeplechase speed, but of jumping low banks, small ditches and stone-walled sheepfolds as safely as possible). 'It is good to take hold of the mane, so that the horse may not be burdened at once by the ground and by the bit'—excellent advice for a bare-back rider using such a bit as Xenophon used. Vary the direction and duration of your rides, 'for this is more interesting for the horse than always doing the same exercises in the same places'.

Xenophon also gives excellent advice on calming a spirited horse (ch. 9): avoid exciting him, as far as possible, and try to settle him by long quiet rides; it is no good trying to tire him out by galloping him. For a sluggish horse (clearly of no interest to Xenophon) 'it is sufficient to recommend the exact contrary of the treatment advised for the spirited one'.

How closely Xenophon, with the somewhat primitive means at his disposal, approached the art of the modern masters, may be disputed. It is notable that, though he gives instructions (7.10–11) for obtaining the correct lead at the gallop, he does not appear to have practised changes of lead. He describes how a horse behaves when showing off in front of other horses, 'especially mares' (10.4)—'He lifts his neck up high, flexes his poll haughtily, picks his legs up freely, and keeps his tail up'[1]—and seeks to develop at the rider's will those gaits that the horse naturally displays 'of his own accord when pleased and enjoying himself'. Chapter 10 of the *Art of Horsemanship* is directed to this end, in order to make a good war-horse 'more magnificent and spectacular to ride'; Chapter 11 to training an exceptional horse to 'lift his body' in order to appear 'brilliant' on parade by 'appearing to do of his own free will the finest action proper to a horse'. Xenophon warns against violent methods; 'pulling at the mouth with the bit, spurring and whipping' are thought by the ignorant to make horses appear brilliant, but such people obtain quite the opposite result to what they intend: 'by pulling their horses' mouths into the air they blind them instead of letting them see where they are going, and by spurring and whipping they bewilder them' (10.1–2). Again (11.6), 'as Simon also remarks, what the horse is compelled to do, he does not understand. Such actions are not beautiful, any more than if one were to teach a dancer by whipping and spurring.' Another warning is given (11.10–11) to the officer who, in displaying his own horsemanship, forgets the squadron at his back, and brings it to a walk, while he himself advances slowly on a horse that 'raises his body highest and most often, in the manner most applauded for High School horses'.

One is tempted to see in these chapters at least the germ of modern High School riding, including a separation between 'airs on the ground' and 'airs above the ground', and some of the great modern authorities support this view. Thus Colonel Alois Podhajsky,[2] while acknowledging that Xenophon's work is only a sketch, deduces from it and from contemporary works of art that ancient horsemen were familiar with such movements as the Piaffe, Passage and Levade. A layman will think twice before questioning such an authority, but it is possible that generosity, and a desire to root his own art in antiquity, have led him to rate

---

[1] Here too a parallel in Shakespeare's *Venus and Adonis* (lines 271ff.) has recently been pointed out, and it has been suggested that Shakespeare's description may actually be derived from Xenophon, through John Astley's *The Art of Riding* (London, 1584) (Ian Donaldson, *Notes and Queries*, NS 19, no. 4 (April 1972) pp. 123–5.

[2] *Die Spanische Hofreitschule* (Vienna, 1948) pp. 14–16.

Xenophon's achievements too highly. Mrs M. A. Littauer[1] perhaps puts the matter more justly: 'Now if we put Xenophon's
text and the art of the period together . . . there is good reason to
believe that in classical times a high, bouncy action was much
favoured at both the trot and the canter, and that probably a form
of rear or series of rears was found very effective in impressing
the multitude during processions on the many religious festivals.
But the frequency with which horses are shown with their noses
in the air [Plate 13*a*], as well as the extreme brevity and vague-
ness of Xenophon's text, should convince us that this was not
real dressage as we know it.'

[1] *The Chronicle of the Horse*, 11 May 1962 (reviewing the present author's
Ancient Greek Horsemanship, Berkeley, 1961). Mrs Littauer has convinced me that
the claims I made for Xenophon in this work were greatly exaggerated: see also
Captain V. S. Littauer, *Horseman's Progress* (Princeton, 1962).

CHAPTER SIXTEEN

Last Years

DIOGENES LAERTIUS (ii. 53) says that after Xenophon was expelled from Scillus he eventually escaped to Corinth with his sons (Philesia is not mentioned: was she already dead?) and settled there. He adds that Xenophon 'sent' his sons to serve with the Athenian army—implying that he did not go to Athens himself—and, on the authority of Demetrius of Magnesia, that he died at Corinth at a considerable age (ii. 56: the date given, 360 B.C., is certainly too early). No doubt Xenophon did visit Athens from time to time after the decree of banishment was repealed, but he probably had few friends left there, and his family property must have been confiscated and sold when he was banished. At Corinth he was perhaps more closely in touch with the friends of his adult life—the Spartiate 'peers'; the mercenary officers who had retired to their Peloponnesian villages; indeed he may have previously formed an acquaintance among the 'best people' at Corinth itself, for whom he shows a strong sympathy in his history (cf. *Hellenica* iv. 4). But it may be supposed that he never felt truly at home; perhaps he had hopes of being invited to Syracuse when in 367 B.C. the old tyrant Dionysius died and philosophy came into fashion for a time at his son's court. Xenophon's *Hieron* is a discussion between a Syracusan ruler of the previous century and Simonides the poet on whether a tyrant, surrounded as he must be by worthless flatterers and denied the pleasures of true friendship and family life, can be happy—commonplaces influenced perhaps by the ninth book of Plato's *Republic*. As the *Hieron* continues, Xenophon, unlike Plato, suggests that after all the tyrant can redeem his own condition and that of his people by enlightened rule. Xenophon is not at his best when discussing general ideas rather than illustrating them by particular examples, and, if the book's purpose was to angle for an invitation to Sicily, Dionysius did not take the bait. We need not believe a story told, with no authority cited, by Athenaeus (x. 427f.) that Xenophon did appear at the court of one Dionysius or the other, and gave him at his own dinner table a lesson on the Socratic theme of eating when hungry and drinking when dry.

Though Xenophon did not settle permanently at Athens, it was to the Athenians that he directed his advice when he felt that his knowledge and experience could be of use. His recommendations for the reform of their cavalry have already been mentioned, and he also wrote a pamphlet on their revenues (*De Vectigalibus*). This was probably one of his last works; it refers (2.7) to the campaign of 362 B.C., with which the *Hellenica* end, and also (5.9) seems, by urging the Athenians to secure the autonomy of the Delphic Oracle and to unite the Greeks against those who are trying to seize the sanctuary, to allude to the Third Sacred War which broke out late in 356 B.C. That Xenophon should advise the Athenians to consult the oracles at Delphi and Dodona before putting his recommendations into practice (6.2) is of course characteristic.

It is possible that Xenophon wrote partly in order to pay an old debt of gratitude by supporting the policies of Eubulus, the statesman who had proposed the repeal of his own banishment some fourteen years earlier (and, 'Istrus says', had moved the decree of banishment too, thirty years earlier still: Diogenes Laertius ii. 59), but we do not know enough about his career[1] to be certain on this point.

But Xenophon gave Athens more than advice. 'When the Athenians voted to help the Lacedaemonians, he sent his sons to Athens to fight on behalf of the Lacedaemonians. [They had been educated at Sparta, as Diocles says in his *Lives of the Philosophers*.] Now Diodorus, without distinguishing himself, came safely home from the battle; and to him was born a son named

[1] For which see G. L. Cawkwell, 'Eubulus', *JHS* 83 (1963) pp. 47–67.

after his brother. But Gryllus was posted to the cavalry (it was the Battle of Mantinea), and after fighting valiantly was killed, as Ephorus relates in his twenty-fifth book. Cephisodorus commanded the cavalry and Hegisileos was general. Epaminondas too fell in this battle. They say that at the very moment when the news came, Xenophon himself was offering sacrifice with a wreath on his head, and when his son's death was announced he put off his wreath. But, when he learned that he had died nobly, he put it on again. And some report that he did not so much as weep, but said that he knew that he had begotten a mortal. And Aristotle says that thousands wrote encomiums and epitaphs for Gryllus, to honour his deed and do pleasure to his father' (Diogenes Laertius ii. 54–5).

The fame of Gryllus was still remembered five hundred years later. Pausanias (i. 3.4) saw, in one of the colonnades of the Athenian market-place, a picture of the Battle of Mantinea, showing 'the cavalry action, in which the best-known figures are, on the Athenian side, Gryllus the son of Xenophon, and, among the Boeotian cavalry, Epaminondas the Theban.' At Mantinea itself (viii. 9.8–10) was a copy of the same picture, and the Mantineans still honoured Gryllus first among those who fought in the battle, his commander Cephisodorus second, and their own Podares third.

Xenophon himself does not name his son in his history (a fact that should be remembered by those who accuse him of exaggerating his own achievements in the *Anabasis*, or omitting, in the second book of the *Hellenica*, the conduct of Socrates because he did not know it). He describes (*Hellenica* vii. 5.15ff.) the forced march of the Athenian cavalry, who, starting from Eleusis, had dinner at the Isthmus, passed through Cleonae (apparently marching by night, without resting), and had just reached Mantinea and been billeted in the houses inside the walls when the news came that Epaminondas, doubling back after a dash upon Sparta that almost took the city 'bereft of defenders like a nestful of fledglings', was upon them with his cavalry. 'Now the Mantineans begged the Athenians to help if they could, for all their herds were outside the walls, and their labourers, and many children and older men of the free population.' (The citizens of military age were no doubt all with the army.) 'When the Athenians heard, they sallied out to the rescue, though neither they nor their horses had yet taken the morning meal ... As soon as they saw the enemy, they grappled with them, passionately longing to preserve the glory inherited from their fathers. And their fight resulted in the rescue of all the property of the Mantineans outside the city, but of their own number there were killed some gallant men, and they killed men who were clearly no less gallant. For no weapon on either side was too short to reach the enemy. The Athenians did not lose possession of the dead on their side, but some of the enemy's dead they returned under truce.' This meant that the Thebans and their allies formally conceded their mastery of the field, and it was no doubt in this action that Gryllus was killed.

Of the great battle that followed, Xenophon writes (*Hellenica* vii. 5.26–7): 'The consequences of this action were contrary to all men's expectation. Almost all Greece joined in the encounter and was ranged on one side or the other. Therefore there was nobody who did not think that, if a battle took place, the victors would rule and the vanquished be subjected. But God so brought it to pass that both sides set up trophies as victors, unopposed by their opponents; both sides as victors returned the enemy's dead under truce; and both as vanquished took back their dead under truce. Both sides claimed the victory, but had evidently gained no advantage in territory, cities or dominion in comparison with the situation before the battle. Indecision and disorder prevailed in Greece even more after the battle than before it.

'Let my history end at this point. Perhaps some other writer will take up the sequel.'

But if history ended in doubt, confusion and disappointment, there were still an old man's daydreams. In the *Cyropaedia* imaginary armies could be trained and manoeuvred according to ideal systems, and fight battles in which the plans of the model general never miscarried. A father could advise his son before sending him to the wars, and welcome him back after a career of victory (*Cyropaedia* i. 6.2ff.; viii. 5.21ff.). And at the end of the hero's life could come a quiet departure to the gods, with children and friends gathered round the deathbed (*Cyropaedia* viii. 7.1ff.). Perhaps a quiet death, in the best home that he had known, was granted to Xenophon after all. The tradition that he died at Corinth has already been mentioned, but, five hundred years later, Pausanias was told another story. 'The Elean guides said that the Eleans recovered Scillus, and that Xenophon was tried before the Olympic Council for receiving the land from the Lacedaemonians, but being pardoned by the Eleans he dwelt securely in Scillus. Moreover a little way from the sanctuary a tomb was shown, with a statue of Pentelic marble on the grave. The neighbours say it is the tomb of Xenophon' (Pausanias v. 6.6—Sir James Frazer's translation).

Some Important Dates

431	Outbreak of Peloponnesian War.
430–425?	Birth of Xenophon.
424	Battle of Delium.
	Socrates distinguishes himself in the Athenian retreat.
421	Peace of Nicias.
413	Renewal of war between Athens and Sparta.
406	Athenian victory at Arginusae.
	Socrates opposes the execution of the Generals.
405	Artaxerxes succeeds to throne of Persia.
	(Late Summer) Lysander destroys Athenian fleet at Aegospotami.
404	(Spring) Surrender of Athens.
	(Autumn) 'Thirty Tyrants' established.
404–3	(Midwinter) Thrasybulus seizes Phyle.
403	(Spring) The 'Thirty' defeated and retreat to Eleusis.
403	(Late Summer) Democratic restoration at Athens.
401	(Spring) Cyrus marches against Artaxerxes.
	(Autumn) Battle of Cunaxa.
	(Autumn–Winter) Retreat of the Ten Thousand.
400	(Early Spring) The Ten Thousand reach the Black Sea.
	(Spring–Autumn) The retreat continued to Byzantium.
	Dispute between Sparta and Persia over the Ionian cities.
	In Europe, Agis of Sparta attacks Elis.
400–399	(Winter) The Ten Thousand in Thrace.
399	(Late Winter) Trial and execution of Socrates at Athens.

(Early Spring) Xenophon brings the remnant of the Ten Thousand (the 'Cyreans') to join the Spartan Thibron in Asia.

Exile of Xenophon from Athens (or in 394 B.C.?).

398–397   War continues in Asia between Sparta and the Persian satraps.

399 or 8   Death of King Agis of Sparta. Agesilaus succeeds, with Lysander's help.

396   Persians plan naval counter-offensive. Agesilaus takes personal command in Asia.

395   Herippidas supersedes Xenophon as commander of the 'Cyreans'. Battle of Sardis.

Death of Tissaphernes.

The Persian fleet under Conon of Athens takes Rhodes.

Persia encourages the enemies of Sparta in European Greece. Lysander killed at Haliartus.

394   Thebes and Athens head coalition against Sparta.

Agesilaus recalled to Europe.

394–387/6   The 'Corinthian War'.

Xenophon continues to serve under Agesilaus, though the Spartans have already granted him Scillus (?).

387/6   The 'King's Peace'. Sparta withdraws from Asia but retains leadership of European Greece.

386–371   Xenophon in retirement at Scillus.

382   The Spartans seize Thebes by treachery.

378   Thebes liberated by Pelopidas.

371   Thebes defeats Sparta at Leuctra.

Xenophon driven from Scillus.

370–369   Athens changes sides and supports Sparta.

Xenophon's banishment repealed. (?)

362   Battle of Mantinea. Death of Xenophon's son Gryllus.

360   (Early Spring) Death of Agesilaus.

356   Outbreak of 'Sacred War'.

After 356   Death of Xenophon.

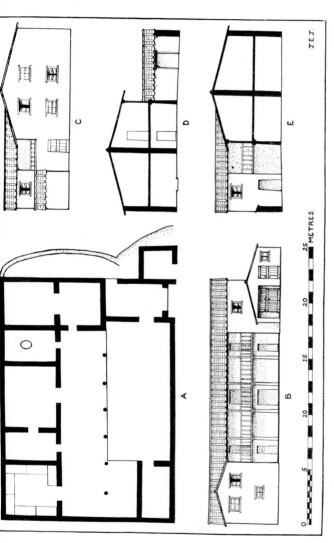

1. *An Attic country house of Xenophon's time.*

The 'Dema House', occupied from c. 420–413 B.C. *Reconstruction and plan, from* Annual of the British School at Athens 57 *(1962) p. 112, by courtesy of the Trustees of the British School at Athens and Dr. J. E. Jones. (pp. 11, 13)*

J.E.J.

3. (*Above*) *Woman acrobat somersaulting over swords.*
From a vase painted in a Greek colony of Southern Italy, c. *350* B.C.
F. Inghirami, Pitture di Vasi Fittili (*Fiesole: 1835*) *vol.* I, *pl. 66.*
(*p. 45*)

2. (*Left*) *Sacrifice.*
Victory hovers above the altar, and pours a wine-offering. The chief
celebrant has already made his libation from the wine-cup in his right
hand. He is named Diomedes—perhaps an Athenian aristocrat of the
Peloponnesian War period, rather than the Homeric hero, to whom the
picture has no obvious reference (*cf. T. B. L. Webster*, Potter and
Patron in Classical Athens (*London: 1972 pp. 51–2*). *The garlanded*
boy who roasts part of the victim on a spit is unnamed.
    From a stamnos (*British Museum E 456*), *by a painter of the*
Group of Polygnotus. By courtesy of the Trustees of the British Museum.
(*p. 13*)

4. a, b. *Coin of Tissaphernes.*

This silver tetradrachm was probably struck c. 411/410 B.C., to pay rowers serving in the Spartan fleet against Athens. The obverse (a) bears the satrap's portrait; the reverse (b) the Athenian owl and olive branch (generally recognized and respected as a coin type), but with the letters ΒΑΣ, for Basileos, of the King, instead of ΑΘΕ for Athenaion, of the Athenians. The owl is countermarked with an Aramaic letter. (p. 67)

5. a, b. *Coin of Pharnabazus.*

Silver tetradrachm, struck at Cyzicus on the sea of Marmara (as the tunny-fish below the warship's prow on the reverse (b) indicates), possibly in 396 B.C., in order to finance the fleet which the Athenian admiral Conon was bringing up to attack the Spartans, or a few years later when Pharnabazus himself sailed with the fleet against Europe. The obverse (a) bears the satrap's 'image and superscription'. The letters are Greek— again implying that the coin was intended to pay Greek mercenaries. On the reverse, the prow of a warship ornamented with an eye and griffin, between dolphins; below, a tunny fish. (p. 67)

These coins are Nos. 621 and 718 in Greek Coins *by C. M. Kraay and Max Hirmer (London: 1966). Photographs by courtesy of Hirmer Verlag, München.*

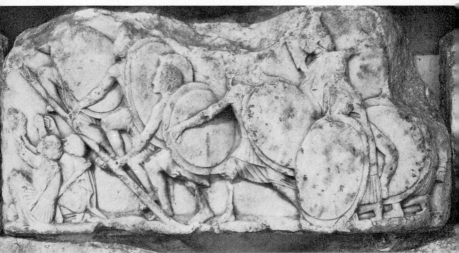

6. a, b. *Details from the Nereid Monument, erected* c. *400 B.C. to a ruler of Xanthus in Lycia, a dependency of the Persian empire, on the south-west coast of Asia Minor. These pieces (also the 'Payava' and 'satrap' sarcophagi illustrated below) were executed by Greek sculptors for 'barbarian' patrons.*

(a) *the ruler, seated under his umbrella of state, receives emissaries who have come to surrender a besieged city. His hoplite bodyguards stand behind him.*

(b) *Greek mercenaries storming a city. The pioneers have placed a ladder against the wall and are steadying it from below, while the hoplites, with characteristic round shields, press forward to the assault. For the man who catches his comrade's shield-rim and tries to push past, cf. Xenophon,* Anabasis *iv.7. 1–12. This frieze apparently commemorates an actual achievement of the dead ruler, but neither he nor it can be identified certainly. By courtesy of the Trustees of the British Museum.* (p. 128)

7. The 'Sarcophagus of Payava'.

A Lycian cavalry commander, c. 400 B.C., charges a party of Greek infantry, whose leader has fallen beneath the Lycian's horse. The heavy cavalry armour combines Greek elements (cuirass, and helmets of the commander's followers), with thigh pieces, which are of Asiatic origin, but were approved by Xenophon in his Art of Horsemanship, ch. 12. By courtesy of the Trustees of the British Museum. (p. 75)

8. The 'Satrap Sarcophagus', now in Istanbul.

The ruler of the Kingdom of Sidon hunting, c. 400 B.C. The hunt probably takes place in the royal 'paradise'. The King and his courtiers (in Persian dress, as Sidon was a Persian dependency) have just wounded a stag with their spears. A panther suddenly breaks in upon the party; the horse on the right shies away and throws its rider, but the King himself leaves the stag, and with spear upraised attacks the more dangerous quarry. By courtesy of Hirmer Verlag, München. (p. 78)

9. *Greek boar-hunt.*

Detail from the 'François Vase' by the Attic artist Kleitias, c. 560 B.C. The heroes Peleus and Meleager face the charging Calydonian boar in the attitude recommended by Xenophon's Treatise on Hunting. Atalanta (distinguished by her fair skin) is immediately behind them. By courtesy of Hirmer Verlag, München. (pp. 174, 184)

10. *Greek infantry and barbarian cavalry.*
The Greek hoplite, on this Attic mixing-bowl by the Orpheus Painter
(Syracuse, Museo Nazionale No. 37175; c. 430 B.C.), springs forward
with determined vigour; by contrast his opponent, an Amazon in Asiatic
dress, sits passively on her horse, her right hand, holding her spear, hang-
ing slack by her side. Her light shield (pelta) has fallen to the ground.
Compare Xenophon's speech (Anabasis iii.2.15–19) on the superiority
of infantry.

  The Greek is 'heroically' nude and wears his helmet pushed to the back
of his head to reveal his face. His attendant wears a short cloak (chlamys)
and hard felt hat (pilos). By courtesy of Hirmer Verlag, München.
(p. 124)

11. *Thracian horseman and infantryman.*
The figures on this Attic mixing-bowl (British Museum E 482) of the mid-fifth century B.C. *wear fox-skin caps and, over their tunics, the heavy woollen cloak described by Xenophon (Anabasis vii.4.3–4). They have high boots and carry two spears: the foot soldier has in addition the* pelta *which give this form of infantry its name. By courtesy of the Trustees of the British Museum. (pp. 86, 139)*

12. Women's activities.

The pictures on this oil-bottle by the Amasis Painter (New York, Metropolitan Museum No. 31.11.10) show wool-working in an Athenian household, c. 540 B.C. On the right of the developed drawing the raw wool is being weighed out; to the left of the centre the finished cloaks or blankets are being folded up and put away; other women are seen taking wool out of baskets, spinning with distaff and spindle, and weaving on the upright loom. One of the weavers passes a shuttle back and forth; other shuttles ready on either side may contain wool of different colours, to produce woven patterns like those of the finished cloth. The second weaver packs the weft tight above her head with a long stick. By courtesy of the Metropolitan Museum of Art, New York (Fletcher Fund: 1931). (pp. 13, 179)

13. a, b. *Athenian horsemen and Greek bit.*
The detail from the inner frieze of the Parthenon (c. 440 B.C.) shows young Athenians riding in the Panathenaic procession. Bits and bridles of bronze were once fastened to the marble, as is shown by the holes drilled to attach them near the horses' polls and at the corners of their mouths. The position of the horses' heads and lower jaws, and the obviously rough transition which is being made by the horse, right of centre, who is being reined back to a walk, indicate the discomfort caused by bits like that shown in (b) (of unknown provenience, but Greek and approximately of Xenophon's time). Both photographs by courtesy of the Trustees of the British Museum. (pp. 15, 188, 191)

Further Reading

THE following list is not intended to be a complete bibliography, merely a note of some of the books on Xenophon that I personally have found most helpful, apart from those mentioned in the footnotes. I have restricted it to books written in English; but no student of Xenophon can escape a debt of gratitude to Edouard Delebecque, and I must also acknowledge the great pleasure and benefit that I have received from Juan Gil's *Jenofonte: Economico* (Madrid, 1967).

This is a bad time to draw up a reading list on Xenophon's historical writings. Professor Sterling Dow and Mr George Cawkwell are both about to produce new works on the *Anabasis*. Mr Cawkwell has seen the first version of my own account of the Battle of Cunaxa, with which he disagrees. I am most grateful to him for his vigorous and well-reasoned criticisms; he has not changed my mind but many readers will no doubt prefer to follow his authority.

Professor James Wiseman promises a new commentary on the *Hellenica*. This is sorely needed, as G. E. Underhill's work on the first two books has long been out of date.

H. W. Parke, *Greek Mercenary Soldiers from the earliest times to the battle of Ipsus* (Oxford, 1933), throws valuable light on Xenophon's military background, though it takes what I consider to be a most unfair view of Xenophon himself.

W. P. Henry, *Greek Historical Writing: a historiographical essay based on Xenophon's Hellenica* (Chicago, 1967), is valuable for its sharp criticism of previous theories on the composition of the Hellenica.

A. H. M. Jones, *Sparta* (Oxford, 1967), and W. G. Forrest, *A History of Sparta, 950–192 B.C.* (London, 1968), both provide useful guidance in a bewilderingly complex field.

On questions of philosophy I cannot pretend to judge, but I believe that W. K. C. Guthrie, *History of Greek Philosophy Vol. III* (Cambridge, 1969) gives a far more just picture of 'Xenophon the Socratic' than does the destructive criticism of A. H. Chroust, *Socrates, Man and Myth: the two Socratic apologies of Xenophon* (London, 1957).

To many readers, 'Xenophon' will mean the *Art of Horsemanship*. M. H. Morgan, *The Art of Horsemanship by Xenophon* (1894, republished London, 1962), is still perhaps the best English translation. Morgan's book also includes an essay on the Greek riding-horse, and useful notes, though the archaeological information is out-dated.

Denison Bingham Hull, *Hounds and Hunting in Ancient Greece* (Chicago, 1964), gives valuable technical information, based on his experiences as a Master of Foxhounds. His translations from the Greek are not reliable, but his shortcomings are less serious in his version of Xenophon's *Cynegeticus*, which is based on that of E. C. Marchant in the Loeb series, than when he is tackling other authors.

Index